I0016783

KNOWLEDGE DISCOVERY IN THE SOCIAL SCIENCES

KNOWLEDGE DISCOVERY IN THE SOCIAL SCIENCES

A Data Mining Approach

Xiaoling Shu

 UNIVERSITY OF CALIFORNIA PRESS

University of California Press

Oakland, California

© 2020 by Xiaoling Shu

Library of Congress Cataloging-in-Publication Data

Names: Shu, Xiaoling, 1968- author.
Title: Knowledge discovery in the social sciences : a data mining approach / Xiaoling Shu.
Description: Oakland, California : University of California Press, [2020] | Includes bibliographical
    references and index.
Identifiers: LCCN 2019024334 (print) | LCCN 2019024335 (ebook) | ISBN 9780520339996 (cloth) |
    ISBN 9780520292307 (paperback) | ISBN 9780520965874 (ebook)
Subjects: LCSH: Social sciences—Research—Data processing. | Data mining.
Classification: LCC H61.3 .S49 2020 (print) | LCC H61.3 (ebook) | DDC 300.285/6312—dc23
LC record available at https://lccn.loc.gov/2019024334
LC ebook record available at https://lccn.loc.gov/2019024335

29 28 27 26 25 24 23 22 21 20
10 9 8 7 6 5 4 3 2 1

To Casey, Kina, and Dong with love and gratitude

CONTENTS

## PART I

KNOWLEDGE DISCOVERY AND DATA MINING IN SOCIAL SCIENCE RESEARCH

Chapter 1

INTRODUCTION

——————

ADVANCES IN TECHNOLOGY—the internet, mobile devices, computers, digital sensors, and recording equipment—have led to exponential growth in the amount and complexity of data available for analysis. It has become difficult or even impossible to capture, manage, process, and analyze these data in a reasonable amount of time. We are at the threshold of an era in which digital data play an increasingly important role in the research process. In the traditional approach, hypotheses derived from theories are the driving forces behind model building. However, with the rise of big data and the enormous wealth of information and knowledge buried in this data mine, using data mining technologies to discover interesting, meaningful, and robust patterns has becoming increasingly important. This alternative method of research affects all fields, including the social sciences. The availability of huge amounts of data provides unprecedented opportunities for new discoveries, as well as challenges.

Today we are confronted with a data tsunami. We are accumulating data at an unprecedented scale in many areas of industry, government, and civil society. Analysis and knowledge based on big data now drive nearly every aspect of society, including retail, financial services, insurance, wireless mobile services, business management, urban planning, science and technology, social sciences, and humanities. Google Books has so far digitalized 4 percent of all the books ever printed in the world, and the process is ongoing. The Google Books corpus contains more than 500 billion words in English, French, Spanish, German, Chinese, Russian, and Hebrew that would take a person eighty years to read continuously at a pace of 200 words per minute. This entire corpus is available for downloading (http://storage.googleapis.com/books/ngrams/books/datasetsv2.html), and Google also hosts another site to graph word usage over time, from 1800 to 2008 (https://books.google.com/ngrams). The Internet Archive, a digital library of internet sites and other cultural artifacts in digital form, provides free access to 279 billion web pages, 11 million books and texts, 4 million audio recordings, 3 million videos, 1 million images, and 100,000 software programs (https://archive.org/about/). Facebook generates 4 new petabyes of data and runs 600,000 queries and one million map-reduce jobs per day. Facebook's data warehouse Hive stores 300 petabytes of data in 800,000 tables, as reported in 2014 (https://research.fb.com/facebook-s-top-open-data-problems/). The GDELT database monitors global cyberspace in real time and analyzes and extracts news events from portals, print media, TV broadcasts, online media, and online forums in all countries of the world and extracts key information such as people, places, organizations, and event types related to news events. The GDELT Event Database records over 300 categories of physical activities around the world, from riots and protests to peaceful appeals and diplomatic exchanges, georeferenced to the city or mountaintop, across the entire world from January 1, 1979 and updated every 15 minutes. Since February 2015, GDELT has brought together 940 million messages from global cyberspace in a volume of 9.4TB (https://www.gdeltproject.org/). A report by McKinsey (Manyika et al. 2011) estimated that corporations, institutions, and users stored more than 13 exabytes of new data, which is over 50,000 times larger than the amount of data in the Library of Congress. The value of global personal location data is estimated to be $700 billion, and these data can reduce costs as much as 50 percent in product development and assembly.

Both industry and academic demands for data analytical skills have soared rapidly and continue to do so. IBM projects that by 2020 the number of jobs requiring data analytical skills in the United States will increase by 15 percent, to more than 2.7 million, and job openings requiring advanced data science analytical skills will reach more than 60,000 (Miller and Hughes 2017). Global firms are focusing on data-intensive sectors such as finance, insurance, and medicine. The topic of big data has been covered in popular news media such as the *Economist* (2017), the *New York Times* (Lohr 2012), and National Public Radio (Harris 2016), and data mining has also been featured in *Forbes* (2015; Brown 2018), the *Atlantic* (Furnis 2012), and *Time* (Stein 2011), to name a few.

The growth of big data has also revolutionized scientific research. Computational social sciences emerged as a new methodology, and it is growing in popularity as a result of dramatic increases in available data on human and organizational behaviors (Lazer at al. 2009). Astronomy has also been revolutionized by using a huge database of space pictures, the Sloan Digital Sky Survey, to identify interesting objects and phenomena (https://www.sdss.org/). Bioinformatics has emerged from biological science to focus on databases of genome sequencing, allowing millions or billions of DNA strands to be sequenced rapidly in parallel.

In the field of artificial intelligence (AI), scientists have developed AlphaGo, which was trained to model expert players from recorded historical games of a database of 30 million game moves and was later trained to learn new strategies for itself (https://deepmind.com/research/alphago/). AlphaGo has defeated Go world champions many times and is regarded as the strongest Go player in the game's history. This is a major advancement over the old AI technology. When IBM's DeepMind beat chess champion Gary Kasparov in the late 1990s, it used brute-force AI that searched chess moves in a space that was just a small fraction of the search space for Go.

The Google Books corpus has made it possible to expand quantitative analysis into a wider array of topics in the social sciences and the humanities (Michel et al. 2011). By analyzing this corpus, social scientists and humanists have been able to provide insights into cultural trends that include English-language lexicography, the evolution of grammar, collective memory, adoption of technology, pursuits of fame, censorship, and historical epidemiology.

In response to this fast-growing demand, universities and colleges have developed data science or data studies majors. These fields have grown from the confluence of statistics, machine learning, AI, and computer science. They are products of a structural transformation in the nature of research in disciplines that include communication, psychology, sociology, political science, economics, business and commerce, environmental science, linguistics, and the humanities. Data mining projects not only require that users possess in-depth knowledge about data processing, database technology, and statistical and computational algorithms; they also require domain-specific knowledge (from experts such as psychologists, economists, sociologists, political scientists, and linguists) to combine with available data mining tools to discover valid and meaningful knowledge. On many university campuses, social sciences programs have joined forces to consolidate course offerings across disciplines to teach introductory, intermediate, and advanced courses on data description, visualization, mining, and modeling to students in the social sciences and humanities.

This chapter examines the major concepts of big data, knowledge discovery in databases, data mining, and computational social science. It analyzes the characteristics of these terms, their central features, components, and research methods.

WHAT IS BIG DATA?

The concept of big data was conceived in 2001 when the META analyst D. Laney (2001) proposed the famous "3V's Model" to cope with the management of increasingly large amounts of data. Laney described the data as of large *volume*, growing at a high *velocity*, and having great *variety*. The concept of big data became popular in 2008 when *Nature* featured a special issue on the utility, approaches, and challenges of big data analysis. Big data has since become a widely discussed new topic in all areas of scientific research. *Science* featured a special forum on big data in 2011, further highlighting the enormous potential and great challenge of big data research. In the same year, McKinsey's report "Big Data: The Next Frontier for Innovation, Competition, and Productivity" (2011) announced that the tsunami of data will bring enormous productivity and profits, adding enthusiasm to this already exciting development. Mayer-Schönberger and Cukier (2012) focused on the dramatic impacts that big data will have on the economy, science, and society and the revolutionary changes it will bring about in society at large.

A variety of definitions of big data all agree on one central feature of this concept: data enormity and complexity. Some treat data that are too large for traditional database technologies to store, access, manage, and analyze (Manyika et al. 2011). Others define big data based on its characteristic four big V's: (1) big *volume*, measured at terabytes or petabytes; (2) big *velocity*, which grows rapidly and continuously; (3) big *variety*, which includes structured numerical data and unstructured data such as text, pictures, video, and sound; and (4) big *value*, which can be translated into enormous economic profits, academic knowledge, and policy insights. Analysis of big data uses computational algorithms, cloud storage, and AI to instantaneously and continuously mine and analyze data (Dumbill 2013).

There are just as many scholars who think big data is a multifaceted and complex concept that cannot be viewed simply from a data or technology perspective (Mauro, Greco, and Grimaldi 2016). A word cloud analysis from the literature shows that big data can be viewed from at least four different angles. First, big data contains information. The foundation of big data is the production and utilization of information from text, online records, GPS locations, online forums, and so on. This enormous amount of information is digitized, compiled, and stored on computers (Seife 2015). Second, big data includes technology. The enormous size and complexity of the data pose difficulties for computer storage, data processing, and data mining technologies. The technology component of big data includes distributed data storage, cloud computing, data mining, and artificial intelligence. Third, big data encompasses methods. Big data requires a series of processing and analytical methods that are beyond the traditional statistical approaches, such as association, classification, cluster analysis, natural language processing, neural networks, network analysis, pattern recognition, predictive modeling, spatial analysis, statistics, supervised and unsupervised learning, and simulation (Manyika et al. 2011). And fourth, big data has impacts. Big data has affected many dimensions of our society. It has revolutionized how we conduct business, research, design, and production. It has brought and will continue to bring changes in laws, guidelines, and policies on the utility and management of personal information.

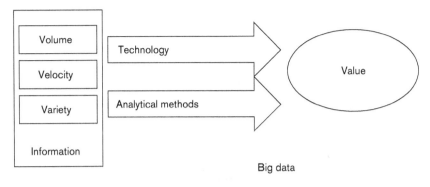

FIGURE 1.1
What Is Big Data?

To summarize, the essence of big data is big volume, high velocity, and big variety of information. As shown in figure 1.1, it also comprises *technology* and *analytical methods,* to transform the information into insights that are worth economic *value,* thus having an impact on society.

WHAT IS KNOWLEDGE DISCOVERY IN DATABASE?

Knowledge discovery in database (KDD) is the nontrivial process of identifying valid, novel, potentially useful, and ultimately understandable patterns in data (Fayyad, Piatesky-Shapiro, and Smyth 1996, 84). It consists of nine steps that begin with the development and understanding of the application domain and ends with actions on the knowledge discovered, as illustrated in figure 1.2.

KDD is a nine-step process that involves understanding domain knowledge, selecting a data set, data processing, data reduction, choice of data mining method, data mining, interpreting patterns, and consolidating discovered knowledge. This process is *not* a one-way flow. Rather, during each step, researchers can backtrack to any of the previous steps and start again. For example, while considering a variety of data mining methods, researchers may go back to the literature and study existing work on the topic to decide which data mining strategy is the most effective one to address the research question.

KDD has already been applied to a variety of fields, including astronomy, investment, marketing, manufacturing, public policy, sports, and telecommunications. An example of KDD system is the Sky Image Cataloging and Analysis Tool (SKICAT), which can automatically analyze, classify, and catalog sky objects as stars or galaxies using machine learning, machine-assisted discovery, and other AI technologies (http://www.ifa.hawaii.edu/~rgal/science/dposs/dposs_frames_skicat.html). Another KDD application is Advanced Scout, which is used by NBA coaching staffs to discover interesting patterns in basketball game data and allows users to relate these patterns to videos (https://www.nbastuffer.com/analytics101/advanced-scout/).

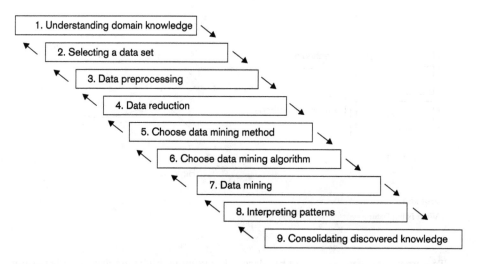

FIGURE 1.2

Components of Knowledge Discovery in a Database.

WHAT IS DATA MINING?

Data mining has two definitions. The narrow definition is that it is a step in the KDD process of applying data analysis and discovery algorithms to produce certain patterns or models on the data. As shown in figure 1.2, data mining is step 7 in the nine steps of the KDD model. It is usually the case that data mining operates in a pattern space that is infinite, and data mining searches that space to find patterns.

Based on this narrow definition of data mining, its techniques and terminology come from three sources. Statistics are the basic source of data mining and bring well-defined techniques to identify systematic relationships between variables. Data visualization, such as histograms and various plots, presents information in visual forms that provide attractive and powerful methods of data exploration. Computational methods include descriptive statistics, correlation, frequency tables, multivariate exploratory techniques, and advanced and generalized linear models. Figure 1.3 shows the three foundations of data mining according to this narrow definition.

AI, another foundation of data mining techniques, contributes to data mining development with information processing techniques based on a human reasoning model that is heuristic. Machine learning represents an important approach in data mining that "trains" computers to recognize patterns in data. An artificial neural network (ANN) consists of structures of a large number of highly interconnected processing elements (neurons) working in unison to solve specific problems. ANNs are modeled after human brains in how they process information, and they learn by example by adjusting to the synaptic connections that exist between the neurons.

The last foundation of data mining is database systems that provide the support platform for information processing and mining. Increases in computing power and advancements in computer science have made it possible to store, access, and retrieve

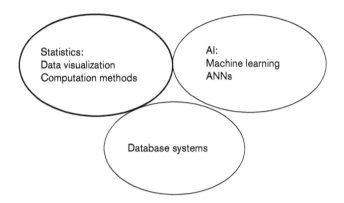

FIGURE 1.3

A Narrow Definition of Data Mining: Three Foundations.

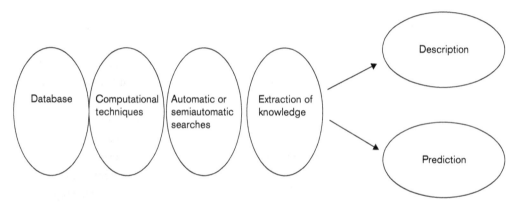

FIGURE 1.4

A Broad Definition of Data Mining.

a huge amount of data, enabling the use of new methods for revealing hidden patterns. These advancements made discoveries of new ideas and theories possible.

The second, and broader, definition of data mining conceptualizes it in a way similar to KDD (Gorunescu 2011). According to this definition, data mining has several components: (1) use of a huge database; (2) computational techniques; (3) automatic or semiautomatic search; and (4) extraction of implicit, previously unknown and potentially useful patterns and relationships hidden in the data. The information expected to be extracted by data scientists are of two types: descriptive and predictive (Larose and Larose 2016). Descriptive objectives are achieved by identifying relations among variables that describe data, and these patterns can be easily understood. Predictive objectives are achieved by using some of the variables to predict one or more of the other outcome variables, thus making it possible to accurately estimate future outcomes based on existing data (Larose and Larose 2016). Figure 1.4 shows the broad definition of data mining.

This book uses the terms *knowledge discovery* and *data mining* interchangeably, according to the broadest conceptualization of data mining. Knowledge discovery and data mining in the social sciences constitute a research process that is guided by social science theories. Social scientists with deep domain knowledge work alongside data miners to select appropriate data, process the data, and choose suitable data mining technologies to conduct visualization, analysis, and mining of data to discover valid, novel, potentially useful, and ultimately understandable patterns. These new patterns are then consolidated with existing theories to develop new knowledge. Knowledge discovery and data mining in the social sciences are also important components of computational social science.

WHAT IS COMPUTATIONAL SOCIAL SCIENCE IN THE ERA OF BIG DATA?

Computational social science (CSS) is a new interdisciplinary area of research at the confluence of information technology, big data, social computing, and the social sciences. The concept of computational social science first gained recognition in 2009 when Lazer and colleagues (2009) published "Computational Social Science" in the journal *Science*. Email, mobile devices, credit cards, online invoices, medical records, and social media have recorded an enormous amount of long-term, interactive, and large-scale data on human interactions. CSS is based on the collection and analysis of big data and the use of digitalization tools and methods such as social computing, social modeling, social simulation, network analysis, online experiments, artificial intelligence to research human behaviors, collective interactions, and complex organizations (Watts 2013). Only computational social science can provide us with the unprecedented ability to analyze the breadth and depth of vast amounts of data, thus affording us a new approach to understanding individual behaviors, group interactions, social structures, and societal transformations.

Scholars have formulated a variety of conceptualizations of CSS. One version argues that there are two fundamental components in CSS: substantive and instrumental (Cioff-Revilla 2010). The substantive, or theoretical, dimension entails complex systems and theories of computer programming. The instrumental dimension includes tools for data processing, mining, and analysis, such as automatic information retrieval, social network analysis, socio-GIS, complex modeling, and computation simulation.

Another conceptualization postulates that CSS has four important characteristics. First, it uses data from "natural" samples that document actual human behaviors (unlike the more artificial data collected from experiments and surveys). Second, the data are big and complex. Third, patterns of individual behavior and social structure

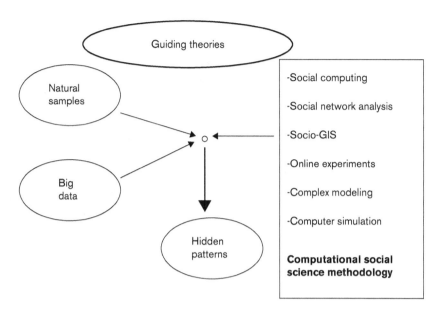

FIGURE 1.5
Computational Social Science.

are extracted using complex computations based on cloud computing with big data-bases and data mining approaches. And fourth, scientists use theoretical ideas to guide data mining of big data (Shah et al. 2015).

Others believe that CSS should be an interdisciplinary area at the confluence of domain knowledge, data management, data analysis, and transdisciplinary collaboration and coordination among scholars from different disciplinary training (Mason, Vaughan, and Wallach 2014). Social scientists provide insights on research background and questions, deciding on data sources and methods of collection, while statisticians and computer scientists develop appropriate mathematical models and data mining methods, as well as the necessary computational knowledge and skills to maintain smooth project progress.

Methods of computational social science consist primarily of social computing, online experiments, and computer simulations (Conte 2016). Social computing uses information processing technology and computational methods to conduct data mining and analysis on big data to reveal hidden patterns of collective and individual behaviors. Online experiments as a new research method use the internet as a laboratory to break free of the confines of conventional experimental approaches and use the online world as a natural setting for experiments that transcend time and space (Bond et al. 2012; Kramer, Guillory, and Hancock 2014). Computer simulations use mathematical modeling and simulation software to set and adjust program parameters to simulate social phenomena and detect patterns of social behaviors (Bankes 2002;

Gilbert et al. 2005; Epstein 2006). Both online experiments and computer simulations emphasize theory testing and development.

As figure 1.5 shows, in CSS researchers operate under the guidance of social scientific theories, apply computational social science methodology to data (usually big data) from natural samples, detect hidden patterns to enrich social science empirical evidence, and contribute to theory discovery.

OUTLINE OF THE BOOK

The book has six parts. Part I, comprising this chapter and chapter 2, explains the concepts and development of data mining and knowledge and the role it plays in social science research. Chapter 2 provides information on the process of scientific research as theory-driven confirmatory hypothesis testing. It also explains the impact of the new data mining and knowledge discovery approaches on this process.

Part II deals with data preprocessing. Chapter 3 elaborates issues such as privacy, security, data collection, data cleaning, missing data, and data transformation. Chapter 4 provides information on data visualization that includes graphic summaries of single, bivariate, and complex data.

Part III focuses on model assessment. Chapter 5 explains important methods and measures of model selection and model assessment, such as cross-validation and bootstrapping. It provides justifications as well as ways to use these methods to evaluate models. This chapter is more challenging than the previous chapters. Because the content is difficult for the average undergraduate student, I recommend that instructors selectively introduce sections of this chapter to their students. Later chapters on specific approaches also introduce some of these model assessment approaches. It may be most effective to introduce these specific methods of model assessment after students acquire knowledge of these data mining techniques.

Part IV is devoted to the methods of unsupervised learning: clustering and association. Chapter 6 explains the different types of cluster analysis, similarity measures, hierarchical clustering, and cluster validity. Chapter 7 concentrates on the topic of associations, including association rules, the usefulness of association rules, and the application of association rules in social research.

Part V continues with the topic of machine learning: supervised learning that includes generalized regression, classification and decision trees, and neural networks. Chapter 8 focuses on models of parameter learning that include linear regression and logistic regression. Chapter 9 covers inductive machine learning, decision trees, and types of algorithms in classification and decision trees. Chapter 10 focuses on neural networks, including the structure of neural networks, learning rules, and the advantages and disadvantages of neural networks.

Part VI ends the book with mining of text data and network data. Chapter 11 focuses on text mining and elaborates the topics of web mining, web crawling and scraping;

web mining of content, structure, and usage; and text mining topics including bag of words, N-grams, and topic models. Chapter 12 elaborates the network/link analysis that uses social network analysis, with various measures of network cohesion, and modes of centrality and prestige in social networks.

Chapters 10 through 12 tackle cutting-edge topics that are emerging as important techniques drawn from a variety of fields to address novel questions. As a result, the materials in these chapters are more cursory than those in others. These approaches—neural networks, network analysis, and text mining—are very broad and involve more advanced methods, so a fuller treatment cannot be provided here. These chapters thus serve as an introductory text for interested students and scholars. I provide a recommended reading list for those who are interested in pursuing these approaches further.

TARGET AUDIENCE AND GUIDE FOR INSTRUCTIONAL USE

The target audience of this book includes a wide range of people with varying backgrounds and readiness: faculty wishing to update or sharpen their skills, graduate students, select undergraduates, and applied data analysts in the nonprofit and corporate sectors. Each group can tailor the content to its individual needs and requirements.

This book is suitable for a variety of courses. It can serve as a textbook for an upper division social science methods course, as an introductory-level textbook for graduate students, as a companion to a traditional statistics textbook in data management or regression modeling, as an ancillary to a more in-depth statistics textbook that would overlap with material presented in chapters 4 through 8, and as a primer for faculty and researchers interested in advanced statistical methods.

Given these various purposes and audiences, below is a guide recommending different teaching plans targeted at different audiences in different courses.

1. An upper division undergraduate course on data mining: chapters 1–8.
2. A graduate course on knowledge discovery: chapters 1–12.
3. A course on machine learning: chapters 5–9.
4. A course on data management: chapters 1–4.
5. Supplementary reading for an undergraduate research methods course: chapters 1–4.
6. Supplementary reading for a graduate statistics course on new and modern methods in data science: chapters 10–12.

Instructors can also tailor the contents to the specific campus or training demands using some combination of chapters, as follows:

- Overview: chapters 1 and 2;
- Data and visualization: chapters 3 and 4;

- Model assessment: chapter 5;
- Unsupervised learning: chapters 6 and 7;
- Supervised learning: chapters 8–10; and
- Advanced approaches in neural networks, social networks, and text mining: chapters 10–12.

SUMMARY

The rapid growth of big data has provided us with new opportunities and challenges in knowledge discovery. To take advantages of these opportunities and resolve these challenges, data analytical skills are in high demand.

Big data has also revolutionized scientific research with the emergence of many inter- and multidisciplinary fields. Computational social science, bioinformatics, the Sloan Digital Sky Survey in astronomy, AlphaGo in artificial intelligence, and the Google Books corpus in language and culture studies have all brought structural transformations in these scientific research communities.

Data mining projects require both knowledge in handling data (i.e., data processing, database technology, statistical and computational algorithms) and domain expertise to detect and discover valid and meaningful knowledge and theory. It is thus important to train students and scholars who possess expertise in fields such as psychology, economics, sociology, political science, and linguistics to acquire data mining skills to work alongside computer scientists and statisticians.

Big data is characterized by big volume, high velocity, and big variety of information. It also entails technologies and analytical methods to transform information into insights that possess economic value and have societal impacts.

Knowledge discovery in database (KDD) is the nontrivial process of identifying valid, novel, potentially useful, and ultimately understandable patterns in data. It consists of nine steps that begin with the development and understanding of the application domain and end with action on the knowledge discovered. The KDD process searches for patterns of interest in a particular representational form or a set of these representations.

Data mining has both a narrow definition and a broad definition. Data mining can be narrowly defined as one step in the KDD process that applies data analysis and discovery algorithms to produce patterns or models on the data. Data mining techniques come from statistics, artificial intelligence, and database systems.

A broader definition of data mining conceptualizes it as similar to the entire process of KDD, which involves use of huge databases, computational techniques, automatic or semiautomatic searches, and extraction of knowledge. The extracted information from data are of two types: descriptions of relationships and patterns in data and predictive estimates of future outcomes based on existing data.

Computational social science is a new interdisciplinary area of research at the confluence of information technology, big data, social computing, and social sciences. It is guided by social science theories, applies computational social science methodology to data that is usually big and from natural samples, detects hidden patterns to enrich social science empirical evidence, and contributes to theory discovery and development.

PRACTICE PROBLEMS

1. Discuss what new opportunities have emerged in your field of research resulting from big data. What types of new research are made possible by this transformation? Can you identify potentially uncharted topics of research in your field using big data?

2. In addition to being big, what are the important features of data in the concept of big data? Does the concept of big data only entail data? If not, what else is included?

3. What is knowledge discovery in database? What are the steps involved in KDD?

4. What is data mining when it is narrowly defined? What are the three foundations of a narrow definition of data mining?

5. What is data mining broadly defined? What are the components in data mining? How do you characterize information extracted from data?

6. What is computational social science? Read Hanna Wallach's 2018 article, "Computational Social Science ≠ Computer Science + Social Data" (https://cacm.acm.org/magazines/2018/3/225484-computational-social-science-computer-science-social-data/fulltext), and discuss why CSS is more than the sum of computer science and social data. What do social scientists bring to this new interdisciplinary area?

REFERENCES

Bankes, Steven C. 2002. "Agent-Based Modeling: Revolution?" *Proceedings of the National Academy of Science of the United States of America* 99 (S3): 7199–7200.

Bond, Robert M., Christopher J. Fariss, Jason J. Jones, Adam D. I. Kramer, Cameron Marlow, Jaime E. Settle, and James H. Fowler. 2012. "A 61-Million-Person Experiment in Social Influence and Political Mobilization." *Nature* 489: 295–98.

Brown, Meta S. 2018. "Data Mining Concepts That Business People Should Know." *Forbes,* July 31. https://www.forbes.com/sites/metabrown/2018/07/31/basics-of-data-mining-that-business-people-should-know/#74504e89515f.

Cioff-Rivilla, Claudio. 2010. "Computational Social Science." *Wiley Interdisciplinary Reviews: Computational Statistics* 2 (3): 259–71.

Conte, Rosaria. 2016. "Computational Social and Behavioral Science." In *New Frontiers in the Study of Social Phenomena,* ed F. Cecconi. New York: Springer.

Dumbill, Edd. 2013. "A Revolution That Will Transform How We Live, Work, and Think: An Interview with the Author of Big Data." *Big Data* 1 (2): 73–77. https://doi.org/10.1089/big.2013.0016.

Economist. 2017. "The World's Most Valuable Resource Is No Longer Oil, but Data." *Economist,* May 6. https://www.economist.com/leaders/2017/05/06/the-worlds-most-valuable-resource-is-no-longer-oil-but-data.

Epstein, Joshua M. 2006. "Remarks on the Foundations of Agent-Based Generative Social Science." In *Handbook of Computational Economics,* vol. 2, 1585–1604. New York: Elsevier. https://www.sciencedirect.com/handbook/handbook-of-computational-economics/vol/2/suppl/C.

Fayyad, Usama, Gregory Piatesky-Shapiro, and Padhraic Smyth. 1996. "Knowledge Discovery and Data Minig: Towards a Unifying Framework." In *Proceedings of the Second International Conference on Knowledge Discovery and Data Mining*, ed. E. Simoudis, J. Han, and U. Fayyad, 82–88. https://www.aaai.org/Papers/KDD/1996/KDD96-014.pdf.

Forbes. 2015. "Data Mining Global News for Economic Uncertainty." *Forbes*, December 14.

Furnas, Alexander. 2012. "Everything You Wanted to Know about Data Mining but Were Afraid to Ask." *Atlantic*, April 3. https://www.theatlantic.com/technology/archive/2012/04/everything-you-wanted-to-know-about-data-mining-but-were-afraid-to-ask/255388/.

Gilbert, Nigel, Matthijs den Besten, Akos Bontovics, Bart G. W. Craenen, Federico Divina, A. E. Eiben, Robert Griffioen, Gyorgy Hévízi, Andras Lõrincz, Ben Paechter, Stephan Schuster, Martijn C. Schut, Christian Tzolov, Paul Vogt, and Lu Yang. 2006. "Emerging Artificial Societies through Learning." *Journal of Artificial Societies & Social Simulation* 9 (2): 9. http://jasss.soc.surrey.ac.uk/9/2/9.html.

Gorunescu, Florin. 2011. *Data Mining: Concepts, Models and Techniques*. New York: Springer.

Harris, Richard. 2016. "Big Data Coming in Faster than Biomedical Researchers Can Process It." National Public Radio, November 28. http://www.npr.org/sections/health-shots/2016/11/28/503035862/big-data-coming-in-faster-than-biomedical-researchers-can-process-it.

Kramer, Adam, D. I., Jamie E. Guillory, and Jeffrey T. Hancock. 2014. "Experimental Evidence Massive-Scale Emotional Contagion through Social Networks." *Proceedings of the National Academy of Sciences* 111 (24): 8788–90.

Laney, Douglas. 2001. "3-D Data Management: Controlling Data Volume, Velocity and Variety." *META Group Research Note*, 6. https://www.scribd.com/document/362987683/3D-Data-Management-Controlling-Data-Volume-Velocity-and-Variety.

Larose, Daniel T., and Chantal D. Larose. 2016. *Data Mining and Predictive Analytics*. New York: Wiley.

Lazer, David, Alex Pentland, Lada Adamic, Sinan Aral, Albert-László Barabási, Devon Brewer, Nicholas Christakis, Noshir Contractor, James Fowler, Myron Gutmann, Tony Jebara, Gary King, Michael Macy, Deb Roy, and Marshall Van Alstyne. 2009. "Computational Social Science." *Science* 323 (5915): 721–23.

Lohr, Steve. 2012. *New York Times*, February 11. https://www.nytimes.com/2012/02/12/sunday-review/big-datas-impact-in-the-world.html.

Mason, Winter, Jennifer Wortman Vaughan, and Hanna Wallach. 2014. "Computational Social Science and Social Computing." *Machine Learning* 95 (3): 257–60.

Manyika, J., M. Chui, B. Brown, et al. 2011. "Big Data: The Next Frontier for Innovation, Competition, and Productivity." McKinsey Global Institute. https://www.mckinsey.com/~/media/McKinsey/Business%20Functions/McKinsey%20Digital/Our%20Insights/Big%20data%20The%20next%20frontier%20for%20innovation/MGI_big_data_exec_summary.ashx.

Mauro, Andrea De, Marco Greco, and Michele Grimaldi. 2016. "A Formal Definition of Big Data Based on Its Essential Features." *Library Review* 65 (3): 122–35. DOI:10.1108/LR-06-2015-0061.

Mayer-Schönberger, Viktor, and Kenneth Cukier. 2013. *Big Data: A Revolution That Will Transform How We Live, Work, and Think*. London: John Murray.

Michel, Jean-Baptiste, Yuan Kui Shen, Aviva Presser Aiden, Adain Veres, Matthew K. Gray, Google Books Team, Joseph P. Pickett, Dale Hoiberg, Dan Clancy, Peter Norvig, Jon Orwant, Steven Pinker, Martin A Nowak, and Erez Lieberman Aiden. 2011. "Quantitative Analysis of Culture using Millions of Digitized Books." *Science* 331: 176.

Miller, Steven, and Debbie Hughes. 2017. "The Quant Crunch: How the Demand for Data Science Skills Is Distributing the Job Market." Burning Glass Technologies, Business-Higher Education Forum, and IBM. https://www-01.ibm.com/common/ssi/cgi-bin/ssialias?htmlfid=IML14576USEN&.

Seife, Charles. 2015. "Big Data: The Revolution Is Digitized." *Nature* 518: 480–81.

Shah, Nihar B., Sivaraman Balakrishnan, Adityanand Guntuboyina, and Martin J. Wainwright. 2017. "Stochastically Transitive Models for Pairwise Comparisons: Statistical and Computational Issues." *IEEE Transactions on Information Theory* 63 (2): 934–59.

Stein, Joel. 2011. "Data Mining: How Companies Now Know Everything about You." *Time,* March 10. http://content.time.com/time/magazine/article/0,9171,2058205,00.html.

Wallach, Hanna. 2018. "Computational Social Science ≠ Computer Science + Social Data." *Communications of the ACM* 61 (3): 42–44.

Watts, Duncan J. 2013. "Computational Social Science: Exciting Progress and Future Directions." *Bridge on Frontiers of Engineering* 43 (4): 5–10.

Chapter 2

NEW CONTRIBUTIONS AND CHALLENGES

K NOWLEDGE DISCOVERY AND DATA MINING bring new opportunities and challenges. They have the potential to revolutionize scientific research as they differ from existing conventional statistical approaches in many ways. This chapter discusses two issues in scientific research and the transformation in social science research brought about by knowledge discovery and data mining: the relationship between theory and data and logical causality versus probability causality. It also considers the challenges arising from these new approaches.

Data mining is not data-driven research. It is a method that combines inductive and deductive processes of knowledge discovery. It does not replace conventional statistical methods, but it can complement them in two ways. First, it provides a new approach and perspective for theory development. Second, it has the potential to provide new solutions to the challenges of conventional methods in uncovering causality.

Data mining provides new technology for knowledge discovery. Before data mining technologies were available, it was difficult for researchers to detect hidden yet meaningful patterns in big data. Data mining provides us with a series of new technologies to assist us in revealing previously hidden patterns, which have the potential to help us innovate and develop new theories, thus promoting revolutionary influences on new theory development in many disciplines. This is the most attractive feature of data mining.

Data mining uses automatic and semiautomatic approaches to identify best-fitting models with the strongest predictive power. Conventional statistical models are often based on manual searches and adjustments of models, which can be time-consuming. Data mining has developed a number of tools to automate the process of searching, computing, and estimating a large number and variety of mathematical and computational models. This can substantially reduce the time and human resources required for the discovery of new knowledge.

Data mining tends to produce models with strong predictive accuracy and with a complex treatment of causal heterogeneity, compared to traditional statistical models. Data mining employs both inductive and deductive approaches, uses and processes diverse data, and emphasizes interactive and heterogeneous causes.

Knowledge discovery and data mining are a comprehensive multidisciplinary area of collaborative research that includes statistics, computer science, machine learning, artificial intelligence, database technology, and pattern recognition. Social scientists, latecomers to this new scientific movement, are starting to use data mining in their research and teaching. Given the new opportunities provided by these new research approaches, social scientists will benefit from teamwork and collaboration across disciplines.

In summary, data mining, as a new frontier of quantitative research, is not led by data or exploratory analysis. It requires strong and deep domain knowledge that is informed by substantive theory. Data scientists without knowledge of social science theories will fall short of accomplishing successful data mining projects because data mining combines both inductive and deductive processes. Data mining is a dialectic process that starts from conceptualizing the latent social patterns discovered from data, developing a new theory or amending the existing theory, using new data, and testing new ideas. This cycle of research can sometimes be accomplished in a single research project. Sometimes the process unfolds separately in different projects or by different researchers, with some using inductive approaches and others using deductive methods. At other times, this process requires a series of projects. Data mining is not a research process dominated by data. It is guided by theories and domain experts with rich knowledge.

THE RELATIONSHIP BETWEEN THEORY AND DATA

Knowledge discovery and data mining is a dialectic research process that combines both deductive and inductive research. It is often mistakenly perceived as "data driven" or exploratory research, and this misconception has made the social science

Galilean approach of scientific methodology

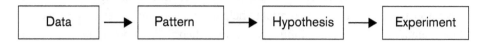

Theory-driven confirmatory hypothesis test

FIGURE 2.1
Two Scientific Methodologies.

research community hesitant in adopting the approach, thus hindering advancements in theory and methods.

THEORY-DRIVEN CONFIRMATORY HYPOTHESES TESTING

The earliest scientific research began with data collection. According to Aristotle's and Bacon's approach to the scientific method, the research process involves collecting data, searching for patterns, and hypothesizing. Later, Galileo (1564–1642) advocated extending this approach to include experiments to test hypotheses, as shown in figure 2.1. The scientific community widely practiced the Galilean approach for three hundred years, until the end of the nineteenth century (Bozdogan 2003).

In the twentieth century, the scientific research community experienced an important shift away from the Galilean method to a theory-driven approach. This new approach advocated that scientists put forth a theory first, then collect experimental data, and then analyze the data to prove or refute that theory. This new approach has been called *theory-driven confirmatory hypothesis testing* (see fig. 2.1).

This confirmatory science has since become an important step in what are often called the seven stages of research. As shown in figure 2.2, these stages are interlinked to form a cycle or loop of scientific research, as follows:

1. Define the research question by understanding the problem thoroughly and translate the questions into meaningful terms according to a theoretical perspective.
2. Carry out a literature review to summarize the pertinent theories and ideas.
3. Formulate specific, concrete, and testable hypotheses that are derived from theories. The logical or empirical consequences of these hypotheses are then subjected to empirical tests.
4. Design research to collect relevant data in an efficient and appropriate way.

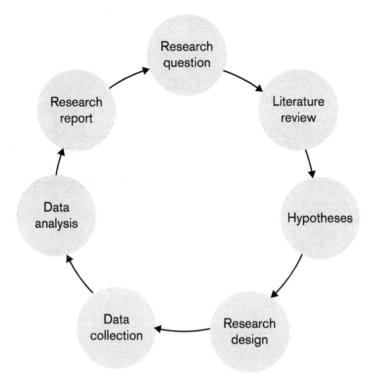

FIGURE 2.2
The Research Process as a Research Loop.

5. Engage in data collection using a variety of approaches, including face-to-face interviews, phone interviews, observation, online or mailed surveys, automatic data documentation, and archival documents.
6. Conduct data analysis, which includes a series of related operations of data cleaning, data coding, editing, manipulation, tabulation, and modeling.
7. Interpret the results and distribute research reports to both the scientific community and the general public. These research reports inspire new research questions and thus initiate another round of research.

THE RELATIONSHIP BETWEEN THEORY AND RESEARCH:
DEDUCTIVE VERSUS INDUCTIVE RESEARCH

The reciprocal relationship between theory and research can be characterized as deductive and inductive research approaches. While the relationship between theory and research differs between the two approaches, they also complement each other. A deductive approach is more fixed and concerned with testing hypotheses, while inductive research is more open-ended and exploratory. Most social research involves both inductive and deductive processes at some point in a given project, and the two processes are often combined to form a cycle from theory to data and back to theory.

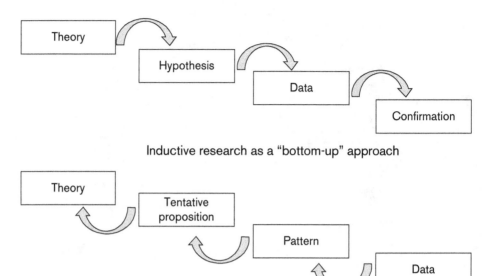

FIGURE 2.3
Deductive and Inductive Research.

The deductive approach is sometimes called a top-down approach in which researchers work from the general theory to the specific data, as illustrated in figure 2.3. Researchers who use a deductive approach start with a theory about their topic of interest. They then derive specific testable hypotheses. They next gather data or observations to test the hypotheses that will lead to confirmation or refutation of the original theory that motivated the entire project.

The inductive approach to research is called a bottom-up approach in which researchers start with specific observations and move to broader generalizations and theories. In inductive research, as illustrated in figure 2.3, researchers begin with collecting data and gathering specific observations and measures. Researchers then look for patterns in the data, formulate tentative hypotheses that could explain these patterns, and finally develop general conclusion or theories.

The use of data mining in research does *not* mean that we are reverting to the Galilean method, in which data lead the theory. Although data mining is sometimes called exploratory research, it would be more appropriate to consider it a combination of both inductive and deductive methods, similar to grounded theory (Holton and Walsh 2017). Grounded theory is a general method that uses systematic research to generate systematic theory. It employs a set of rigorous research procedures on matters of data collection and analysis to develop conceptual categories. Although qualitative researchers use this approach more often, it is not exclusively a qualitative method.

The method can be applied to numerical data, conversations, videos, images, texts, observations, spoken words, and so on. Grounded theory is a research tool that enables researchers to seek out and conceptualize the latent social patterns and structures in a specific research field through the process of constant comparison. This process encompasses both inductive and deductive dimensions of research. Researchers first use an inductive approach to generate substantive patterns from the data. From this newly developed theory, they design new research, collect data, analyze data, and test the theory. This latter stage comprises the deductive phase of the grounded theory process.

Both inductive and deductive approaches can be used in a single project. For example, when researchers use data from open-ended questions or from online posts, they must code and recode a large amount of text data (tens or hundreds of thousands or millions of entries) and summarize them according to themes or topics. One approach is to randomly sample a small portion from this large data set, using an inductive method of unsupervised learning to automatically identify themes or groups that emerge from the data. They then use supervised learning to derive decision rules to learn how these differentiations are determined. They then use theories and empirical knowledge from the field to modify these decision rules and recode some of the cases if needed. Last, they apply these revised decision rules in a deductive manner to code the remaining cases, which could number in the tens of thousands or millions. This way, the data inform research about meaningful and valid patterns while the researcher provides substantive guidance in formulating decision rules to identify hidden patterns in the data. This process incorporates both inductive and deductive research.

DIALECTIC RELATIONSHIP BETWEEN THEORY AND DATA IN KNOWLEDGE DISCOVERY AND DATA MINING

Similar to the grounded theory method, the scientific field of data mining has also developed and matured by carefully trying to guard against the pitfalls of data-driven approaches. Efforts to establish the knowledge discovery process (KDP) model were initiated in academia in the mid-1990s when the data mining field was taking shape. Researchers defined rigorous procedures to guide users of data mining tools in knowledge discovery. The two most prominent process models were developed in 1996 (Fayyad, Piatesky-Shapiro, and Smyth 1996) and 1998 (Anand and Büchner 1998), respectively. The 1996 KDP model developed by Fayyad and colleagues consists of nine steps:

- Understanding domain knowledge: This involves reviewing the literature and learning relevant prior knowledge. Researchers also formulate the goals of discovered knowledge. Since the process is iterative, there may be revision and fine-tuning of this step as the process proceeds.

- Selecting a data set: Researchers select a subset of variables and data points that will be used to perform data mining or knowledge discovery tasks. This often involves using existing data to select a desired subset.
- Data preprocessing: Researchers remove outliers, deal with missing values and data imputation, and conduct data transformation or standardization if needed.
- Data reduction: Researchers find useful composite measures or latent constructs by applying dimension reduction and transformation methods.
- Data mining method: Researchers choose a particular data mining method, such as classification, regression, or clustering.
- Data mining algorithm: Researchers select methods to discover patterns in the data and decide which models and parameters may be appropriate.
- Data mining: Researchers generate patterns using a particular data mining approach, such as classification rules, decision trees, regression models, or trends.
- Interpreting patterns: Researchers create visualizations of the discovered patterns and extracted models.
- Consolidating discovered knowledge: Researchers incorporate the discovered knowledge into the current knowledge base, documenting and reporting the knowledge to the scientific community. This may involve checking and resolving conflicts with existing knowledge or theories.

This process is iterative, and a number of loops between any two steps are usually executed. Later KDP models have all been built based on this initial model. For example, a six-step model was developed later to fit with academic research (Cios et al. 2007):

1. Understanding the problem domain: The research problem is defined and the project goals are identified. Important knowledge and terminology of the subject areas are learned. Problems are translated into data mining objectives, and data mining tools are selected.
2. Understanding the data: The researchers collect data and decide which data will be used. Again, domain knowledge is needed to guide these activities. Researchers check data for completeness and redundancy and so on.
3. Preparing the data: This step involves sampling, running correlation and significance tests, and data cleaning. It also includes data processing by using feature selection and extraction algorithms to reduce dimensionality, derive new attributes by discretization, and summarize data.

4. Data mining: Researchers use various data mining methods to derive knowledge from processed data.
5. Evaluation of the discovered knowledge: Evaluation includes understanding the results, checking whether the discovered knowledge is novel and interesting, interpreting the results by domain experts, and checking the impact of the discovered knowledge. Only approved models are retained, and the entire process is revisited to identify which alternative actions could have been taken to improve the results.
6. Use of the discovered knowledge: This final step consists of planning where and how to use the discovered knowledge, including extending it to other domains. Implementation of the discovered knowledge is monitored and documented. The discovered knowledge is deployed.

The Cios model describes these multiple steps in knowledge discovery and data mining. It also emphasizes the iterative aspects of the process based on the experience of users. Figure 2.4 displays the components and interconnections among them. It highlights the following backtracking steps:

1. Understanding the data → understanding the problem domain: Additional domain knowledge is needed to better understand the data.
2. Preparation of the data → understanding of the data: Additional information about the data is needed in order to guide the choice of specific data processing algorithms.
3. Data mining → understanding of the problem: When the selected data mining methods generate unsatisfactory results, the project's goals need to be modified.
4. Data mining → understanding of data: When the data are poorly understood and result in incorrect selection of a data mining method and subsequent failure, there is a need to return to step 1, understanding the data.
5. Data mining → preparation of data: When a specific data mining method requires a specific data preparation, there is a need to return to the previous step and organize and prepare the data accordingly.
6. Evaluation of the discovered knowledge → understanding of the problem: When the discovered knowledge is invalid due to incorrect understandings or interpretations or incorrect design or understandings of problem restrictions, requirements, or goals, the entire KD process must be repeated.
7. Evaluation of the discovered knowledge → data mining: When the discovered knowledge is not novel, interesting, or useful, the solution is to choose a different data mining tool and repeat the data mining step.

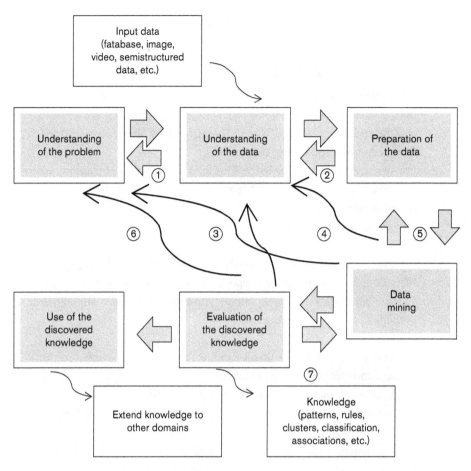

FIGURE 2.4
The Knowledge Discovery Process Model.

CHALLENGES IN CAUSALITY

The knowledge discovery and data mining approach sheds new light on causality. A fundamental task in scientific inquiry is to identify cause and effect. Causal relations can be characterized as counterfactual relations, for example, "X occurred and Y occurred and in the circumstance Y would not have occurred if X had not" (Mackie 1974). When causal relations are described as counterfactual relations, a cause is both necessary and sufficient in the production of its effect (Beauchamp 1974; Bunge 1979; Mackie 1974). This "sufficient in the circumstances" in the counterfactual sense means that "if Y had not been going to occur, X would not have occurred" (Mackie 1974).

TWO STRUCTURES OF CAUSES: CONJUNCTIVE PLURALITY
AND DISJUNCTIVE PLURALITY

Almost all causes consist of multiple factors that are jointly necessary and sufficient. This plurality of causes has two structures: conjunctive plurality of causes and

Conjunctive plurality of causes

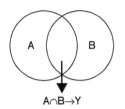

Disjunctive plurality of causes

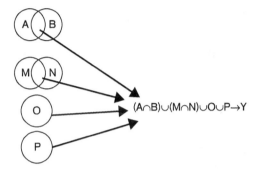

FIGURE 2.5
Conjunctive and Disjunctive Plurality of Causes.

disjunctive plurality of causes (Bunge 1979). The first, conjunctive plurality of causes, occurs when various factors, symbolized by A and B, must be present jointly to produce an effect Y, as shown in figure 2.5. Thus, Y occurs whenever some conjunction of A and B (symbolized as A∩B) occurs, but Y does not occur when only A or B occurs. For example, a short circuit (A) that occurs close to combustible materials (B) form jointly necessary and sufficient conditions for a house fire (Y), which can be expressed as A∩B→Y. Similarly, a burning candle (M) can ignite combustibles (N), and the joint presence of candle and combustibles will cause a house fire, thus expressed as M∩N→Y.

The second, disjunctive plurality of causes, is often identified as genuine "multiple causation" or "independent causes." Disjunctive plurality of causes occurs when the effect is produced by each of several factors alone, and each of these factors is an independent cause such that occurrence of two or more factors does not alter the effect (Bunge 1979; Mackie 1965, 1974; Skyrms 1980). For example, there are multiple causes of house fires, and each of these causes can independently produce a house fire. These causes may include a short circuit and presence of combustibles (A∩B), or a burning candle with combustibles (M∩N), or arson (O), or an uncontained grease fire (P), or other causes such as lighting. This is expressed as P[y|(A∩B)∪(M∩N)∪O∪P∪...] = 1, whereby all of these multiple independent causes jointly account for all the house fires in the field, thus a probability of 1 for Y (house fire) to occur. The bottom graph in figure 2.5 displays disjunctive plurality of causes.

The combination of conjunctive and disjunctive plurality of causes shows that causes are multiple factors that are jointly necessary and sufficient (Bunge 1979). This approach of identifying causes as jointly necessary and sufficient conditions is quite common among historical sociologists, who often identify joint causes. For instance, in her highly influential and seminal book on the Chinese, French, and Russian Revolutions, Theda Skocpol proposed a deterministic theory of revolution. Her theory included two jointly sufficient causes that, when satisfied, guarantee the outcome of revolutions (Skocpol 1979). She made a strong prediction that whenever these two conditions of "crisis of state" (A) and "pattern of class dominance" (B) were jointly present, they would lead to revolution. According to her, a "crisis of state" is often provoked by international factors, such as increasing economic or security competition from abroad, and "patterns of class dominance" determine which group will rise up to exploit the revolutionary situation. This can be expressed as $P[Y|A \cap B] = 1$ such that whenever A and B are both present, revolution Y will occur, so A and B are jointly necessary and sufficient conditions for revolution.

SINGLE CAUSES IN SOCIAL SCIENCE RESEARCH

Although causes are almost always a combination of conjunctive and disjunctive plurality of causes, conventional statistical approaches are more willing to identify a single cause, even though single causes rarely if ever produce an effect. Social scientists do so for two reasons. First, we are more willing to say that a *single* event, particularly one that is intrusive or disruptive, caused the effect than a standing condition. This is because what is viewed as abnormal or wrong is more likely to arouse people's causal interest. Things that are part of the ongoing concern or standing situation that are perceived as normal, proper, or right are often not seen as part of the causal package. For example, although a spark and combustible materials are jointly necessary and sufficient conditions for a fire, we are more likely to say that a spark rather than flammable material is the cause of a fire.

Second, the determination of causal relevance depends critically on context because the causal judgment reflects the degree to which a variable is different from "a background" (Einhorn and Hogarth 1986). Thus, the research focus determines the breadth of the causal field, and the number and salience of alternative causes are either included or eliminated as a result of this determination. For example, when the police investigate a house fire, they tend to focus on the source of the spark (candle, short circuit, arson, etc.) that ignited the fire. However, if material scientists searching for fire-retardant materials are looking into a house fire in a series of experiments with different materials, they are more likely to see the surrounding materials as a source of the house fire because the flammable ones lead to combustion. For another example, if researchers of instructional methods are told that a large number of students have failed a math class, they tend to focus on the instructional approach as responsible for these failures. However, if sociologists are analyzing these results, they tend to view the school's and the students' disadvantageous socioeconomic status and limited social resources as the causes of poor academic performance.

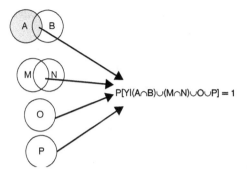

FIGURE 2.6
A as an INUS Condition.

A single predictor that we often identify and test in statistical analyses in the social sciences is neither a necessary nor a sufficient condition for the effect. Rather, a single predictor that has often been erroneously labeled as a "cause" is an INUS condition: "an Insufficient but Nonredundant part of an Unnecessary but Sufficient condition" (Mackie 1974). This is demonstrated in figure 2.6. For example, in the situation of a house fire whereby $P[y|(A \cap B) \cup (M \cap N) \cup O \cup P \ldots] = 1$, a conventional statistical model estimates a single cause, A (short circuit), as the predictor of the house fire. Since both A and B need to be present simultaneously for Y to occur (A and B are joint sufficient conditions) and A alone is not a sufficient condition for Y, conventional statistical models are derived from probabilistic theories of causality. Researchers use statistical models to predict the probability of Y occurring when A is present in the form of the main effect of A after the effects of other variables are controlled for.

The data mining approach moves us closer to the logical causes than the probabilistic models of causality that we currently use in conventional statistics. Conventional statistical models tend to analyze the average impact of explanatory variables on all the cases, largely ignoring causal heterogeneity when the same causes may generate differential outcomes to different groups with different combinations of other conditions. Data mining considers a larger number of joint and interactive causes. As result, the data mining approach substantially improves the predictive power of models over traditional single-cause models.

CAUSALITY IN KNOWLEDGE DISCOVERY AND DATA MINING

Data mining contributes to the discovery of causality in multiple ways. Although data mining will never replace confirmatory analysis of model building and is not contrary to this approach, it provides innovative ways of conceptualization that are conducive to theory development and knowledge discovery. Social science research using conventional statistical approaches tends to emphasize some specific causal mechanisms as a way to test one or few theories, while data mining is concerned with offering a thorough or complete account for the event under investigation. It is often the case that using one or two theories can only provide partial explanations for the outcomes and does not exhaust all the explanations. Thus, conventional statistical models emphasize a small number of explanations consisting of simple functional forms because these models are thought of as straightforward, parsimonious, elegant, and theoretically appealing. On the other hand, data mining is interested in providing a full account of the event or outcome of interest to the extent permitted by the data in order to provide maximum accuracy in prediction for the future. This approach does not shy away from a rich analysis of multiple, complicated, and nuanced explanations as they all contribute to the strong explanatory power of the resulting model.

As a result, knowledge discovery and data mining are different from conventional statistical approaches commonly used in the social sciences in multiple ways. Data mining emphasizes complex causal heterogeneity, whereas conventional social science research focuses on the simple main effects of interesting predictors. Data mining considers a variety of nonlinear and joint effects, whereas conventional approaches stress linear main effects. Data mining tends to estimate complex and elaborate models, whereas conventional statistical models seek parsimonious (simple and effective) models. Data mining aims at maximizing a model's predictive power, whereas conventional approaches highlight the estimation of predictor coefficients. Data mining provides methods capable of analyzing non-numerical data such as text, images, and voice; this type of analysis used to fall outside the scope of conventional statistical analysis and belonged to the realm of qualitative methods. These comparisons are meant to inform researchers of the pros and cons of these approaches. They do not intend to project a judgment that one method is superior over the other.

To establish a causal relationship, domain experts should be able to elaborate on the causal mechanism based on the associations between variables discovered from data. Both conventional statistical approaches and data mining play the same role in the process of scientific research: they provide information on correlations among variables or associations among entities. In addition, data mining can efficiently filter complex and multiple correlations among variables to help us identify complexity, interactions, and heterogeneity in the causal relationship. Data mining does not challenge the conventional model-building approach. Rather, it plays an important complementary role in improving model goodness of fit and enriching our discovery.

COMPLEX CAUSAL HETEROGENEITY

Seldom do conventional statistical models consider conjuncture (joint effects among two or more variables) or causal heterogeneity. Although it is possible to estimate the joint effects of several variables by including interaction terms between two or more predictors (Aiken and West 1991; Berry, Golder, and Milton 2012; Brambor, Clark, and Golder 2006; Jaccard and Turrisi 2003), a majority of studies in sociology estimate only the main effects of explanatory variables (e.g., Elwert and Winship 2010). Social science research thus generally ignores effect heterogeneity and estimates only main effects as an approximation of the average effects. To do so, it also avoids the pitfall of computational complexity in estimating large numbers of multiple-way interaction terms. With m explanatory variables, a model will generate $C_m^p = \frac{m!}{p!\,(m-p)!}$ interactions, with p = p-way interaction. For example, a model with 10 explanatory variables has 45 two-way interactions, 120 three-way interactions, 210 four-way interactions, and 252 five-way interactions! There are also six-, seven-, eight-, nine-, and ten-way interactions. Because it is time-consuming to inspect each of these interaction effects in conventional statistical models, it is no wonder that these effects are largely ignored.

Knowledge discovery and data mining techniques have automated the process of searching and evaluating joint and heterogeneous causes. New data mining techniques can swiftly generate and estimate thousands of interactions and combinations among predictors to improve the prediction of outcome variable. One approach, association rule mining, is very good at identifying associations among combinations of attributes. Association rules are generated in the form of multivariate associations. They provide novel or unexpected combinations of prior conditions that co-occur before the outcomes or the target variables. Discovering such combinations directs researchers to investigate interesting joint effects among explanatory variables (see chap. 7). Another method, decision tree programs such as Chi-squared Automatic Interaction Detection (CHAID) (Magidson 1993) and Classification and Regression Tree (CART), apply multivariate methods with a classification capacity and automatically consider large numbers of combined effects among predictors to improve the prediction models (see chap. 9). A third approach, neural networks, also automatically generate functions equivalent to interactions or combined effects among predictors within their algorithms to substantially increase the predictive power of their models (see chap. 12).

Data mining also provides the tools of supervised and unsupervised learning to classify the data and detect causal heterogeneity such that different predictor variables are applied to different sub-populations. For example, an unsupervised learning approach revealed four primary waves of Mexican immigrants, some of which had never before been detected (Garip 2017). These groups include a male-dominated migration in the earliest period, young men from more well-off families during the 1980s, women joining families in the United States in the late 1980s and 1990s, and a generation of more educated, urban migrants in the late 1990s and early 2000s. For each of these waves of immigration, different pulling and pushing factors are involved in these migrants' actions. These diverse groups and the different theories that account for their immigration shed light on causal heterogeneity in the Mexican immigration process. These findings resolve some of the ongoing theoretical debates over whether instead of being universal, theories should be applied selectively to different population segments at different historical times. It is no wonder that earlier research that tested migration theories on all Mexican immigrants without recognizing their causal heterogeneity was destined to produce confusing evidence. Often, theories are bound by the type of population, the larger context, and the historical period.

NONLINEAR AND JOINT EFFECTS

In conventional statistical models, interval variables are used in generalized linear models as linear functions, with the exception of only a few well-known variables that function curvilinearly, such as age (quadratic), GDP (ln), and income (ln). For most continuous variables, the default function is linear unless the researcher has strong theoretical or empirical evidence to believe otherwise. This is the case for several reasons. First, it is rather cumbersome to present and explain this nonlinear pattern resulting from converting a variable on a continuous interval scale into a series of dummy variables. As a result, researchers using conventional statistical models usually choose a simple linear effect over use of a series of variables, particularly when the variable is a control that is not theoretically interesting. Second, it takes time and effort to carefully evaluate each explanatory variable and its functional form with the outcome variables, especially when the number of explanatory variables is large. Researchers often choose not to engage in such an exhausting endeavor. And third, conventional statistics often use either a correlation or variable/covariance matrix to summarize an entire data set. The matrix representation assumes a linear relationship among the variables whereby one-unit increases of one variable are associated monotonically with changes in another variable. Although this gross simplification of data has simplified data storage and porting, it has serious implications for modeling. By ignoring nonlinear relationships among variables, one loses the ability to capture complex relationships among variables.

Data mining provides many automatic or semiautomatic tools to aid researchers' search for nonlinear relations and increase model prediction accuracy. Data mining procedures can automatically generate breakpoints for continuous independent variables in order to capture a nonlinear effect between the dependent and independent variables (see chap. 3). For example, SPSS (a standard statistical package) now provides automatic binning and discretization of variables that reflect nonlinear effects. Binning by predictive value involves partitioning the variable based on predictive values of a target variable. This is called optimal binning because it is optimal in predicting a particular outcome variable. CART also has a binning procedure, called optimal binning or entropy-based discretization, to handle nonlinear relations. These software programs choose the boundaries for each bin to differentiate the cases in each bin from the other bins in terms of their functions on the outcome variable (Witten, Frank, and Hall 2011). This helps to increase the prediction accuracy of each of the explanatory variables and thus the power of the entire model. In addition, data mining provides visualization tools that can view the relationship among variables from any angle with any rotation to detect nonlinear relations. Tools such simple graphs, scatterplots, 3D graphs, and other visualizations can be rotated and inspected from any angle. These visualization tools allow researchers to see how values of an outcome variable are affected jointly by changes in the value of other variables in a model.

MODEL COMPLEXITY AND COMPLETENESS TO
INCREASE MODEL PREDICTION

Conventional statistical analyses use the principle of parsimony to select models. A parsimonious model maximizes the amount of explained variance in the outcome variable with as few predictors as possible. As a result, this approach emphasizes the fit between model and data and the efficiency of models. Goodness-of-fit measures how well a model describes the relations in the data under examination. For example, for generalized additive mixed models using the classic Gaussian for the errors, we conduct a likelihood ratio test. When comparing two models, researchers use the Aikake Information Criterion (AIC) or the Bayesian Information Criterion (BIC) to compare the goodness-of-fit between two models (see chap. 5). When comparing nested models, researchers use likelihood ratio tests or a chi-squared or an F test, which controls whether the extra predictors really improve the model. The guiding principle is to have effective models with a small set of explanatory variables, with each contributing a substantial amount of the variance in the outcome variable.

Data mining is primarily interested in whether the model adequately predicts new data. To achieve this purpose of successful prediction, models can be complex, large, and computationally costly. The most typical method to evaluate models for prediction purposes is cross-validation (see chap. 5). Researchers divide data into a number of training sets to build the model and a testing set to verify if the model can predict the outcomes. To measure the prediction accuracy, researchers use mean squared differences between the observed and predicted values. Using each of the training sets, researchers repeat this multiple times and calculate the mean squared difference over all iterations to calculate a general value of the standard deviation. This allows researchers to compare two models on their prediction accuracy using standard statistical techniques such as t-tests or ANOVA. For discrete outcomes, data mining uses a number of measures calculated from a confusion table to evaluate model performance and select classification schemes. Accuracy, error rate, sensitivity, and specificity are measures of specific dimensions of models, while the product of sensitivity and specificity gives an overall measure of model performance. Cost-benefit matrices are used in conjunction with confusion tables to carry out profit calculations and evaluate model performance. Data mining also derives a series of curves (i.e., cumulative response curve, life chart, ROC curve, and recall-precision curve) from the confusion table and cost-benefit matrix to aid in measuring model performance. These measures of model performance pay scant attention to the size and complexity of models and thus tend to not penalize those models that are large and convoluted.

MODEL PREDICTION POWER

When using conventional statistical models, social and behavioral scientists emphasize the effects of individual predictors and their relationship with the outcome variable. Because they value understanding of the causal mechanisms between the predictors and the outcome variable as the paramount research interest, the analysis and interpretation concentrate on the predictor coefficients, including their size and significance level. This kind of model tends to leave out large amounts of unexplained variance that often come from missing causal variables as well as measurement error and missing data. However, the goodness-of-fit model is not a primary concern for these researchers (Breiman 2001), so models with low measures of goodness of fit are tolerated. It is therefore not uncommon to find articles in leading social science journals with models of modest or low predictive power, such as 25 percent or less of the variance explained (Attewell and Monaghan 2015). Even models with coefficients of determination (R^2) less than .10 have been accepted. For example, most individual-level models in published work on gender attitudes account for only 3.5~10.5 percent of the variance (Shu 2004).

Data mining, on the other hand, emphasizes accuracy in model prediction. Data mining grew out of AI's preoccupation with applied predictive models, such as prediction of insurance fraud, illness diagnoses, and pattern recognition (Shu 2003). An important measure of success in these models is their ability to accurately predict outcomes in real world application. To achieve this purpose, data mining uses a variety of approaches to make predictions more accurate. For example, machine learning enables dynamic intelligent systems with the ability to learn from data and generate models to best predict the outcome. Agent-based models construct globally intelligent systems based on the interaction between individual agents. Neural networks often outperform multiple regression and other multivariate techniques in estimating outcomes (Shu 2003). By combining different methods to maximize the overall predictive power, data mining uses a variety of tools from machine learning, AI, database, and statistics to provide much more predictive power than conventional statistical models.

VARIETY OF DATA (TEXT, IMAGES, VIDEO, VOICE, ETC.)

Conventional statistical analyses are based primarily on survey data in which variables take on numerical values. Data of other forms, such as text or interview data, have often been considered qualitative data that fall in the realm of qualitative research. These researchers use enormous amounts of time to immerse themselves in the qualitative data to manually identify patterns and regularities. When these data sets are of small size, this labor-intensive approach is sufficient to process and analyze data. However, when the data become large, variables multiply, and the dimensions grow complicated, it is impossible for human eyes, ears, and brains to quickly recognize and detect patterns and relationships. Institutional records, personal accounts, and communication between and among people are in the format of text, voice, or image data. The internet and various online communities contain vast amounts of text and pictures in the form of web pages, Facebook updates, WeChat Moments, Twitter feeds, e-mails, blogs, and Instagram pictures, among others. It is often the case that large amounts of text, image, and voice data have been left untapped because they are considered unmanageable or unanalyzable by social scientists who lack the necessary tools to process and examine these invaluable data.

Data mining provides tools to preprocess unstructured data and a variety of methods and models to mine non-numerical data such as text mining and linguistic analysis. These types of data are complicated, with varying lengths, uncertain order, and messy structure (e.g., ungrammatical sentences, misspellings, unexpected abbreviations, random punctuations, domain-specific terminologies, and context). Because of these issues, preprocessing data plays a vital role in converting inputs into data formats conducive to data mining algorithms. Data mining algorithms can treat individual words as terms (bags of words), include sequences of adjacent works as terms (n-gram sequences), recognize common named entities (name entry extraction), and model the set of topics as clusters of words (topic models). For example, mining news streams can be used to predict the stock market (Provost and Fawcett 2013).

DATA MINING CHALLENGES

Although data mining can remedy some deficiencies of traditional statistical approaches in identifying meaningful patterns in data, it also faces new challenges and problems. We need methods to enjoy the advantages of this big data while addressing their deficiencies.

CONVENIENCE SAMPLES

Data mining often uses data that are from "natural" samples, neither census nor well-designed probability samples. Conventional statistical approaches are based on statistical inference from probability samples designed by careful sampling. With the ever-increasing online activities, large data can be obtained from existing online databases, such as online purchase records, Facebook interactions, WeChat moments, fitness records from tracking devices, GPS records, credit card purchases, Uber or Lyft trips, insurance claims, and so on. These data sets are usually records of nonrandom human activities, and they are called "convenience samples."

These natural data also evolve with social and historical dynamics, thus reflecting different "population" sampling schemes. For example, the Google Books corpus does not represent an unbiased sampling of the culture of the time as publications (fiction and scientific) have been increasingly dominated by scientific and academic writings rather than popular works since the 1900s. It is therefore necessary to first identify and distinguish the popular and scientific components in the Google Books corpus in order for it to be informative about cultural and linguistic evolution versus the evolution of scientific norms. In addition, these works also reflect a delay between their appearance in print and their popularity with the public, as well as their authors' prolificacy (Pechenick, Danforth, and Dodds 2015).

Although large data sets are readily available from various online databases, they are neither population censuses nor well-designed probability samples. It is unknown whether they are representative of the population or what the probability is for each member of the population to be included in the sample. As a result, traditional significance tests are not suitable for these convenience samples.

Data mining employs several methods to handle these issues, including replication, cross-validation, bootstrapping, and nonparametric methods. Replication involves using different types of data to test, verify, and modify the model to prevent overfitting and guarantee its reliability and generalizability. Cross-validation divides data sets into training samples, tuning samples, and testing samples (see chap. 5). Researchers use training samples to train the model, tuning samples to adjust and modify the model, and testing samples to verify the model. Multiple rounds of cross-validation may be performed using different sample partitioning, and the results are averaged over the rounds. Bootstrapping is a resampling method in which a series of new samples are generated from a convenience sample uniformly and with replacement. The multiple estimates from this series of samples are either averaged (for regression) or voted (for classification) to generate combined results, including confidence interval and significance tests. This approach is often used in neural networks, classification and regression trees, and linear regression (Breiman 1996). Nonparametric methods do not assume that the structure of a model is fixed. Rather, the model grows in size to accommodate the complexity of the data. Typically in these techniques, individual variables are assumed to belong to parametric distributions, and assumptions are also made about connections among variables. On the other hand, nonparametric models are more flexible and can be widely used on a variety of data distributions. Some supervised and unsupervised learning schemes, such as association rules (see chap. 7), decision trees (see chap. 9), and neural networks (see chap. 10), are nonparametric statistical applications that impose few assumptions on the sample data. They thus provide a wider scope of application.

CAUSAL MECHANISMS

Some data mining models remain opaque about the complex relationships between variables. This is the case with neural networks and decision trees when the latter are large and complex. Although data mining can provide a great deal of prediction power using model construction, some of these models are so complex that it is unclear in what ways the input variables are connected with the output. Data mining approaches build rules that develop joint occurrence ratios between the predictors and the outcomes, indicative of the co-occurrence mechanism and the strength among variables. These co-occurrences or associations strongly suggest the possibility of causation and the causal mechanism. However, other data mining methods do not share this property. As a result, the connection between empirical evidence from the data and the theoretical framework to establish causal relationships is unattainable. For example, a complex multilayer neural network can be very successful in predicting outcomes, but often it sheds little light on the causal process and the relative influences of each variable on the outcome (although some software programs, e.g., SPSS, now provide such a function to estimate the relative importance of variables). As powerful as their predictive power in dealing with a variety of data and information, especially with regard to pattern recognition, some AI models process the relationship between predictors and outcomes in a "black box." The actual causal mechanisms, including which predictors act, in what ways, and by how much, are usually invisible. To make these AI models useful for social science research, it is important that we make the causal processes in them perceptible and meaningful as the primary interest of social science research is the detection of important predictors, their functions in this process, and insights into the causal mechanism.

SUMMARY

Knowledge discovery and data mining is a dialectic research process that combines both deductive and inductive research. The inductive approach is a "bottom-up" process in which researchers start with observations and move to broader generalizations and theories. The deductive approach is a top-down process in which researchers work from the general theory to the specifics of data and hypothesis testing. This approach is similar to the grounded theory method, which encompasses an inductive phase whereby researchers observe data and generate substantive patterns and a deductive component in which researchers derive hypotheses from this newly developed theory and use data to test them.

The scientific field of data mining has developed and matured into its current status by carefully guarding against the pitfalls of a purely data-driven approach. Researchers have defined rigorous procedures, known as the knowledge discovery process model, to guide researchers in using data mining tools in knowledge discovery. Among these models, the KDP model by Fayyad, Piatesky-Shapiro, and Smyth (1996) is worth noting. Another KDP model more applicable for academic research was later developed by Cios et al. (2007).

There are two types of causes: logical and probability. Logical causes consist of a combination of conjunctive plurality of causes and disjunctive plurality of causes. These causes are multiple factors that are jointly necessary and sufficient. Probability causes are single causes that are neither necessary nor sufficient conditions for the effects. Such single causes are erroneously labeled "causes" because they are an insufficient but nonredundant part of an unnecessary but sufficient (INUS) condition. Conventional statistical models are derived from probabilistic theories of causality to identify probable causes by predicting the probability of an effect occurring when a single cause is present, in the form of its main effect after the effects of other variables are controlled for. Data mining approaches move us closer to the logical cause paradigm, in which a larger number of joint and interactive causes are considered simultaneously.

Knowledge discovery and data mining differ from traditional statistical analysis in several ways. The data mining approach has automated the process of searching for and evaluating joint and heterogeneous causes. It also provides tools to classify the data and detect causal heterogeneity for different segments of the population.

Data mining provides many automatic or semiautomatic tools that aid researchers' search for nonlinear relations to increase model prediction accuracy. For example, it can automatically generate breakpoints for continuous independent variables to capture a nonlinear effect. It can also partition an independent variable based on the predictive value of the target variable. Data mining provides data visualization tools that can rotate graphs to help detect nonlinear relations.

Data mining is primarily interested in the ability of a model to accurately predict new data, and it pays less attention to model parsimony. To achieve this goal of predictive accuracy, data mining builds models that are complex and large and often with costly computations, in contrast to conventional statistical models' emphasis on maximizing the amount of variance explained with as few predictors as possible.

Data mining uses a variety of approaches to maximize the amount of variance accounted for. Machine learning enables intelligent systems to learn from data and generate models to best predict the outcome. Neural networks use complex, multiple layers of computation to produce results that best approximate the data. These models generally pay scant attention to model parameters as theoretically meaningful component of the models. Sometimes these parameters are so many and so complexly interconnected that interpretation of their effects is impossible. This is in contrast to traditional statistical models' attention to parameter estimation and inattention to the total proportion of variance accounted for.

Data mining provides tools to preprocess unstructured data and a variety of models to mine non-numerical data. Preprocessing data that are complicated, with varying lengths, with uncertain order, and with messy structures, is necessary to convert them into formats conducive to mining algorithms. This enables researchers to mine a large variety of non-numerical data, including text, images, and voice data that have remained previously untapped by social science research.

Data mining suffers from several challenges. It often uses data that are convenience samples with unclear relationships with the population. However, it uses cross-validation, bootstrapping, and nonparametric methods to handle these concerns.

Some data mining models do not provide insights into the nature of the relationships between the input and the output variables. These models are so large and complex that gaining empirical evidence from the analysis to establish a clear theoretical framework of the nature of the causal relationship is impossible. When building these types of models, attention should be directed to models that are perceptible and meaningful with regard to the role of the input variables.

PRACTICE PROBLEMS

1. Draw flowcharts to describe the Galilean model of scientific methodology and the theory-driven confirmatory hypothesis test. Discuss the differences between these two models.

2. What is the cycle of the research process? How many steps are involved? What are they? Identify a research topic of interest to you. Describe the steps in the research process. What do you accomplish in each of these steps?
3. What is inductive research? What is deductive research? Draw a top-down model and a bottom-up model to explain.
4. Name the six steps in the model developed by Cios et al. (2007) for academic research of knowledge discovery projects. Describe the relationships among these six steps.
5. Explain conjunctive plurality. Use an example to demonstrate.
6. Explain disjunctive plurality. Use an example to demonstrate.
7. Why is it the case that causes are both conjunctive plurality causes and disjunctive plurality causes?
8. Why do social scientists prefer single causes? What is the relationship between a single cause and causes that are a combination of conjunctive plurality and disjunctive plurality causes?
9. In order to establish a single cause, what approach do researchers take?
10. What is conjuncture and causal heterogeneity? How do you estimate them in models? Is it easy to do so?
11. How does data mining handle nonlinear functions?
12. What strategy does data mining take to increase model predictive accuracy?
13. What factors do data mining models emphasize that are considered unimportant in conventional statistical analysis?
14. What are data mining's contributions to the analysis of non-numerical data?
15. To what type of samples are data mining approaches often applied? What are the challenges of using this type of sample, and how do researchers address them?
16. About what do neural network models fail to inform researchers? Are there ways to deal with this problem?

REFERENCES

Aiken, Leona S., and Stephen G. West. 1991. *Multiple Regression: Testing and Interpreting Interactions*. Newbury Park, CA: Sage.

Anand, Sarabjot S., and Alex.G. Büchner. 1998. *Decision Support through Data Mining*. London: Financial Times Management.

Attewell, Paul, and David B. Monaghan. 2015. *Data Mining for the Social Sciences: An Introduction*. Berkeley: University of California Press.

Beauchamp, Tom. 1974. *Philosophical Problems of Causation*. Encino, CA: Dickenson Publishing Co.

Berry, William, Matt Golder, and Daniel Milton. 2012. "Improving Tests of Theories Positing Interaction." *Journal of Politics* 74: 653–71.

Bozdogan, Hamparsum. 2003. *Statistical Data Mining and Knowledge Discovery*. Boca Raton, FL: Chapman and Hall / CRC.

Brambor, Thomas, William Roberts Clark, and Matt Golder. 2006. "Understanding Interaction Models: Improving Empirical Analyses." *Political Analysis* 14: 63–82.

Breiman, Leo. 1996. "Bagging Predictors." *Machine Learning* 24 (2): 123–40.

———. 2001. "Statistical Modeling: The Two Cultures." *Statistical Science* 16 (3): 199–231.

Bunge, Mario. 1979. *Treatise on Basic Philosophy. Part IV: A World of Systems*. Dordrecht: Reidel.

Cios, Krzysztof J., Witold Pedrycz, Roman W. Swiniarski, and Lukasz A. Kurgan. 2007. *Data Mining: A Knowledge Discovery Approach*. New York: Springer.

Einhorn, Hillel J., and Robin M. Hogarth. 1986. "Judging Probable Cause." *Psychological Bulletin* 99 (1): 3–19.

Elwert, Felix, and Christopher Winship. 2010. "Effect Heterogeneity and Bias in Main-Effects-Only Regression Models." In *Heuristics, Probability and Causality: A Tribute to Judea Pearl*, ed. R. Dechter, H. Geffner, and J. Halpern, 327–36. Milton Keynes, U.K.: College Publications.

Fayyad, Usama, Gregory Piatesky-Shapiro, and Padhraic Smyth. 1996. "Knowledge Discovery and Data Mining: Towards a Unifying Framework." In *Proceedings of the Second International Conference on Knowledge Discovery and Data Mining*, ed. E. Simoudis, J. Han, and U. Fayyad, 82–88. https://www.aaai.org/Papers/KDD/1996/KDD96-014.pdf.

Garip, Filiz. 2017. *On the Move: Changing Mechanisms of Mexico-U.S. Migration*. Cambridge, MA: Harvard University Press.

Holton, Judith A., and Isabelle Walsh. 2017. *Classic Grounded Theory: Applications with Qualitative and Quantitative Data*. Thousand Oaks, CA: Sage.

Jaccard, James, and Robert Turrisi. 2003. *Interaction Effects in Multiple Regression*. 2nd ed. Thousand Oaks, CA: Sage.

Mackie, John Leslie. 1965. "Causes and Conditions." *American Philosophical Quarterly* 2 (4): 245–64.

———. 1974. *The Cement of the Universe: A Study of Causation*. Oxford: Oxford University Press.

Magidson, Jay. 1993. "The Use of the New Ordinal Algorithm in CHAID to Target Profitable Segments." *Journal of Database Marketing* 1: 29–48.

Pechenick, Eitan Adam, Christopher M. Danforth, and Peter Sheridan Dodds. 2015. "Characterizing the Google Books Corpus: Strong Limits to Inferences of Socio-Cultural and Linguistic Evolution." *PLoS ONE* 10 (10): e0137041. https://doi.org/10.1371/journal.pone.0137041.

Provost, Foster, and Tom Fawcett. 2013. *Data Science for Business: What You Need to Know about Data Mining and Data-Analytic Thinking*. Beijing: O'Rilly Media Inc.

Shu, Xiaoling. 2003. "Artificial Intelligence." In *The Sage Encyclopedia of Social Science Research Methods*, ed. M. Lewis-Beck, A. Bryman, and T. F. Liao, 27–28. Thousand Oaks, CA: Sage.

———. 2004. "Education and Gender Egalitarianism: The Case of China." *Sociology of Education* 77 (4): 311–36.

Skocpol, Theda. 1979. *States and Social Revolutions: A Comparative Analysis of France, Russia and China*. New York: Cambridge University Press.

Skyrms, Brian. 1980. *Causal Necessity: A Pragmatic Investigation of the Necessity of Laws*. New Haven, CT: Yale University Press.

Witten, Ian H., Eibe Frank, and Mark A. Hall. 2011. *Data Mining: Practical Machine Learning Tools and Techniques*. 3rd ed. Burlington, MA: Elsevier.

PART II

DATA PREPROCESSING

———

Chapter 3

DATA ISSUES

BEFORE EACH DATA MINING PROJECT, we may need to collect data, uphold the code of ethics, ensure data confidentiality, evaluate the quality of the data, clean data, handle missing data, and perform transformations of variables. To prepare data for data mining, the raw data need to undergo the preprocessing steps of data cleaning and data transformation. Unprocessed raw data may contain information that may be problematic (i.e., obsolete, redundant, or containing values that are inconsistent with common sense) or missing. Unprocessed raw data may also contain outliers or data in forms that are not conducive for data mining models.

DATA PRIVACY, SECURITY, AND ETHICS
IN DATA MINING

Data mining, similar to any other approach that uses data gathered from people, is subject to a series of ethical concerns. Besides the common issues confronting researchers who conduct research on human subjects, data mining practitioners confront additional complexities. Data mining researchers must be fully aware of these serious ethical implications and act responsibly concerning the data and the application of certain data mining approaches.

The code of ethics shared by data practitioners covers data privacy, data integrity, and the rights of human subjects. When researchers gain consent prior to data collection, informants have the right to know how their data will be used, the purpose of the research, the procedures that will be used to guard their confidentiality and integrity, and their rights and redress options.

Data mining can encounter complex situations in which the code of ethics is compromised. Data could be used in ways far beyond the original purpose intended. Researchers need to know the conditions under which the data were collected and the scope to which they are allowed to apply the data. For example, campus ID cards might document faculty and student campus purchases, cafeteria consumption, library loans, campus building entries and exits, and so on. This information should not be available to the campus ethics committee to surveil the recreational reading tastes of faculty or students, or to campus vendors to increase their sales, or to publishers to recommend new books.

The advancement of data mining techniques makes it difficult to anonymize data, so researchers run the risk of compromising data confidentiality. Even when data are released to the public after having taken precautions such as stripping identifying information (names, birthdates, addresses, email addresses, or Social Security numbers), it is still possible for individual records to be recognized by combining all information and patterns to reveal the individual's identity. For example, some researchers have permission to use randomized cellular phone GPS data to analyze patterns of traffic flow in a city in order to study urban design. Although all phone owners' information—including phone numbers, names, birthdates, and credit card and bank account numbers—has been removed, it is still possible to identify individuals' home and work addresses based on their day- and nighttime movement patterns.

One major data mining function is to classify or differentiate people. Some classifications are considered acceptable, such as using race or gender for medical diagnosis and treatment. Based on research using data from medical databases, African Americans, Asians, and Hispanics were seen to receive aspirin from emergency medical services in the setting of suspected acute coronary syndrome (ACS) at higher rates than non-Hispanic whites (Tataris, Mercer, and Govindarajan 2015). But using data mining results to discriminate against people based on their race/ethnicity, gender, religion, sexual orientation, or disability in providing access to loans, jobs, or housing is not only unethical but also illegal. In addition, it is unethical to use proxy variables, such as neighborhood as a proxy for social class and race/ethnicity, to differentiate people in providing access to valued social and economic resources.

Enormous amounts of online data provide both new opportunities and new ethical concerns. Before researchers scrape data from web pages, they should not assume that the data are public, and they need to make certain that they are allowed to access the data. It is imperative that researchers verify with the Terms of Service (TOS) of the site. When web pages prohibit "programmatic" access to their sites and block your account or IP address or limit the number of visits or operations per day, researchers face an ethical dilemma between respecting the site owners' wishes and the urge to pursue research efficiency and needs.

Some website owners treat data obtained from their site as a commodity with monetary value to be sold for profit. While the amount of data captured and traded has increased exponentially, the chance of ethical violation has also grown tremendously. Although it is the obligation of those companies who own, sell, or purchase the data to protect data privacy by making users anonymous and being legally responsible for the contents of data release, they sometimes fail to do so. In addition, these purchasing companies are legally allowed to trade data to a third or fourth company that may or may not fulfill these obligations. Researchers who use these data face a high likelihood of privacy violations. In addition, the chance of these data being used for purposes other than what was originally agreed on has grown tremendously. One example is the Facebook–Cambridge Analytica data scandal that demonstrated the peril of online data mining. Cambridge Analytica, a U.K.-based data analytics firm, gained access to user information from more than 50 million Facebook users. It reportedly acquired data from Facebook through a personality test and then tapped the information to build psychographic profiles not only of the original users who gave consent but also of their Facebook friends who did not consent to such data collection. This information was later used for a different purpose, according to reports, to identify personalities of American voters and influence their behaviors in the 2016 presidential election. This was a breach of the original data collection consent in which Facebook users who agreed to let Cambridge Analytica gather their information were not informed about this data usage for the purpose of political campaigning and profiling their voting tendencies.

DATA CLEANING AND MISSING DATA

Data sets may contain erroneous or missing information that can plague data analysis. The pattern of the data that are missing varies, and this variation determines the method we use to address the issue of missing data. To deal with missing data, there are a few common approaches.

The most common method is to delete or ignore the record with missing data in the analysis. This approach is reasonable when the missing data occur randomly. If the pattern of missingness is systematic, however, deleting the case will lead to a biased subset of data that will then result in biased estimates. Another issue plaguing this approach when using *listwise deletion* (i.e., discarding all cases with any missing values) is that it may end up deleting the majority of cases if cases with any one variable missing are eliminated even if the proportion of missing data for each individual variable is low. An alternative approach that uses the correlations among the maximum number

TABLE 3.1   **MISSING DATA FROM THE GENERAL SOCIAL SURVEY 1977–2014**

RS RELIGIOUS PREFERENCE

		Frequency	Percent	Valid Percent	Cumulative Percent
Valid	Protestant	23416	55.4	55.7	55.7
	Catholic	10267	24.3	24.4	80.1
	Jewish	815	1.9	1.9	82.0
	None	5427	12.8	12.9	94.9
	Other	773	1.8	1.8	96.8
	Buddhism	156	.4	.4	97.1
	Hinduism	76	.2	.2	97.3
	Other Eastern	34	.1	.1	97.4
	Moslem/Islam	117	.3	.3	97.7
	Orthodox Christian	105	.2	.2	97.9
	Christian	723	1.7	1.7	99.6
	Native American	26	.1	.1	99.7
	Internondenominational	128	.3	.3	100.0
	Total	42,063	99.5	100.0	
Missing	System	195	.5		
Total		42,258	100.0		

of pairs of variables with nonmissing data, called *pairwise deletion*, is also problematic. There is the potential inconsistency that the covariance matrix and the correlations and other statistics are based on different but overlapping subsamples of a larger sample. Because of these concerns, multiple data replacement schemes have been used.

One of the most common data replacement approaches is to replace the missing value with a measure of central tendency (i.e., mean and mode for numerical and categorical variables, respectively). The potential problems with this method are that we underestimate the standard error of the sampling distribution, thus making the confidence intervals for statistical inference overoptimistic and that these measures of central tendency, mean or mode, may not be the most typical value for the variable among the missing. For example, in the data gathered for the General Social Survey 1977–2014, as shown in table 3.1, the mode for Respondent's Religious Preference is "Protestant." This data replacement approach would replace the 195 missing cases with "Protestant," which may be inaccurate; the people with missing values might have chosen not to answer the question because their religions were not listed, because they were transitioning from one religion to another, or because they practiced a combination of religious beliefs.

A different replacement approach is to substitute the missing value with a random value generated from the distribution of the variable. This way, the measures of central tendency and standard deviation remain close to the original data. However, the resulting record of random values may not make sense for a particular record. For example, a random value replacement procedure might put a random income value of $14,000 for a case because it fits with the mean and standard deviation of the variable. However, if this respondent is a professional pilot with a college education and twenty years of work experience, the randomly generated income would not seem to fit with his or her profile.

A third approach is to replace the missing value with imputed values based on the other characteristics of the case. For categorical variables, logistic regression or any classification algorithm can be used to impute missing values. For continuous variables, multiple regression models with good predictors of the missing data are appropriate for imputing missing values. When there are several variables with missing values, a pattern of missingness may be identified, and recursive programming may be used to impute missing values in succession from the variable with the least missing data to the variable with the most missing data (Marini, Olson, and Ruben 1980).

Multiple imputation provides a useful strategy for dealing with missing values. Instead of filling in a single value for each missing case, multiple imputation replaces each missing value with a set of plausible values that represent the uncertainty about the value to impute (Little and Rubin 2002). These multiple imputed data sets are then analyzed by using standard procedures for complete data, and the results from these analyses are then combined to generate the final estimates.

This procedure of multiple imputation has become one of the standard features of many software programs. For example, SPSS provides a command, "Analyze > Multiple Imputation > Impute Missing Data Values . . ." to impute multiple values for missing data for variables (https://www.ibm.com/support/knowledgecenter/en/SSLVMB_ 24.0.0/spss/mva/idh_idd_mi_variables.html). Users can specify the number of imputations to compute (the default is 5). The output data set consists not only of the original case data with missing data but also of a set of cases with imputed values for each imputation. For example, if the original data set has 1,000 cases, and you choose to have 5 imputations for each missing variable, the resulting data set will have 6,000 cases. This output data set includes all variables in the input data set. The procedure automatically defines the variable for which imputations are performed as a split variable. If splits are in effect when the procedure executes, the output data set includes one set of imputations for each combination of values of split variables.

Stata's **mi** command provides a range of multiple imputation methods for the analysis of incomplete data. mi provides both the imputation and the estimation steps (https://www.stata.com/features/overview/multiple-imputation/). Its estimation step includes both estimation on individual data sets and pooling the multiple data sets in one easy-to-use procedure. It also provides procedures to examine the pattern of missing values in the data. It enables us to use flexible imputation methods by providing nine univariate imputation methods that can be used as building blocks for multivariate imputation using chained equations, as well as multivariate normal (MVN).

R provides five different packages on missing data imputation. 1) MICE (Multivariate Imputation via Chained Equations) is one of the commonly used package by R users (https://cran.r-project.org/web/packages/mice/mice.pdf). It creates multiple imputations to take care of uncertainty in missing values. It assumes that the missing data are Missing at Random (MAR). It imputes data on a variable-by-variable basis by specifying an imputation model per variable. 2) Package Amelia also performs multiple imputation by generating imputed data sets to deal with missing values (https://cran.r-project.org/web/packages/Amelia/Amelia.pdf). It is enabled with a bootstrap-based EMB algorithm, which makes it faster and more robust to impute many variables including cross sectional and time series data. It assumes that all variables in a data set have Multivariate Normal Distribution (MVN) and that missing data are random in nature. 3) Package missForest uses a random forest algorithm (https://cran.r-project.org/web/packages/missForest/missForest.pdf). It is a nonparametric imputation method applicable to various variable types while not making explicit assumptions about functional form of f (any arbitary function). It builds a random forest model for each variable, then uses the model to predict missing values in the variable with the help of observed values. It yields OOB (out of bag) imputation error estimates and provides a high level of control on the imputation process. It has options to return OOB separately (for each variable) instead of aggregating over the whole data matrix. 4) Package Hmisc allows mean imputation using additive regression, bootstrapping, and predictive mean matching (https://cran.r-project.org/web/packages/Hmisc/Hmisc.pdf). In bootstrapping, different bootstrap resamples are used for each of the multiple imputations. It fits a flexible additive model, which is a nonparametric regression method, on samples taken with replacements from original data to predict missing values based on nonmissing values. It assumes linearity in the variables being predicted. 5) The mi (Multiple imputation with diagnostics) package provides several features for dealing with missing values (https://cran.r-project.org/web/packages/mi/mi.pdf). It builds multiple imputation models to approximate missing values and uses the predictive mean matching method.

DATA TRANSFORMATION (NORMALIZATION, STANDARDIZATION)

Some algorithms and methods require that the variables be normalized because there are large variations in the ranges among different variables. As the data in table 3.2 show, some variables are measured as small fractions, such as infant mortality rates, which range from .0020 to .1602, while others are very large numbers, such as GDP per capita, which ranges from $255 to $116,613. For some data mining algorithms, variables with larger variability will have undue dominance over variables with smaller ranges. For example, if we use both national infant mortality rates and GDP per capita together in a mining procedure, GDP per capita would tend to have a much larger influence on the results. Therefore, it is important to normalize the variables in data mining

TABLE 3.2   **ILLUSTRATING DATA NORMALIZATION AND STANDARDIZATION**

COUNTRY INDICATORS IN 2014

Showing partial data with 20 cases, extracted from the World Development Database http://databank.worldbank.org/data/home.aspx

Country Name	Fertility	GDP per Capita	Life Expectancy	Population	Mortality (ages 0–5)
Aruba	1.66	.	75.45	103,441	0.0029
Andorra	.	.	.	72,786	0.0939
Afghanistan	4.84	634	60.37	31,627,506	0.1622
Angola	6.08	.	52.27	24,227,524	0.0144
Albania	1.78	4564	77.83	2,894,475	0.0378
United Arab Emirates	1.78	43,963	77.37	9,086,139	0.0129
Argentina	2.32	12,510	76.16	42,980,026	0.0147
Armenia	1.53	3,874	74.68	3,006,154	.
American Samoa	.	.	.	55,434	0.0084
Antigua and Barbuda	2.08	13,432	75.94	90,900	0.0039
Australia	1.86	61,980	82.25	23,470,118	0.0037
Austria	1.44	51,122	81.34	8,545,908	0.0329
Azerbaijan	2.00	7,886	70.76	9,535,079	0.0846
Burundi	5.95	286	56.69	10,816,860	0.0042
Belgium	1.75	47,328	80.59	11,231,213	0.1021
Benin	4.77	903	59.51	10,598,482	0.0924
Burkina Faso	5.52	713	58.59	17,589,198	0.0395
Bangladesh	2.18	1,087	71.63	159,077,513	0.0109
Bulgaria	1.48	7,851	75.41	7,223,938	0.0065
Bahrain	2.06	24,855	76.68	1,361,930	0.0124
. . .	. . .	. . .	. . .	. . .	. . .

projects so that the measurement scales are standardized and the effect of each variable on the outcome is considered equally. This way, data mining algorithms such as neural networks or K-means algorithms that measure distances between cases can appropriately map out cases without the undue influences of variables with large measurement units.

Summary statistics of this data set are presented in table 3.3.

Z-SCORE STANDARDIZATION

Z-score standardization is a commonly used approach to convert variables from their original measurement units to values based on standard deviations. This method is appropriate when the variables under investigation are of different physical characteristics or different quantities, the numerical values representing these variables are on different measurement scales, and the variables with high values should be considered

TABLE 3.3   **DESCRIPTIVE INFORMATION FOR DATA IN TABLE 3.2**

	DESCRIPTIVE STATISTICS				
	N	Minimum	Maximum	Mean	Std. Deviation
GDP per capita	192	255	116613	14540.43	20799.778
Mortality (ages 0–5)	199	.0020	.1622	.033062	.0333500
Life expectancy at birth	206	48.93	83.98	71.4187	8.39310
Fertility birth per woman	207	1.21	7.60	2.7681	1.37387
Total population	221	9893	7,259,691,769	89,243,178.91	528,982,668.410

more important in the analysis. This makes it possible to compare variables of different natures or characteristics using different measurement units. This method is particularly useful for methods that are based on the distance between data points in a multidimensional space defined by multiple predictor variables of different magnitudes. For examples, Principle Components Analysis (PCA) characterizes groups of cases, or clouds of data points, based on their relative positions in a multidimensional space defined by the multiple variables under analysis. Since variables with large numerical values contribute more to the variance, they thus dominate the solution, overpowering the effects of other variables based on measures of smaller magnitudes.

This rescaling takes the difference between the value $\bar{y}$ and the mean and converts this difference into the number of standard deviations from the mean, S_y or Z-score.

$$Z = \frac{y - \bar{y}}{S_y}$$

For example, using the data from Afghanistan in table 3.2, the Z-scores for GDP per capita and the child mortality rate are the following, respectively:

$$Z_{GDP} = \frac{634 - 14540.43}{20799.778} = -.67$$

$$Z_{Mortalinty} = \frac{.1622 - .033062}{.0333500} = 3.87$$

For Australia, the Z-scores for GDP per capita and the child mortality rate are the following, respectively:

$$Z_{GDP} = \frac{61780 - 14540.43}{20799.778} = 2.27$$

$$Z_{Mortality} = \frac{.0037 - .033062}{.0333500} = -.88$$

```
*Z-score normalization in SPSS 23. Codes are automatically generated.
*It saves normalized variables in the data file with same variable names but start-
ing the normalized variables with Z.
DESCRIPTIVES VARIABLES = GDPpercapita mortality
/SAVE.
```

RANGE NORMALIZATION

Range normalization is a scaling scheme that converts a variable into a proportion within its range between the minimum and maximum. It measures a variable as a proportion out of the entire range of possible values, so the normalized variable is between [0, 1].

$$N_{Range}(y) = \frac{y - \min(y)}{range(y)}$$

Again, taking Afghanistan from the example above, its range-normalized scores for GDP per capita and the child mortality rate are the following, respectively:

$$N_{Range}(GDP) = \frac{634 - 255}{116613 - 225} = .0035$$

$$N_{Range}(Mortality) = \frac{.1622 - .002}{.1622 - .002} = 1$$

For Australia, the range-normalized scores for GDP per capita and the child mortality rate are the following, respectively:

$$N_{Range}(GDP) = \frac{61980 - 255}{116613 - 225} = .5305$$

$$N_{Range}(Mortality) = \frac{.0037 - .002}{.1622 - .002} = .0106$$

```
*Automatic Data Preparation in SPSS 23. Codes are automatically generated.
*Transform-> Prepare Data for ModelingADP
/FIELDS INPUT=GDPpercapita mortality
/PREPDATETIME DATEDURATION=NO TIMEDURATION=NO EXTRACTYEAR=NO EXTRACTMONTH=NO
EXTRACTDAY=NO
EXTRACTHOUR=NO EXTRACTMINUTE=NO EXTRACTSECOND=NO
/SCREENING PCTMISSING=NO UNIQUECAT=NO SINGLECAT=NO
/ADJUSTLEVEL INPUT=NO TARGET=NO
/OUTLIERHANDLING INPUT=NO TARGET=NO
/REPLACEMISSING INPUT=NO TARGET=NO
/REORDERNOMINAL INPUT=NO TARGET=NO
/RESCALE INPUT=MINMAX(MIN=0 MAX=1) TARGET=NONE
/TRANSFORM MERGESUPERVISED=NO MERGEUNSUPERVISED=NO BINNING=NONE SELECTION=NO
CONSTRUCTION=NO
/CRITERIA SUFFIX(TARGET='_range' INPUT='_range')
/OUTFILE PREPXML='C:\Users\xshu\AppData\Local\Temp\spss23216\spssadp_automatic.tmp'.
TMS IMPORT
/INFILE TRANSFORMATIONS='C:\Users\xshu\AppData\Local\Temp\spss23216\spssadp_
automatic.tmp'
MODE=FORWARD (ROLES=UPDATE)
/SAVE TRANSFORMED=YES.
EXECUTE.
ERASE FILE='C:\Users\xshu\AppData\Local\Temp\spss23216\spssadp_automatic.tmp'.
```

DECIMAL SCALING

Decimal scaling is an approach used to convert a variable into a range of -1 and 1 using the number of digits from the largest absolute value.

$$N_{Decimal}(y) = \frac{y}{10^n}$$

where n is the number of digits in the variable of interest with the maximum absolute value.

For Afghanistan, the decimal scales for GDP per capita and the child mortality rate are the following, respectively:

$$N_{Decimal}(GDP) = \frac{634}{10^6} = .000634$$

$$N_{Decimal}(Mortality) = \frac{.1622}{10^0} = .1622$$

For Australia, the Z-scores for GDP per capita and the child mortality rate are the following, respectively:

$$N_{Decimal}(GDP) = \frac{61780}{10^6} = .061780$$

$$N_{Decimal}(Mortality) = \frac{.0037}{10^0} = .0037$$

TRANSFORMATION INTO A NORMAL DISTRIBUTION

Some algorithms and methods require that variables have normal distributions. A normal distribution is a bell-shaped, normal, continuous probability distribution that centers on a mean μ and standard deviation σ. A standard normal distribution of Z is a normal distribution with a mean of 0 and a standard deviation of 1.

To evaluate whether a variable is normally distributed, graphs such as histograms are commonly used. Figure 3.1 illustrates the distribution of three variables: GDP per Capita, Child Mortality, and Life Expectancy at Birth. The first two variables are right-skewed, while the last is left-skewed.

More rigorous statistical tests are also used to evaluate whether a distribution deviates significantly from a normal distribution. The most commonly used tools are a simple examination of skewness and kurtosis. Additional measures include P-P plots and inferential tests of normality, such as the Kolmorogov-Smirnov or Shapiro-Wilk's W test. We focus on skewness.

Skewness estimates the extent to which a distribution is symmetrical.

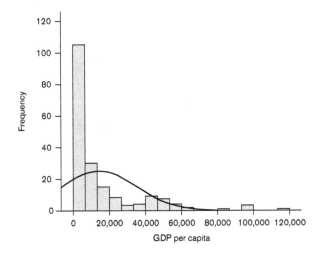

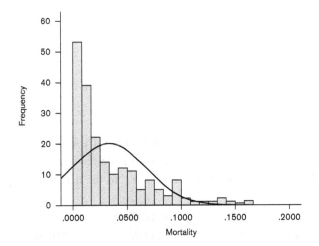

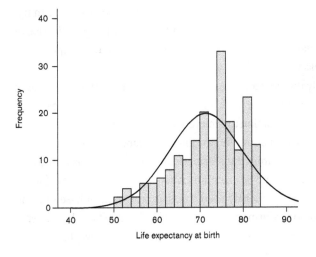

FIGURE 3.1
Original Distribution of GDP per
Capita, Child Mortality (ages 0–5),
and Life Expectancy.

TABLE 3.4 **MEASURES OF SKEWNESS**

	STATISTICS		
	GDP per Capita	Mortality (ages 0–5)	Life Expectancy at Birth
Mean	14540.43	.033062	71.4187
Median	5723.76	.018500	73.4332
Std. Deviation	20799.778	.0333500	8.39310
Skewness	2.334	1.435	–.703
Std. Error of Skewness	.175	.172	.169
Kurtosis	6.001	1.670	–.266
Std. Error of Kurtosis	.349	.343	.337
Minimum	255	.0020	48.93
Maximum	116613	.1622	83.98

- A completely symmetrical distribution has a skewness of 0.
- An asymmetrical distribution with a long tail to the right (skewed to the right) has a positive skew.
- An asymmetrical distribution with a long tail to the left (skewed to the left) has a negative skew.

Statistics packages report a statistic called the standard error for the skewness score. This allows a simple rule of thumb to be applied. If you divide skewness by its standard error and the result is greater than ±1.96, it suggests that the data are not normally distributed.

The skewness measures in this example are 2.334 for GDP per Capita, 1.435 for Child Mortality, and –.703 for Life Expectancy, as shown in table 3.4. When divided by their corresponding standard errors, all three measures are larger than ±1.96, indicating that the distributions of these three variables are not normal. Consistent with figure 3.1, skewness is positive for both GDP per Capita and Child Mortality, indicative of a positive skew with large values, while skewness is negative for Life Expectancy, revealing a negative skewness with small values.

To make the data normally distributed, we need to eliminate the skewness and make the distribution symmetrical. To do so, we perform data transformations. The most commonly used methods of data transformation to achieve symmetry are the natural log or log transformation, square root transformation, and the inverse square root transformation.

Log transformation(s). Logarithmic transformations are actually a class of transformations, and a range of bases should be examined when attempting log transformations (Osborne 2002). The most frequently used bases are the natural base of e and the log base of 10. Before log transformation, the variable also needs to be adjusted so that the minimum is 1 or larger. Both figure 3.2 and table 3.5 show that the log

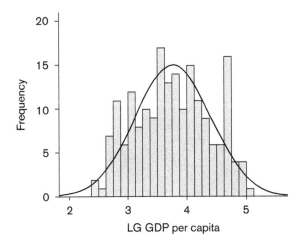

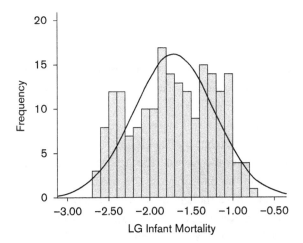

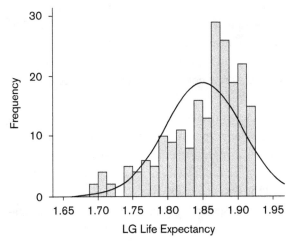

FIGURE 3.2
Log Transformed Distribution of GDP
per Capita, Mortality, and Life
Expectancy.

TABLE 3.5   MEASURES OF SKEWNESS FOR LOG-TRANSFORMED VARIABLES

| | STATISTICS | | |
	LGgdg	LGmortality	LGlifeexp
Mean	3.7534	−1.7206	1.8506
Median	3.7573	−1.7328	1.8659
Std. Deviation	.63746	.48861	.05401
Skewness	−.003	−.112	−.945
Std. Error of Skewness	.175	.172	.169
Kurtosis	−.857	−1.059	.265
Std. Error of Kurtosis	.349	.343	.337
Minimum	2.41	−2.70	1.69
Maximum	5.07	−.79	1.92

transformation has normalized GDP per Capita and Mortality as the ratio between the skewness and the standard error of skewness is smaller than ±1.96 but has failed to transform the Life Expectancy variable into a normal distribution: its distribution is still quite left skewed and the ratio between the skewness and the standard error of skewness is −5.59.

Square root transformation. We can also use the square root of the original variable to correct its skewness. For a negative number, a constant must be added to move the minimum value of the distribution above 0 (Osborne 2002). This transformation is often thought of as most appropriate for normalizing data that are counts of occurrences. Both figure 3.2 and table 3.6 show that although square root transformations of these three variables have reduced their skewness, these distributions are still skewed, as indicated by the ratio between their skewness and the standard error of skewness that is larger than ±1.96.

Inverse transformation. The inverse transformation computes 1/y and makes very small numbers very large and very large numbers very small. This is a class of transformations, including square root inverse and inverse of other powers. As shown in figure 3.4 and table 3.7 in the ratios of skewness and the standard error of skewness that are larger than ±1.96, the inverse transformation is not effective for these three variables as all remain fairly skewed.

Box-Cox transformation. Box-Cox transformation uses a class of power transformations that raise numbers to an exponent or power. The procedure identifies an appropriate exponent λ to use to transform data into a normal shape. The λ value indicates the power to which the original variable should be raised. The Box-Cox power transformation searches until the best value is found.

The Box-Cox transformation is another general approach of variable transformation. It uses the following equation to transform variable x:

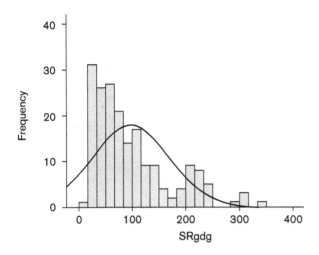

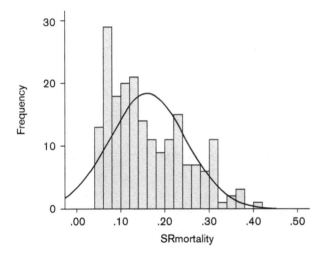

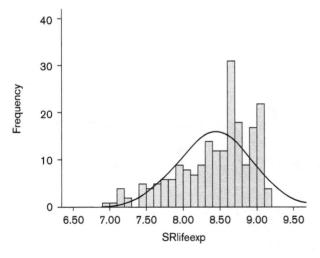

FIGURE 3.3
Square Root Transformed
Distribution of GDP per Capita,
Mortality, and Life Expectancy.

TABLE 3.6 **MEASURES OF SKEWNESS FOR SQUARE ROOT TRANSFORMED VARIABLES**

	STATISTICS		
	SRgdg	SRmortality	SRlifeexp
Mean	97.4567	.1603	8.4356
Median	75.6389	.1360	8.5693
Std. Deviation	71.19705	.08602	.50969
Skewness	1.209	.667	−.821
Std. Error of Skewness	.175	.172	.169
Kurtosis	.861	−.477	−.025
Std. Error of Kurtosis	.349	.343	.337
Minimum	15.97	.04	7.00
Maximum	341.49	.40	9.16

TABLE 3.7 **MEASURES OF SKEWNESS FOR INVERSE TRANSFORMED VARIABLES**

	STATISTICS		
	IVSgdp	IVSmortality	IVSlifeexp
Mean	.0172	8.4753	.1190
Median	.0132	7.3521	.1167
Std. Deviation	.01259	4.81258	.00762
Skewness	1.229	.879	1.074
Std. Error of Skewness	.175	.172	.169
Kurtosis	.992	−.206	.608
Std. Error of Kurtosis	.349	.343	.337
Minimum	.00	2.48	.11
Maximum	.06	22.36	.14

$$f(BC) \begin{cases} \dfrac{(x^{\alpha} - 1)^2}{\alpha}, for\ \alpha \neq 0 \\ \ln x, for\ \alpha = 0 \end{cases}$$

We may choose a range of values for to identify the best-fitting transformation.

When we use $\alpha = 0$, then $f(BC) = \ln x$, or

When we use $\alpha = .5$, then $f(BC) = \dfrac{(x^5 - 1)^2}{.5}$, or

When we use $\alpha = 1$, then $f(BC) = (x - 1)^2$, or

When we use $\alpha = 1.5$, then $f(BC) = \dfrac{(x^{1.5} - 1)^2}{1.5}$, or

When we use $\alpha = 2$, then $f(BC) = \dfrac{(x^2 - 1)^2}{2}$, etc.

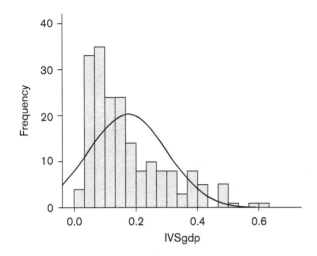

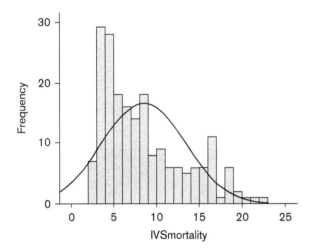

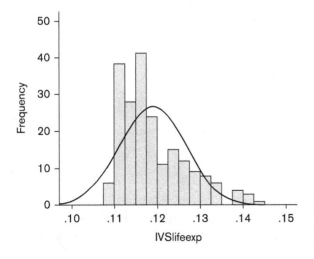

FIGURE 3.4
Inverse Transformed Distribution of
GDP per Capita, Mortality, and Life
Expectancy.

We use the method of maximum likelihood to find the optimal value of α. SPSS 25.0 has an ADP (Automated Data Preparation) function that automatically transforms a continuous variable using the Box-Cox transformation into a new one that has an approximately normal distribution with a mean and standard deviation to be specified by the user. The defaults are 0 and 1, respectively.

As shown below, SPSS automatically identifies $\alpha = 1.5$ for Life Expectancy, $\alpha = 0$ for GDP per Capita, and $\alpha = -3$ for Mortality. As shown in figure 3.5 and table 3.8, these transformations have all standardized the three variables with a mean of 0 and a standard deviation of 1. The skewed distributions have improved, particularly for Life Expectancy, but the two variables GDP per Capita and Mortality remain rather skewed as demonstrated by the ratio between the skewness and the standard deviation of skewness. The ln transformation of these latter two variables was successful in reducing skewness but these variables were not standardized by the ln transformation.

```
* Interactive Data Preparation in SPSS 25. Codes are automatically generated.
* Transform->Prepare Data for Modeling->Interactive->Settings: Rescale Fields->
* Rescale a continuous target with a Box-Cox transformation to reduce skew
COMPUTE lifeexpectancyatbirth_boxcox = (((1/37.5986517939305)*(((((lifeexpectancy-
atbirth-47.9347317073171)**1.5)-1)/1.5)-79.0980045716101))+0).
VARIABLE ROLE
/NONE lifeexpectancyatbirth
/TARGET lifeexpectancyatbirth_boxcox
/INPUT GDPpercapita mortality.
EXECUTE.
COMPUTE GDPpercapita_boxcox = (((1/1.74697400357554)*(LN(GDPpercap
ita-254.04456957319)-8.47370536838262))+0).
VARIABLE ROLE
/NONE GDPpercapita
/TARGET GDPpercapita_boxcox
/INPUT mortality lifeexpectancyatbirth.
EXECUTE.
*Interactive Data Preparation.
COMPUTE mortality_boxcox = (((1/0.027289644769925)*(((((mortality-
(-0.998))**(-3))-1)/(-3))-0.0274536829122099))+0).
VARIABLE ROLE
/NONE mortality
/TARGET mortality_boxcox
/INPUT lifeexpectancyatbirth GDPpercapita.
EXECUTE.
FREQUENCIES VARIABLES=GDPpercapita_boxcox mortality_boxcox lifeexpectancyatbirth_
boxcox
/STATISTICS=STDDEV MINIMUM MAXIMUM MEAN MEDIAN SKEWNESS SESKEW KURTOSIS SEKURT
/HISTOGRAM NORMAL
/ORDER=ANALYSIS.
```

BINNING VARIABLES

In preparing data for analysis, we sometimes need to change a variable from a numerical one into discrete categories for several reasons. One consideration is that a

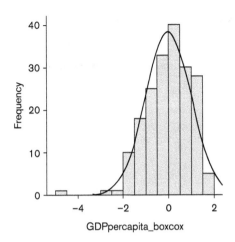

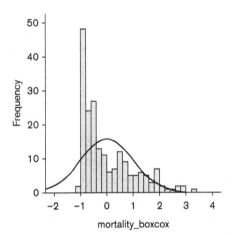

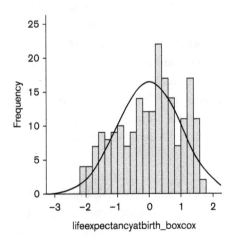

FIGURE 3.5
Box-Cox Transformed Distribution of GDP per Capita,
Mortality, and Life Expectancy.

TABLE 3.8   MEASURES OF SKEWNESS FOR BOX-COX TRANSFORMED VARIABLES

	STATISTICS		
	GDPpercapita_boxcox	mortality_boxcox	lifeexpectancy_boxcox
Mean	.0000	.0000	.0000
Median	.0757	−.4208	.1615
Std. Deviation	1.00000	1.00000	1.00000
Skewness	−.784	1.167	−.318
Std. Error of Skewness	.175	.172	.169
Kurtosis	1.944	.621	−.869
Std. Error of Kurtosis	.349	.343	.337
Minimum	−4.85	−1.01	−2.10
Maximum	1.83	3.39	1.72

distribution on a continuous variable is not normal, such as the distribution is skewed or bi- or multimodal or "chunky" or "lumpy." Another reason is that the relationship between an explanatory variable and an outcome variable is nonlinear. A third reason is that for some variables it is substantively meaningful to break them into discrete categories rather than treat them as continuous. A fourth reason is that the algorithms that we will use prefer discrete rather than continuous variables.

Partitioning a numerical variable into a series of discrete ordered categories (called bins or bands) is called binning a variable. In other words, we convert a continuous variable into a categorical variable. There are six common methods for binning numerical variables: binning based on meaning, binning based on equal width, binning based on equal frequency, binning by clustering, and binning by predictive value.

IBM SPSS version 25 provides *Optimal Binning* modules that automatically or semiautomatically bin variables. It is a supervised method for discretizing a variable whereby the cut points are chosen to optimize the target variable with a nominal variable. This procedure first sorts cases internally on the original variable. It then uses forward binning algorithms to begin within all cases in a single bin. It next inserts cut points to divide the sample into progressively smaller bins until a stopping criterion is reached. It applies backward binning algorithms with each unique scale value defined as a bin. Last, it merges bins until a stopping criterion is reached. *Visual Binning* allows users more supervision by providing visualization of the variable distribution and the interactive locations of potential cut points to assist with decision making.

BINNING BASED ON MEANING

Binning based on meaning of the variable divides a numerical variable into k numbers of groups with the values entailed in each group having a meaning-equivalent group in the domain field. For example, a variable of number of years of education can be

TABLE 3.9   **A DATA SET OF INCOME AND**
SENSE OF HAPPINESS (N = 20)

ID	Income	Happiness
1	15,789	2
2	17,492	2
3	26,047	3
4	27,406	3
5	36,989	4
6	37,008	5
7	37,008	5
8	37,009	5
9	38,037	6
10	39,584	7
11	41,836	8
12	42,502	8
13	44,385	8
14	47,928	8
15	48,000	8
16	48,658	8
17	68,097	9
18	80,094	9
19	91,596	9
20	250,000	10

divided into seven categories representing levels of education: Elementary school: $0 \leq x \leq 6$; Junior high school: $6 < x \leq 9$; Senior high school: $9 < x \leq 12$; Some college: $12 < x < 16$; College: $x = 16$; and Graduate school: $x > 16$.

BINNING BASED ON EQUAL WIDTH

Binning based on equal width groups a numerical variable into k number of categories of equal width, where k is decided by the analyst or researcher. For example, it is common to group age measured in calendar year into age groups with an interval of 10 years (0–9, 10–19, 20–29, 30–39, 40–49, 50–59, 60–69, 70–79, 80–89, 90–99, 100–109, etc.). When the data are skewed or have outlier(s), this approach could be problematic. When this is the case, some of the categories have few records while other categories could be composed of large proportions of the sample.

Below are examples to illustrate these points and show how we can convert a continuous variable into a categorical one under different approaches. A small sample (n = 20) of individuals' annual incomes and their sense of happiness (1–10) have records as illustrated in table 3.9.

In this data set of 20 records, suppose a researcher decides to partition the variable into 4 categories of equal distance on the variable Annual Income (fig. 3.6a). The four categories are divided by the four lines on the vertical axis marked as Annual Income from First Job:

a. Lowest: $0 \leq x < 62{,}500$, with 16 cases (1 to 16);
b. Low: $62{,}500 \leq x < 125{,}000$, with 3 cases (17 to 19);
c. High: $125{,}000 \leq x < 187{,}500$, with no case;
d. Highest: $187{,}500 \leq x \leq 250{,}000$, with 1 case (20).

```
* Visual Binning in SPSS 25. Codes are automatically generated.
* Transform->Visual Binning->Equal Width Intervals
* Income.
RECODE Income (MISSING=COPY) (LO THRU 62500=1) (LO THRU 125000=2) (LO THRU
187500=3) (LO THRU HI=4) (ELSE=SYSMIS) INTO IncEW.
VARIABLE LABELS IncEW 'Income (Binned)'.
FORMATS IncEW (F5.0).
VALUE LABELS IncEW 1 '= 62500' 2 '62501 - 125000' 3 '125001 - 187500' 4 '187501+'.
VARIABLE LEVEL IncEW (ORDINAL).
EXECUTE.
```

BINNING BASED ON EQUAL FREQUENCY

Binning based on equal frequency divides a numerical variable into k number of categories of equal frequency; that is, each has n/k number of cases with n equal to the total sample size. For example, we often divide our data into quartiles or quintiles, which are either four or five categories of an equal number of cases in each group. Although each category now has the same number of cases, the width to which each category spans could vary greatly. Some categories can contain a very narrow range of values; others, a wide range.

In this data set of 20 records, suppose a researcher decides to partition the variable into 4 categories of equal frequency on the variable Annual Income (fig. 3.6b). The four categories are divided by the four lines on the horizontal axis marked as Case Number:

a. Lower Quartile: $0 \leq x \leq 27{,}809$, with 5 cases (1 to 5);
b. Second Quartile: $27{,}809 < x \leq 39{,}584$, with 5 cases (6 to 10);
c. Third Quartile: $39{,}584 < x \leq 51{,}978$, with 5 cases (10 to 15);
d. Upper Quartile: $51{,}978 < x \leq 250{,}000$, with 5 cases (15 to 20).

```
* Visual Binning SPSS 25 - codes are automatically generated
* Transform->Visual Binning->Equal Percentile Based on Scanned Cases:
* Number of Cut points: 3, Width(%): 25

* Income.
RECODE Income (MISSING=COPY) (LO THRU 36998.5=1) (LO THRU 40710=2) (LO THRU
48329=3) (LO THRU HI=4) (ELSE=SYSMIS) INTO IncEF.
```

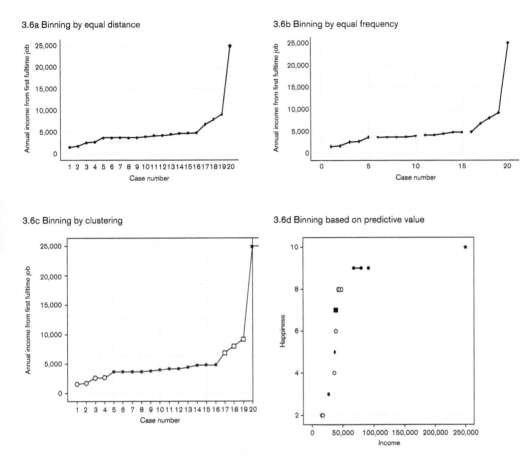

3.6a Binning by equal distance

3.6b Binning by equal frequency

3.6c Binning by clustering

3.6d Binning based on predictive value

Binned input variable income based on guide variable happiness

◁ Income < 26,047
♦ 26,047 <= Income < 36,989
▽ 36,989 <= Income < 37,008
♦ 37,008 <= Income < 37,037
○ 37,037 <= Income < 35,584
■ 35,584 <= Income < 41,836
◊ 41,836 <= Income < 68,097
● 68,097 <= Income < 250,000
★ 250,000 <= Income
— Interpolation line

FIGURE 3.6
Binning Methods.

```
VARIABLE LABELS IncEF 'Income (Binned)'.
FORMATS IncEF (F5.0).
VALUE LABELS IncEF 1 '' 2 '' 3 '' 4 ''.
VARIABLE LEVEL IncEF (ORDINAL).
```

BINNING BY STANDARD DEVIATION

Binning by standard deviation discretizes a numerical variable into its Z value. We standardize the variable by subtracting the mean $(y - \bar{y})$ and dividing this result by the standard deviation S_y. We then round it down to whole numbers.

$$y* = \frac{(y - \bar{y})}{S_y}$$

```
* Visual Binning in SPSS 25. Codes are generated automatically
* Transform->Visual Binning->
* Cutpoints at Mean and Selected Standard Deviations Based no Scanned Cases

*Income.
RECODE Income (MISSING=COPY) (LO THRU 3993.86153250908=1) (LO THRU
53773.25000000001=2) (LO THRU 103552.638467=3) (LO THRU HI=4) (ELSE=SYSMIS) INTO
InSD.
VARIABLE LABELS InSD 'Income (Binned)'.
FORMATS InSD (F5.0).
VALUE LABELS InSD 1 '' 2 '' 3 '' 4 ''.
VARIABLE LEVEL InSD (ORDINAL).
EXECUTE.
```

BINNING BY CLUSTERING

Binning by clustering uses a clustering approach to calculate the optimal partitioning of the sample. For example, researchers may use k-means clustering to group the cases based on their distance from each other (see chap. 6 for discussion of cluster analysis). This partition is an "optimal" partition of data into k clusters, while the number of clusters is chosen by the researcher.

In this data set of 20 records, suppose a researcher decides to partition the variable into 4 categories using k-means clustering to group the cases based on small distance from cluster members and large distance from nonmembers (fig. 3.6c). The four categories are divided by the four different colors indicating the cluster for each dot (case):

a. Cluster 1: $15,784 \leq x \leq 27,406$, 4 cases (1 to 4);
b. Cluster 2: $36,989 \leq x \leq 48,658$, 12 cases (5 to 16);
c. Cluster 3: $68,097 \leq x \leq 91,596$, 3 cases (17 to 19);
d. Cluster 4: $x = 250,000$, 1 case (20).

BINNING BY PREDICTIVE VALUE

Binning by predictive value partitions the variable based on the value of a target variable that it is intended to predict. Because the binning is specific to the dependent variable, if we choose a different dependent variable, a very different binning group will be generated. This is called optimal binning because it is optimal in predicting a particular outcome variable.

Income variable is binned in the following way that is related to the dependent variable of Happiness. This binning result is illustrated in figure 3.6d.

a. Income 1: $x < 26,047$, 2 cases (1 to 2);
b. Income 2: $26,047 \leq x < 36,989$, 2 cases (3 to 4);

c. Income 3: 36,989 ≤ x < 37,008, 1 case (5);

d. Income 4: 37,008 ≤ x < 38,037, 3 case (6 to 8);

e. Income 4: 38,037 ≤ x < 39,584, 1 cases (9);

f. Income 5: 39,584 ≤ x < 41,836, 1 case (10);

g. Income 6: 41,836 ≤ x < 68,097, 6 case (11 to 16);

h. Income 7: 68,097 ≤ x < 250,000, 3 cases (17 to 19);

i. Income 8: x ≤ 250,000, 1 case (20).

```
* EQUALFREQ Optimal Binning in SPSS 25.
* Transform-> Optimal Binning: Variables to Bin: Income, Optimize Bins with
Respect to: Happiness
OPTIMAL BINNING
/VARIABLES GUIDE=Happiness BIN=Income SAVE=YES (INTO=Income_bin)
/CRITERIA METHOD=MDLP PREPROCESS=EQUALFREQ (BINS=1000) FORCEMERGE=0
LOWERLIMIT=INCLUSIVE
LOWEREND=UNBOUNDED UPPEREND=UNBOUNDED
/MISSING SCOPE=PAIRWISE
/PRINT ENDPOINTS DESCRIPTIVES ENTROPY.
```

SUMMARY

Before each data mining project, we need to collect data, uphold the code of ethics, ensure data confidentiality, evaluate the quality of the data, clean data, handle missing data, and perform transformations of variables.

The code of ethics includes data privacy, data integrity, and the rights of human subjects. In addition to common ethical issues arising in research on human subjects, data mining faces further complexities. Data should not be used beyond the original purpose for which the informants grant consent. Data mining techniques make it difficult to anonymize data, so researchers should take special precautions to shield data confidentiality to protect informant identities. The results of data mining analyses should not be used to discriminate against people based on race/ethnicity, sex, religion, sexual orientation, or disability. Scraping data from websites should follow the terms of service.

There are multiple ways to handle missing data. When the missing data occur randomly, deleting them is reasonable. An alternative to deletion is data replacement, which might involve replacing the missing value with a measure of central tendency, a random value generated from the value distribution, imputed values based on other characteristics of the case, and multiple imputation of a set of plausible values.

Some algorithms and methods require variable normalization and standardization. Variable standardization methods include Z-score standardization, range normalization, and decimal scaling. To normalize skewed variables, we use methods of mathematical functions such as log transformation, square transformation, inverse transformation, and Box-Cox transformation.

Binning converts a variable from numerical to discrete. We use methods of binning based on meaning, equal width, equal frequency, standard deviation, clustering, and predictive value.

PRACTICE PROBLEMS

1. What is the code of ethics shared by data practitioners? Which code of ethics did Facebook–Cambridge Analytica violate in their data scandal?
2. When is deleting or ignoring missing data acceptable?
3. How many approaches are there to replacing missing data? Discuss their advantages and disadvantages.
4. Why is it necessary to normalize variables?
5. Based on information in table 3.2, find the following values and fill in table P3.1
   A) Z normalized,
   B) range normalized, and
   C) decimal scaling
   For the following variables:
   Fertility, GDP per Capita, Life Expectancy, Population, and Morality Rate
   For the following countries:
   Albania, United Arab Emirates, Argentina, Belgium, and Bangladesh

TABLE P3.1   **VARIABLE TRANSFORMATIONS**

	Fertility			GDP per capita			Life Expectance			Population			Mortality		
	A	B	C	A	B	C	A	B	C	A	B	C	A	B	C
Albania															
United Arab Emirates															
Argentina															
Belgium															
Bangladesh															

6. What are the statistical tests commonly used to evaluate whether a distribution deviates significantly from a normal distribution?
7. What are the most commonly used methods of data transformation to achieve symmetry? Explain how each transformation is achieved.
8. Explain why we need to bin variables from continuous to discrete. How many ways are there to bin a variable?
9. Bin the variable age based on meaning using information from table P3.2.

TABLE P3.2 **VARIABLE BINNING**

ID	Age	# of Viral Infections Have Ever Had
1	1	3
2	2	4
3	4	6
4	8	10
5	10	16
6	16	23
7	18	42
8	22	44
9	29	43
10	36	56
11	38	57
12	45	60
13	49	58
14	50	50
15	54	60
16	58	70
17	62	76
18	68	80
19	72	82
20	76	88

10. Using the data from Problem 9 and a statistical software program if needed, bin the variable of age based on the following:
   a. Equal width;
   b. Equal frequency;
   c. Standard deviation;
   d. Clustering;
   e. Predictive value of the number of infections.

REFERENCES

Little, Roderick J., and Donald Rubin. 2002. *Statistical Analysis with Missing Data.* 2nd ed. New York: Wiley.

Marini, Margaret Mooney, Anthony R. Olsen, and Donald B. Rubin. 1980. "Maximum Likelihood Estimation in Panel Studies with Missing Data." *Sociological Methodology* 11: 314–57.

Osborne, Jason. 2002. "Notes on the Use of Data Transformations." *Practical Assessment, Research & Evaluation* 8 (6). http://PAREonline.net/getvn.asp?v=8&n=6. Retrieved December 2, 2005.

Stuart, Alan, and Keith Ord. 2010. *Kendall's Advanced Theory of Statistics.* Vol. 1: *Distribution Theory.* 6th ed. New York: Wiley.

Tataris, K. L., M. P. Mercer, and P. Govindarajan. 2015. "Prehospital Aspirin Administration for Acute Coronary Syndrome (ACS) in the USA: An EMS Quality Assessment Using the NEMSIS 2011 Database." *Emergency Medicine Journal* 32 (11): 876–81. doi:10.1136/emermed-2014-204299.

Chapter 4

DATA VISUALIZATION

DATA VISUALIZATION INVOLVES THE GRAPHIC presentation of data to understand their structure and significance. Large and complex data that are expressed in tabular form can often hide patterns and correlations, and these are easier to recognize when the data are represented visually. Numerical data also cannot provide the context of quantitative relationships that can help us compare and contrast them effectively. Presenting data in a visual form greatly facilitates this process. Data visualization involves making many choices about how to present the data. Researchers decide on a combination of points, lines, areas, sizes, colors, positions, axes, and grid lines to construct different types of charts that vary in complexity and composition. These charts are capable of describing different types of data and portraying different angles of analysis. When making decisions about data presentation, we need to consider the data type, our analytical purpose, the key components of different chart types, and principles that distinguish effective visualizations from less effective ones.

The ultimate purpose of data visualization is to help us understand data. To achieve this, data visualizations should possess the following three qualities. First, charts should clearly communicate the values of data under study. Charts should make it easy for readers to decode various shapes, sizes, and colors; convert visual representations into values; and estimate the relationships between different values. Second, charts should help readers understand the significance of the values in the chart. This involves making design choices that clarify what meaning readers should draw from the visual display of captions, colors, titles, and other annotations. Third, data visualization helps readers understand what the chart contributes to existing knowledge. Charts should reflect what we already know or do not know about particular quantitative relationships in the existing literature. New charts should purposefully shed light on new knowledge or insights.

Data visualizations are of two types: explanatory and exploratory. Explanatory visualization not only provides viewers with a visual portrayal of the data but also reveals new insights about the relationship between variables. The purpose of explanatory visualizations is to lead viewers through a process of understanding by providing key links in interpreting and drawing hidden meanings from the data. Explanatory visualization requires that the researcher have sufficient knowledge about the topic under study and be capable of identifying the most relevant, interesting, and worthwhile insights. In contrast, exploratory visualization aims at helping viewers discover their own insights. This process involves interrogating and manipulating the data. This process is both interactive and iterative, allowing users to modify their view of a graph, filter central traits of interest, change parameters, or rotate the view.

The process of data visualization contains four steps in planning and implementation: formulating the brief, working with data, establishing editorial thinking, and developing design solutions (Kirk 2016). Researchers start with planning, defining, and initiating the project, then move on to gathering or accessing information and preparing their data. They next decide on what they will show to readers. The last step is to develop the most effective design to produce graphs that illustrate important features of the data.

One key step in the design process involves understanding the levels of data measurement. Data are often expressed in the form of variables, or characteristics that vary for different cases. Data are distinguished as either qualitative or quantitative variables. These variables are further differentiated into Nominal, Ordinal, Interval, and Textual.

TYPES OF VARIABLES
QUALITATIVE AND QUANTITATIVE DATA
When the elements of a variable are classified according to some characteristics, this variable is qualitative. It is also called a categorical variable. Examples of qualitative variables are marital status, religious affiliation, political party affiliation, state of

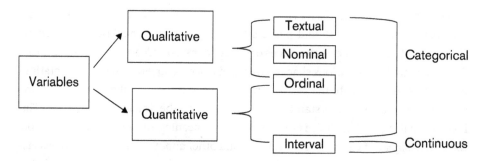

FIGURE 4.1
Types of Variables.

residence, attitudes toward gun control, and beliefs about immigration policies. Qualitative variables can be further distinguished as nominal or textual. Nominal data are measured in categories that allow users to label and distinguish values without ranking them. Nominal data allow for neither natural ordering in terms of magnitude or volume nor any numerical calculations to be carried out. In contrast, ordinal variables can be ranked in a particular order, although one still cannot carry out meaningful arithmetic manipulations on ordinal variables. Examples of ordinal variables are the highest educational degree achieved, income brackets, and attitudes toward gun control (ranging from strongly support to strongly oppose). Although nominal and ordinal data cannot be arithmetically manipulated, there exists another class of quantitative variables—interval variables—that allow for arithmetic manipulation.

DISCRETE AND CONTINUOUS VARIABLES

A variable with a countable number of values is a discrete variable, where each value is a separate point with spaces between them. The vast majority of variables in the social sciences are discrete, including variables such as occupation, college major, number of children born, and number of homicides. A variable that takes an infinite number of values is a continuous variable, where possible values form a continuum with no space between them. Examples of continuous variables are distance (in miles), income (in dollars), and weight (in pounds). Figure 4.1 illustrates how variables are classified as qualitative and quantitative variables; how they are further divided into textual, nominal, ordinal, and interval variables; and how they are differentiated as categorical and continuous variables.

GRAPHIC SUMMARY OF SINGLE VARIABLES

For categorical variables, a bar chart is the best representation of absolute or relative frequency. The bars do not touch each other in order to indicate the discrete nature of these values. In addition, all the bars in a bar chart are based on the same measurement scale, so the heights of the bars indicate the relative frequency distribution among the

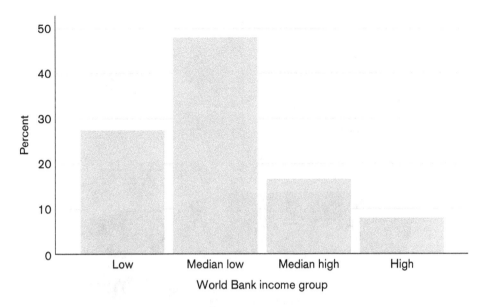

FIGURE 4.2
Bar Chart of World Bank Country Income Groups.

categories. Figure 4.2 is a bar chart illustrating the distribution of countries among income groups. The data are from Country Indicators in 2014, extracted from the World Development Database (http://databank.worldbank.org/data/home.aspx). We define the high-income group as having GDP per capita higher than $50,000 (50K), the second highest income with GDP per capita between 16K and 50K, the third group between 2K and 16K, and the poorest group as below 2K. Less than 10 percent of the countries are high income with GDP exceeding 50K, while close to 30 percent and 50 percent of the countries are low and median low income, respectively, with GDP less than 16K. The other countries, less than 20 percent, have a median high income in the range of 16K to 50K.

The frequency distribution of a categorical variable can also be expressed as a pie chart that divides a circle into slices, with the size of each slice proportional to the relative frequency of the associated category. Figure 4.3 shows the same information as the bar chart but in the format of a pie chart.

A histogram represents the relative frequency distribution for a quantitative variable using connected bars. However, because the number and width of the bars determine the shape of histograms, we should practice caution when interpreting histograms. Each bar represents a decision to group a range of values, which is a simple form of data smoothing. How and why these values are grouped together influences the shape of the histogram. Figure 4.4 is a histogram of GDP per capita showing a distribution with a long right tail.

A stem-and-leaf plot illustrates the shape of the data distribution similarly to a histogram while maintaining the original data values in the display, sometimes

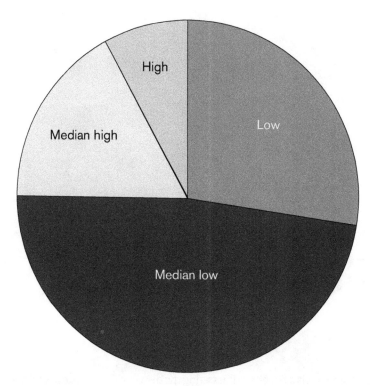

FIGURE 4.3
Pie Chart of World Bank Country Income Groups.

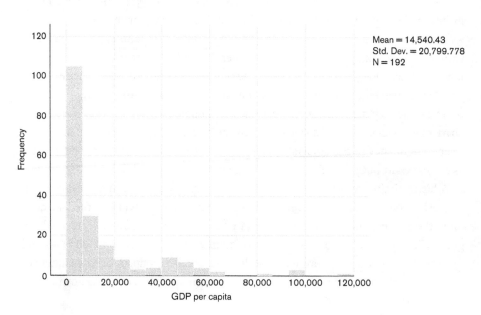

Mean = 14,540.43
Std. Dev. = 20,799.778
N = 192

FIGURE 4.4
Histogram of GDP per Capita.

TABLE 4.1   STEM-AND-LEAF PLOT OF GDP PER CAPITA

GDP per capita Stem-and-Leaf Plot

Frequency	Stem & Leaf
52.00	0 . 0000000000000000000000000000011111111111111111111111111
25.00	0 . 2222222223333333333333333
21.00	0 . 444444444444455555555555
18.00	0 . 666666667777777777
4.00	0 . 8899
12.00	1 . 000000001111
5.00	1 . 22233
7.00	1 . 4445555
2.00	1 . 66
4.00	1 . 8899
3.00	2 . 011
2.00	2 . 22
3.00	2 . 444
2.00	2 . 77
1.00	2 . 9
.00	3 .
.00	3 .
1.00	3 . 5
2.00	3 . 67
28.00 Extremes	(>=37793)

Stem width:	10000
Each leaf:	1 case(s)

approximately. The stem units are usually the first digit of the values; the leaf units are defined as the second digit of the values. In table 4.1, the stem units in the left column represent 10,000s and the leaf units in the right column are 1,000s. "1.2" represents $12,000 GDP per capita, and the line "1.22233" indicates three cases of $12,000 and two cases of $13,000.

A box plot is a graphic representation of both the center and the variation of a distribution. It consists of a center box that represents the middle 50 percent of the cases, ranging from the lower quartile to the upper quartile (also called the interquartile range, or IQR), and two whiskers, representing a length of 1.5 times the IQR. Cases outside the reach of the whiskers are outliers. Box plots also indicate the locations of the median and the mean. The box plot therefore allows for a quick graphic examination of data sets. It overcomes one of the shortcomings of histograms, that is,

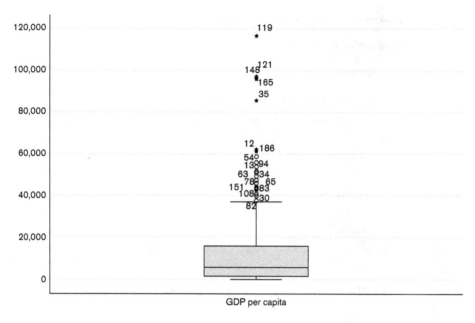

FIGURE 4.5
Box Plot of GDP per Capita.

that the number and width of bars can heavily influence their shape. The box plot also takes less space than a histogram and is thus particularly useful for comparing several subpopulations or examining changes over time. Figure 4.5 is a box plot showing the distribution of GDP per capita. This distribution is skewed toward the upper end, with a long upper whisker and a few outliers beyond the upper whisker.

VISUALIZATIONS OF BIVARIATE DATA
A number of graphic representations can be used to visualize the relationship between two variables. The relationship between a categorical variable and a quantitative variable can be summarized with a series of histograms with identical measurement scales and group division schemes. Figure 4.6 is a series of histograms showing life expectancy (a quantitative variable) by income group (a categorical variable). This graph appears to show that as national income increases, the average life expectancy increases ande the variance decreases. However, this graph does not display group averages and takes up quite a bit of space.

To simplify the presentation, we might create bar charts classified by the categorical variable, with the height of the bars showing the average value for each subgroup. Variation in the height of the bars demonstrates the relationship between the categorical and quantitative variables. Figure 4.7 is a bar chart showing the average life expectancy for each income group. It appears to reflect a positive linear association between income and life expectancy.

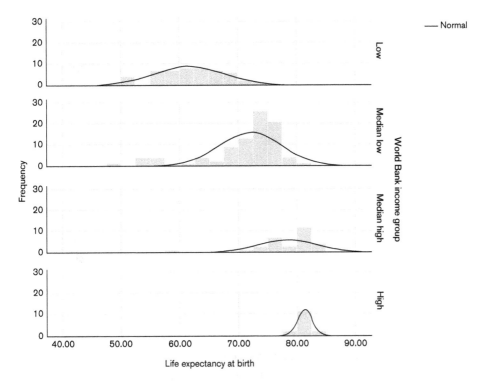

FIGURE 4.6

Histograms of Life Expectancy by World Bank Income Group.

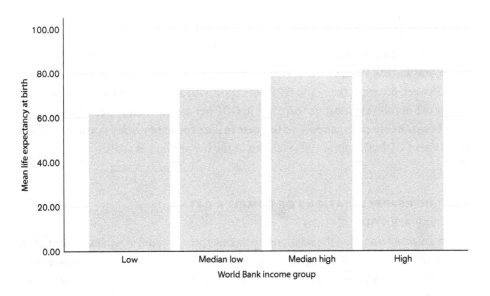

FIGURE 4.7

Bar Chart of Life Expectancy by World Bank Income Group.

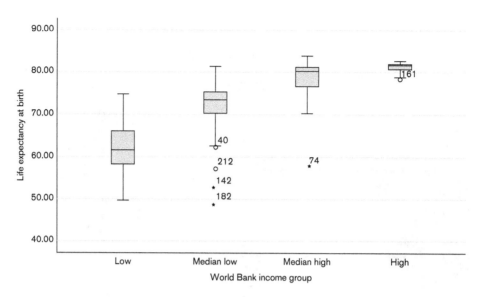

FIGURE 4.8

Box Plot of Life Expectancy by World Bank Income Groups.

Alternatively, instead of histograms we could create a series of box plots to represent the relationship between a categorical and a quantitative variable. These plots can show both the center and the spread of the distribution in very little space. Figure 4.8 illustrates the relationship between income levels and life expectancy. Median life expectancy increases with income, while the whiskers are longer in the lower income groups and shorter in the higher income groups, indicating that the variance of life expectancy decreases with income.

We use a scatter plot to illustrate the relationship between two quantitative variables. Scatter plots graph each (x, y) point on a Cartesian plane, with the x axis on the horizontal and the y axis on the vertical. Figure 4.9 shows a scatter plot of the relationship between life expectancy and GDP per capita with an extrapolation line describing the nature of this relationship. Increases in GDP per capita at the lower levels provide large boosts in life expectancy. This increase in life expectancy slows down in the middle range of GDP per capita and levels out at the highest end of GDP.

GRAPHIC REPRESENTATIONS OF COMPLEX DATA

MULTIVARIATE VISUALIZATION

When we want to analyze the relationship among three or more variables, we can use a variety of approaches. Some approaches are similar to those used for bivariate relations, while others are new ways to depict data. One of the former approaches is a series of scatter plots describing relationships among three or more variables. Figure 4.10 contains a series of six scatter plots illustrating the association among three variables

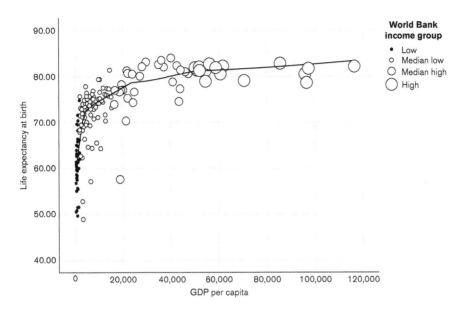

FIGURE 4.9

Scatter Plot of Life Expectancy by GDP per capita.

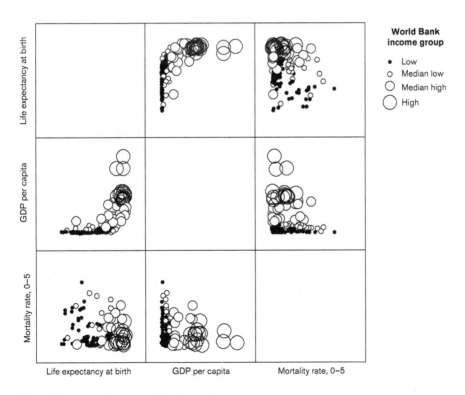

FIGURE 4.10

Scatter Plot of Relationship between Life Expectancy, GDP per Capita, and Infant Mortality Rate.

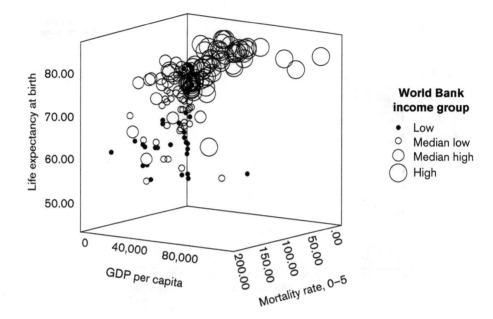

FIGURE 4.11

3D Scatter Plot of Relationship between Life Expectancy, GDP per Capita, and Infant Mortality Rate.

and allows us to inspect all the pairs of correlations simultaneously. Alternatively, we can inspect these relationships among three variables in an interactive 3D scatter plot that can be rotated and visualized from any angle, as illustrated in figure 4.11.

When analyzing a two-way classification of a variable on ordinal scale, we may consider a series of stacked bars. Figure 4.12 shows changes in attitudes toward premarital sex in China by birth cohort and historical period. By stacking the bars for an ordinal variable, the graph elegantly shows the changing pattern by birth cohorts: younger cohorts express more liberal views about premarital sex than do older cohorts. Comparing across the four panels provides insight into changes over the four survey years. In this case, attitudes generally become more liberal over this period.

NETWORK VISUALIZATION

Network visualization is concerned with describing relationships and connections between actors, or nodes, in a network. The nature of the visualization depends on the goals of the analysis and emphasizes different features of the network, such as actors and links, relationship strength, structural properties, diffusion patterns, network transformations, network maps, and communities. Researchers use color, positon, size, and shape to represent these qualities of the network. A number of software programs provide the capacity to visualize networks. For example, R provides packages such igraph, sna, network, visNetwork, threejs, NetworkD3, ndtv, and others. Figure 4.13 shows the same 100-node network in different layout options (sphere vs. randomly

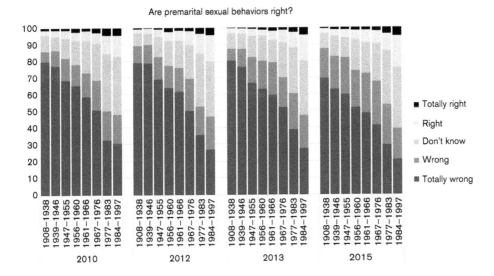

FIGURE 4.12

Stacked Bars of Cohort and Period Variations in Attitudes toward Premarital Sex in China as an Ordinal Scale.

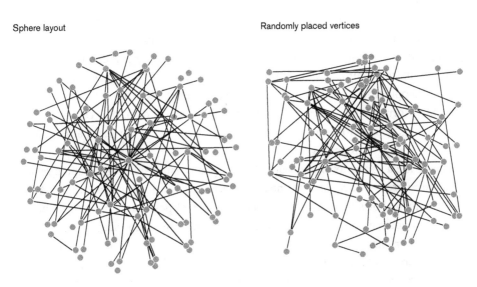

FIGURE 4.13

A 100-Node Network in Different Layouts.

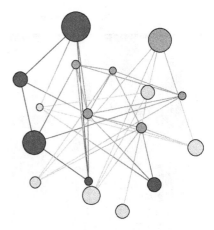

FIGURE 4.14
A Network with Colored (by Type) Nodes of
Varying Sizes (Centrality).

placed vertices) after using the sample_pa() function to generate a simple graph of 100 nodes (actors in the network).

In addition to setting up the network layout, we can color the nodes based on a classification scheme. Figure 4.14 is an example of a layout with all nodes colored based on the type of node and in sizes proportional to their network centrality (network positions indicative of status and prominence).

MAP VISUALIZATION

Map graphs are useful for analyzing spatial patterns. To make a map, researchers need information about the shape of the geographic area. For example, in R, Leaflet and ggmap provide background maps from Google. There are several R libraries providing information for common country boundaries. A third source of geospatial information for people who are studying a specific area is from the web, under the shapefile or GeoJSON format. Once researchers obtains the geospatial data, they can use ggplots for drawing, Leaflet for interactive presentation, or other R libraries/packages (e.g., Ggplot, Ggmap, Cartography) to make maps.

There are a variety of other maps. A choropleth map displays geographic regions that are colored, shaded, or patterned to reflect spatial variations in a variable. A connection map shows the connections between several positions on a map. A bubble map has bubble markers with sizes proportional to some numerical variable. Figure 4.15 is a choropleth map demonstrating the spatial pattern of infant mortality rates, using different colors to illustrate global variations in infant mortality rates.

Using connection maps and network graphs, we can generate links between different spatial locations. For example, figure 4.16 shows the connecting flights between major U.S. airports. This was generated in R using map packages to add a map of the United States, then mark points on the map for the major airports. Using flight data, the coordinates of the shortest arc between starting and ending cities were generated. Then each arc was plotted over the map.

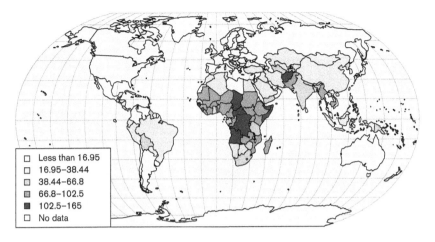

FIGURE 4.15
Choropleth Map of Infant Mortality Rate on a Global Scale.

FIGURE 4.16
Connection Map of Flights between Major U.S. Airports.

WORD CLOUDS

Word clouds are an approach to summarizing the major keywords in a speech or text by giving greater prominence to words that appear more frequently in the source. We can modify word clouds with different fonts, layouts, and color schemes.

Many software programs are capable of processing text files and generating word clouds. For example, the R packages tm, wordcloud, and RColorBrewer may be used to read text files. R can convert text files into a corpus that can be processed by the tm

FIGURE 4.17

Word Cloud Summarizing Keywords and Their Frequencies in This Chapter.

package. Then we can clean the file using the tm package to process the text by stripping white space, converting uppercase letters to lowercase, removing common English words such as *the*, and removing numbers and punctuation. After specifying the layout of the word cloud, including the difference in font size between the largest and smallest words, the upper limit on the number of words in the cloud, the percentage of text that is vertically oriented, and the colors to be used, we can generate a collection of words representing the topics covered as well as their relative prominence or frequency in the text. Figure 4.17 is a word cloud showing the topics covered in this chapter and their relative prominence, as measured by the frequency of their appearance. It is not surprising that in a chapter dedicated to data visualization, the most prominent words are *data, variable(s), visualization,* and *figure*.

SUMMARY

Graphic data presentation provides information for readers to compare and analyze a large number of data points. Effective data visualizations should possess three features: (1) a graph should communicate the basic information clearly; (2) it should facilitate mental conversion of numbers and values into meaningful knowledge; and (3) it should purposefully shed light on new insights.

There are two types of data visualization: explanatory and exploratory. Explanatory visualization starts with existing knowledge, paints a visual portrayal of the data, provides interpretive links, and reveals hidden patterns in the data. Exploratory visualization involves manipulating and interrogating data to potentially discover new insights.

When designing a data visualization, the first key step is to understand the levels of data measurement. We differentiate between qualitative and quantitative variables. Qualitative variables are textual, nominal, and sometimes ordinal; quantitative variables are interval and ordinal. Besides a small number of variables that are continuous, most variables are categorical or discrete.

Graphic representations of single variables include bar charts (for categorical variables) and histograms (for continuous variables), pie charts, stem-and-leaf plots, and box plots. To illustrate the association between two variables, there are a number of data visualization methods. For example, we can construct a series of histograms and box plots to show the values of the first variable organized by different values of the second variable. Scatter plots are also an effective approach for analyzing bivariate relationships. For multivariate relationships, we can use a series of scatter plots for continuous variables or a series of stacked bar charts, box plots, or histograms that are grouped by a third variable.

Network visualizations present connections between a number of actors in a network to highlight some features of their relationships. For research on spatial patterns, map graphs combine statistical information with geospatial data such as the shape of a continent, country, county, or city.

Word clouds are a graphic representation of the major keywords in a text that give more prominence to more frequent words.

PRACTICE QUESTIONS AND ADDITIONAL WORK

1. What are the advantages of data visualization over tabulation of data?
2. What is data visualization?
3. In order to achieve effective data visualization, what qualities should a graph possess?
4. What are the two different purposes of data visualization? What are the different steps and objectives involved in these different types of data visualization?
5. What are the four steps in data visualization?

6. What is a variable? What is a qualitative variable? What is a quantitative variable? What is a discrete variable? What is a continuous variable? What are textual, nominal, ordinal, and interval variables? What are categorical and continuous variables? How would you measure and visually represent the relationships among these different types of variables?

7. Locate a data set of interest and identify a target variable. Generate a bar chart (categorical variable) or a histogram (continuous variable). Compare the graph with a frequency distribution table and discuss what additional information the graph provides that is not visible from the table.

8. Find a continuous variable in this data set and produce a box plot and a histogram for this variable. Compare the box plot, histogram, and frequency distribution table, identifying differences and similarities among these three graphs.

9. Perhaps you are interested in whether this variable varies by race, gender, age group, or income group. Find a categorical variable in the same data set that may affect the variable you analyzed in Question 8. Construct a series of histograms and box plots showing the values of the first variable by values of the new categorical variable. What do you learn from these graphs? How are changes in the first variable related to changes in the second variable?

10. Use the same continuous variable from Question 8 and a second continuous variable from the same data set to construct a scatter plot. What relationship do you observe from this graph?

11. Find a third variable that is also continuous and construct a matrix of scatter plots. What are the relationships of the third variable with the first two? Discuss how the third variable may change the nature of the relationship between the first two variables.

INFORMATION ON R AND R STUDIO

Networks Visualization

R igraph

https://cran.r-project.org/web/packages/igraph/igraph.pdf
http://igraph.org/r/doc/aaa-igraph-package.html
Download and install the package
install.packages("igraph")
Load package
library(igraph)

SNA

https://cran.r-project.org/web/packages/sna/sna.pdf
Download and install the package
install.packages("sna")

```
## Load package
library(sna)
```

network
https://cran.r-project.org/web/packages/network/network.pdf
```
## Download and install the package
install.packages("network")
## Load package
library(network)
```

visNetwork
https://cran.r-project.org/web/packages/visNetwork/visNetwork.pdf
```
## Download and install the package
install.packages("visNetwork")
## Load package
library(visNetwork)
```

threejs
https://cran.r-project.org/web/packages/threejs/threejs.pdf
```
## Download and install the package
install.packages("threejs")
## Load package
library(threejs)
```

NetworkD3
https://cran.r-project.org/web/packages/networkD3/networkD3.pdf
```
## Download and install the package
install.packages("networkD3")
## Load package
library(networkD3)
```

ndtv
https://cran.r-project.org/web/packages/ndtv/vignettes/ndtv.pdf
```
## Download and install the package
install.packages("ndtv")
## Load package
library(ndtv)
```

Map Visualization

Leaflet
https://cran.r-project.org/web/packages/leaflet/leaflet.pdf

```
## Download and install the package
install.packages("leaflet")
## Load package
library(leaflet)
```

ggmap

https://cran.r-project.org/web/packages/ggmap/ggmap.pdf
```
## Download and install the package
install.packages("ggmap")
## Load package
library(ggmap)
```

ggplot

https://cran.r-project.org/web/packages/ggplot2/ggplot2.pdf
```
## Download and install the package
install.packages("ggplot")
## Load package
library(ggplot)
```

Cartography

https://cran.r-project.org/web/packages/cartography/cartography.pdf
```
## Download and install the package
install.packages("cartography")
## Load package
library(cartography)
```

Word Cloud

wordcloud

https://cran.r-project.org/web/packages/wordcloud/wordcloud.pdf
```
## Download and install the package
install.packages("wordcloud")
install.packages("rcolorbrewer")
## Load package
library(wordcloud)
library(rcolorbrewer)
```

APPENDIX

R (3.5.1) CODES FOR CREATING A WORD CLOUD from chapter 3 of this book

```
install.packages("RColorBrewer")
install.packages ("tm")
```

```
install.packages ("wordcloud")
install.packages("SnowballC")
library(RColorBrewer)
library(tm)
library(wordcloud)
speech = "C:\Users\xshu\Documents\Ch3.txt"
modi_txt = readLines(speech)
modi<-Corpus(VectorSource(modi_txt))
modi_data<-tm_map(modi,stripWhitespace)
modi_data<-tm_map(modi_data,tolower)
modi_data<-tm_map(modi_data,removeNumbers)
modi_data<-tm_map(modi_data,removePunctuation)
modi_data<-tm_map(modi_data,removeWords, stopwords("english"))
tdm_modi<-TermDocumentMatrix (modi_data)
TDM1<-as.matrix(tdm_modi)
v = sort(rowSums(TDM1), decreasing = TRUE)
wordcloud (modi_data, scale=c(5,0.5), max.words=100, random.order=FALSE, rot.
per=0.35, use.r.layout=FALSE, colors=brewer.pal(8, "Dark2"))
```

REFERENCES

Kirk, Andy. 2016. *Data Visualization: A Handbook for Data Driven Design*. Thousand Oaks, CA: Sage.

## PART III

MODEL ASSESSMENT

Chapter 5

ASSESSMENT OF MODELS

DATA MINING EXTRACTS NEW, MEANINGFUL, and valid patterns from data. It is thus very important to evaluate alternative models that have a different fit with the data and may be consistent with different "theories" about the data. Goodness-of-fit measures and testing are important elements of any analysis because our models represent hypotheses derived from theoretical ideas about the processes that have generated the data. If our model fits with the data in some statistical or scientific sense, we thus conclude that the data are not inconsistent with the hypotheses and that the model appears adequate. We then believe that the data are generated from a process consistent with what the theory hypothesized and that this result lends support to our theory.

In machine learning, it is imperative that we use a training data set, a testing data set, and sometimes a data set to validate the model. These data sets are usually independent when there are sufficient data. This is an important feature of the data mining method as the data used tend to be "natural" or "convenience" samples that do not fulfill assumption of probability samples. When the data are too small to afford independent samples, we can use various methods of cross-validation. Cross-validation provides a variety of methods to divide a single sample into two or three data sets for training, testing, or validation. Instead of splitting the total data into parts in cross-validation, bootstrapping draws training data and testing data from the total data set, allowing for the possibility that the same cases are used in both the training set and the testing set.

When evaluating numerical prediction, we use mean squared error (MSE), root mean squared error (RMSE), and mean absolute error (MAE). Akaike's information criterion (AIC) and the Bayesian information criterion (BIC) are methods to compare a series of statistical models that are not necessarily nested models. Both AIC and BIC rank all alternative models and provide a relative measure of model goodness-of-fit. They all provide some measurement of the error between the predicted value and the actual value. These measures are used in cluster analysis (chap. 6), linear regression (chap. 8), and neural network (chap. 10).

For discrete outcomes, we use a number of measures calculated from a confusion table to evaluate model performance and select classification schemes. These include accuracy, the error rate, sensitivity, specificity, and the product of sensitivity and specificity as an overall measure of model performance. In addition, combining cost-benefit matrices with confusion tables provides profit as an evaluation of model performance. We can also derive a series of curves from the confusion table and cost-benefit matrix to aid in measuring model performance: cumulative response curve, lift chart, ROC curve, and recall precision curve. These measures of model performance are used in evaluating association (chap. 7).

TRAINING AND TESTING

For machine learning problems, we work with both training and testing data sets. We train a classification scheme to minimize the amount of error in allocating cases in different categories. We know that it is effective with regard to the data we used to train it; however, this is not satisfactory. We are more interested in its future performance on new data. We want to know if we can generalize our model to other data, settings, and time periods. In order to test the performance of a classifier on new data, we need to evaluate its performance on a new set of independent data that has played no part in the original estimation. This new set of independent data is called the testing set, and the data used to train the classifier is called the training set.

It is important that the testing set be a new and independent data set, totally unused in the creation of the classifier. We can easily achieve this when the data available are large. For example, we may take data collected from one occasion or location to train the classifier. Then we might use data collected from another occasion or location to test the classifier. The performance of the classifier on the testing set will be a good indicator of how well it will perform in the future. We generally benefit from larger samples as they enable us to have independent training and testing sets, and they provide us with a more accurate estimation.

Sometimes researchers use three independent data sets when the data are sufficiently large. They use the first data set to create a basic structure based on one or more learning schemes. This is the training set. They use the second data set to optimize the parameters in the structure or to choose among a number of learning schemes. This is the validation set. Last, they use the third set to test the validity and performance of the final, optimized classifier. All three data sets are usually independent.

CROSS-VALIDATION

When the available data are insufficiently large to be split into independent training and testing sets, we use cross-validation to make the most out of limited data. Small samples constrain the amount of data that can be used for training, validation, and testing. One method for training and testing on small samples is called the holdout method, where researchers split a single data set into several parts: one for training, one for validation (if required), and one for testing. In practice, it is common to split a sample into two halves, one half for training and the other half for testing. If validation is expected, the data will be divided into three parts: one-third for training, one-third for validation, and one-third for testing.

Data sets used for training and testing should be representative. If cases of a certain class are omitted from the training set and appear only in the testing set, the learning process will produce a biased classification scheme that will perform poorly on the testing set (which includes all the cases of the omitted class). To avoid this type of problem and achieve representative data sets, there are two approaches. One approach is the stratified holdout, which ensures that researchers sample in a way that ensures each class is present in both the training and the testing set. However, this approach provides only basic protection against representation issues in training and testing sets. The stratified holdout method requires researchers to already have knowledge of the number of relevant classes, which is not always possible. Often researchers discover the relevant classes at later stages of the research process.

Cross-validation overcomes the requirement of prior knowledge by using random data multiple times for training and testing sets. Researchers first decide on a number of "folds," or partitions, of the data. If we decide on a fold of three, then we would divide the data into three groups of approximately equal size. We would conduct the training-testing cycle three times, each time using one-third of the data for testing and two-thirds for training. Cross-validation is complete when each case has been used once in testing. This method is called threefold cross-validation.

TENFOLD CROSS-VALIDATION

When working with a single, fixed-size sample, the standard method of developing a classification scheme and predicting its errors is a learning technique called tenfold cross-validation. This approach randomly divides the data into ten portions and ensures that each portion is a representative subset of the total sample. It then uses nine-tenths of the data for training and reserves the remaining one-tenth for testing. Although researchers still debate the best approach to divide the data into what number of portions, tenfold cross-validation is generally regarded as the standard method. There is both theoretical and practical evidence in support of this position (Witten, Frank, and Hall 2011). Just like the threefold cross-validation described above, tenfold cross-validation proceeds in multiple stages, each time using a different one-tenth of the data as the testing set and the remaining data for training. As a result, the learning takes place ten times, each time with a different data set of nine-tenths of the total data (although these data sets overlap substantially). The resulting ten classifiers have different parameter and error estimates. We calculate the average of these estimates to produce the final parameter and error estimates.

LEAVE-ONE-OUT CROSS-VALIDATION

Besides tenfold cross-validation, an attractive alternative is called leave-one-out cross-validation. This is a simple n-fold cross-validation where n is the number of cases, or instances, in the data set. The learning scheme is trained n times on all the cases except for one left-out case that rotates each time. Then the scheme is judged by the remaining one test case, giving a score of one for success and zero for failure. The average of all such scores across all n learning schemes indicates the average error estimate. This approach allows researchers with small data sets to maximize the amount of data for training in each round, thus improving the accuracy of the estimate.

BOOTSTRAPPING

Bootstrapping is an alternative to cross-validation based on the procedure of sampling with replacement. Bootstrapping treats the existing sample as a population and samples it with replacement to form a training set. For a reasonably large data set, the training set might contain 63.2 percent of the total number of cases, while the testing set contains 36.8 percent. Because these two sets are sampled with replacement, both sets will have some cases that are used in both training and testing. This is the approach of the .632 bootstrap. The procedure is repeated several times, each time using 63.2 percent of the total cases for training and 36.8 percent for testing. Researchers then calculate the average of all results as the final estimates. The error estimation can be represented by the formula $e = \frac{\Sigma(.632 * e_{training} + .368 * e_{testing})}{m}$ where m is the number of repetitions in the bootstrapping procedure.

EVALUATION OF NUMERICAL ESTIMATION AND PREDICTION

When using models to estimate and predict numerical values, we generate a predicted value of the target variable, $\hat{y}$, and the actual value of the target variable is represented by y. We can assess the accuracy of a model by examining the residual, or error, between the predicted value and the actual value $(y - \hat{y})$. Based on this residual measure, we may choose among a series of performance indices for numeric predictions.

Mean Squared Error. Mean squared error (MSE) is calculated as the average squared error between the predicted and actual values. MSE is the most commonly used measure of model performance. It is mathematically well behaved and is thus regarded as the easiest to manipulate mathematically. MSE is calculated with the formula

$$MSE = \frac{\Sigma(y - \hat{y})^2}{n - p - 1}$$

where n is the total number of cases in the model, and p is the number of model variables. Some versions of the formula use n instead of $(n{-}p{-}1)$ as the denominator (Witten, Frank, and Hall 2011). This difference can be ignored when the sample size is very large.

Root Mean Squared Error. Root mean squared error (RMSE) is the square root of the MSE between the predicted and actual values:

$$RMSE = \sqrt{\frac{\Sigma(y - \hat{y})^2}{n - p - 1}}$$

Mean Absolute Error. Mean absolute error (MAE) is the average of the errors. MAE has an advantage over MSE and RMSE, as the latter two tend to exaggerate the effect of outliers because squared errors are much larger for outliers than for other data points. MAE treats all errors evenly based on their size and calculates absolute errors for all the points:

$$MAE = \sqrt{\frac{\Sigma|y - \hat{y}|}{n - p - 1}}$$

COMPARISON OF ALTERNATIVE MODELS
WITH AIC AND BIC INDICES

Both AIC and BIC are criteria for selecting a model from a finite set of models. When fitting models, there is a trade-off between model goodness-of-fit and the number of parameters used. So AIC and BIC measures are used to achieve a balance between model size and complexity and its explanatory power, more in line with the conventional statistical principle of model parsimony. By adding parameters, it is possible to increase the likelihood without the risk of decreasing it. However, too many parameters may result in overfitting. Both BIC and AIC attempt to resolve this dilemma by introducing a penalty for the number of parameters included in the model. BIC uses a larger penalty term than AIC.

AKAIKE'S INFORMATION CRITERION

AIC makes it possible to compare a series of statistical models. These models can be based on different samples of different sizes and different parameters. AIC ranks all alternative models from best to worst. It is a relative measure, in that it ranks all the models and identifies the "best" one, but it cannot provide information on the absolute quality of these models. If all of the models are poor, AIC can help us identify the best among a group of poor models. In addition to selecting the strongest model using AIC, researchers need to evaluate the relationship between the variables in the model and the outcome variable to ensure the strength of the association (Akaike 1981; Sakamoto, Ishiguro, and Kitagawa 1986).

The basic formula for Akaike's information criterion is defined as

$$AIC = 2k - 2\ln(L)$$

where k is the number of model parameters, that is, the number of variables in the model plus 1 for the intercept. Ln(L) is a measure of model fit, its log likelihood. The higher the ln(L), the better the fit. All widely available statistical software programs provide ln(L).

When the sample size is small relative to the number of model parameters (i.e., fewer than 40 cases per model parameter), there is a substantial probability that AIC will select overfitted models with too many parameters. To address this potential problem, we use AIC_c, which provides a correction for small sample sizes:

$$AIC_c = AIC + \frac{2k^2 + 2k}{n - k - 1}$$

where n is the sample size, and k is the number of model parameters.

When comparing multiple models, we use the difference in AIC or AIC_c (ΔAIC) to make decisions. The ΔAIC is the relative difference between two models, Model i and Model min, which is the "true" best model generated by the data:

$$\Delta AIC = AIC_i - AIC_{min}$$

We then calculate $e^{\frac{-\Delta AIC}{2}}$. This provides the relative likelihood of the model i (Akaike 1981; Burnham and Anderson 2004). The relative likelihood is closely related to the likelihood ratio. However, the likelihood-ratio test is valid only for comparisons of nested models, whereas AIC has no such restriction. We can use $e^{\frac{-\Delta AIC}{2}}$ as in relative likelihood tests on models that are not nested.

BAYESIAN INFORMATION CRITERION

BIC is similar to AIC. It provides a method for comparing a series of statistical models that are not necessarily nested and may be based on different samples of different sizes and of different parameters. Similar to the AIC, the BIC ranks all alternative models and provides a relative measure of model fit. Also similar to AIC, BIC cannot evaluate the absolute quality of these models. We need to ensure the association between the model and the predicted variable by evaluating their relationships directly, and then we can use BIC to select the strongest model among all successful models. Despite all of the above similarities, BIC differs from AIC in that it imposes a different penalty for the number of parameters considered. For AIC the penalty is 2k, whereas for BIC the penalty is ln $(n)k$.

The formula for Bayesian information criterion is defined as

$$BIC = \ln{(n)}k - 2 \ln(L)$$

where L is the maximized likelihood function of the model, n is the number of data points, and k is the number of model parameters. Similar to AIC, we would select the model with the largest value of the criterion.

EVALUATION OF CLASSIFICATIONS

For classifications, we use a number of measures to evaluate model performance and select classification schemes. We can also derive a series of curves to aid in measuring model performance (Japkowicz and Shah 2011).

ACCURACY AND ERROR RATE

Accuracy. Accuracy is a measure of the proportion of correct classifications made by the model. The error rate is the proportion of incorrect classifications across all cases. In a two-class classification scheme, as shown in table 5.1, a model may generate four possible outcomes: (1) the true positives (TP) correctly classify the positive cases; (2) the true negatives (TN) correctly classify the negative cases; (3) there is a false positive (FP), where a case has been classified as Yes but is actually not in the class; and (4) there is a false negative (FN), where a case is classified as not being in the class but turns out to be a member. The *true positive rate* is the ratio between TP and AP (actual positive). The *false positive rate* is the ratio between FP and AN (actual negative). Table 5.1 illustrates a confusion matrix that shows the possible outcomes of a classification model by how a member of one class is confused for a member of another. In this way, different types of correct classifications and errors are identified.

The overall **accuracy** or **success rate** is a measure of the proportion of correct classifications. It is the number of total correct classifications divided by the total number of cases in the classification:

$$Success\ Rate = Accuracy = \frac{TP + TN}{TP + FP + FN + TN} = \frac{TN + TP}{n}$$

Error Rate. The error rate is the proportion of incorrect classifications across all cases. It is the ratio between the number of total incorrect classifications and the total number of cases in the classification:

$$Error\ Rate = 1 - Accuracy = 1 - \frac{TP + TN}{TP + FP + FN + TN} = \frac{FP + FN}{n}$$

TABLE 5.1   CONFUSION MATRIX SHOWING POSSIBLE OUTCOMES IN A TWO-CLASS
CLASSIFICATION MODEL

		Prediction		
		Yes	No	Total
Actual Class	**Yes**	True Positive (TP)	False Negative (FN)	Actual Positive (AP)
	No	False Positive (FP)	True Negative (TN)	Actual Negative (AN)
	Total	Predicted Positive (PP)	Predicted Negative (PN)	n

TABLE 5.2   A SAMPLE TWO-CLASS CLASSIFICATION MODEL FOR ACCURACY AND ERROR RATE

		Prediction		
		Yes	No	Total
Actual Class	**Yes**	720	80	800
	No	2	198	200
	Total	722	278	1000

For the sample data in table 5.2, we can calculate accuracy and error rate using these equations:

$$Success\ Rate = Accuracy = \frac{TP + TN}{n} = \frac{720 + 198}{1000} = .918$$

$$Error\ Rate = 1 - Accuracy = 1 - .918 = .082$$

SENSITIVITY, SPECIFICITY, FALSE-POSITIVE RATE, AND FALSE-NEGATIVE RATE

Sensitivity. A good classification should be able to achieve high proportions of correctly identified cases in a class. This proportion is called the sensitivity rate:

$$Sensitivity = \frac{TP}{AP} = \frac{TP}{TP + FN}$$

If we use this formula on data from table 5.2, the $Sensitivity = \frac{TP}{AP} = \frac{720}{800} = .90$. This model correctly identifies 90 percent of the cases in the class.

Specificity. A good model should not only successfully identify most of the cases that belong in the class; it should also successfully identify most of the cases that do not belong in the class. Specificity is the proportion of correctly identified cases that are nonmembers of the class:

$$Specificity = \frac{TN}{AN} = \frac{TN}{FP + TN}$$

If we use this formula on data from table 5.1b, the *Sensitivity* = $\frac{TN}{AN} = \frac{198}{200}$ = .99. This model correctly identifies 99% of the cases that are nonmembers of the class.

Sometimes these two measures are used to form a single measure of the overall model performance. This measure is the product of sensitivity and specificity:

$$Sensitivity \times Specificity = \frac{TN}{AN} \times \frac{TP}{AP} = \frac{TN \times TP}{(FP + TN)(TP + FN)}$$

Based on this equation, *Sensitivity* × *Specificity* = .90 × .99 = .891%.

False-Positive Rate and False-Negative Rate. The false-positive rate and false-negative rate are additive inverses of specificity and sensitivity, respectively. They are both indicative of the errors committed by a model:

$$False\ Positive\ Rate = 1 - Specificity = 1 - \frac{TN}{AN} = \frac{FP}{FP + TN}$$

$$False\ Negative\ Rate = 1 - Sensitivity = 1 - \frac{TP}{AP} = \frac{FN}{TP + FN}$$

Again, if we use these formulas on data from table 5.1b, the *False Positive Rate* = 1 – *Specificity* = 1 – .99 = .01. The false positive rate is very low at 1 percent, showing that the model incorrectly identifies only 1 percent of all nonmembers of the class as members of the class. The *False Negative Rate* = 1 – *Sensitivity* = 1 – .90 = .10. The false negative rate is 10 percent, indicating that the model incorrectly classifies 10 percent of all the members of the class as nonmembers.

PROPORTIONS OF TRUE POSITIVES AND FALSE POSITIVES

Proportion of True Positives (PTP). This is the proportion of true positives out of all predicted positives. It is also called **precision** because it measures how precise the model is in correctly predicting true positives:

$$PTP = \frac{TP}{PP} = \frac{TP}{FP + TP}$$

Applying this equation to data in table 5.1b, the *Proportions of True Positives* = $\frac{TP}{PP} = \frac{720}{722}$ = .997. This model correctly predicts true positives 99.7 percent of the time that it predicts positives.

Proportion of False Positives. The proportion of false positives (PFP) is the additive inverse of the PTP. It measures the proportion of incorrectly identified positives, or false positives, out of all the positives identified by the model:

$$PFP = 1 - PTP = \frac{FP}{PP} = \frac{FP}{FP + TP}$$

According to this equation and data from table 5.2, *PFP* = 1 − *PTP* = 1 − .997 = .003. Among all the positives identified by the model, only 0.3 percent are false positives.

The proportion of true negatives (PTN) is the proportion of true negatives out of all predicted negatives. It measures the degree to which the model correctly predicts true negatives:

$$PTN = \frac{TN}{PN} = \frac{TN}{FN + TN}$$

Using the data in table 5.1b, this equation yields $PTN = \frac{TN}{PN} = \frac{198}{200}$ = .99. This model therefore correctly predicts true negatives 99 percent of the time that it identifies negatives.

The proportion of false negatives (PFN) measures the proportion of false negatives out of all predicted negatives. It indicates the degree to which the model incorrectly predicts that cases are nonmembers of a class when they actually are members. It is the additive inverse of the PTN:

$$PFN = 1 - PTN = \frac{FN}{PN} = \frac{FN}{FN + TN}$$

Again, using the data in table 5.1b and this equation, PFN = 1 − PTN = 1 − .99 = .01. The proportion of false negative is 1 percent, indicating that out of all the negatives predicted, the model incorrectly identifies only 1 percent of the cases.

COST-BENEFIT ANALYSIS
The advantage of using a confusion matrix is that it distinguishes between two types of errors: false positives and false negatives. These errors often differ in importance and risk to the people or organizations involved. This is very important for real-world applications. For example, if a biological trace determination model determines that an individual's biological sample is consistent with biological evidence at a crime scene, a false positive will be costly both to the wrongfully convicted individual and to the justice system. In this case, a false positive is costlier than a false negative. On the other hand, if a medical diagnostic model incorrectly identifies an individual as having a form of cancer that is curable at an early stage, the cost of a false positive may be outweighed by the cost of a false negative. A false positive may cost the patient mental anguish and additional tests, but a false negative will prevent the patient from early detection and cost them an important chance to receive effective treatment at an early stage of disease development. It is thus necessary to consider the cost and benefit of each decision when calculating the performance of a classification model. The costs and benefits are in the same decision rows and column as the confusion matrix in table 5.3. Correct decisions yield benefits b(TP) and b(TN) for true positives and true

TABLE 5.3   **A GENERAL COST-BENEFIT MATRIX**

		Prediction		
		Yes	No	
Actual Class	Yes	b(TP)	c(FN)	AP
	No	c(FP)	b(TN)	AN
		PP	PN	n

TABLE 5.4   **A COST-BENEFIT MATRIX FOR A HYPOTHETICAL REMEDIAL PROGRAM**

		Prediction	
		Yes	No
Actual Class	Yes	$100,000	$0
	No	−$1,000	$0

negatives, respectively. Incorrect decisions pose costs $c(FP)$ and $c(FN)$ for false positives and false negatives, respectively.

For example, a school district might use a classification system to determine which students will benefit from a remedial program. Table 5.4 shows the cost-benefit matrix of these decisions. A *true positive* is a student who will benefit from the remedial program and has also been identified as such. The student ends up costing less time and money to be trained for the remainder of their career, so the total benefit is $100,000. A *false positive* occurs when the district classifies a student as needing the program when they actually do not. The cost is -$1,000 for the time and cost of implementing the program. A *true negative* is a student who does not need the program and has been identified as such, so the benefit is $0. A *false negative* is a student who has been identified as not needing the program but would have benefited from it if provided the opportunity. In this case, no money or time is spent, so there is no cost or benefit. The cost is $0. (Less commonly, this may be considered a loss of $100,000.)

Given the confusion matrix, the rates we can calculate from the confusion matrix, and the cost-benefit matrix, we can construct an expected profit equation as follows:

$$E(Profit) = p(AP)[p(TP)b(TP) + p(FP)c(FP)] + p(AN)[p(TN)b(TN) + p(FN)c(FN)]$$

The first part of the equation shows the expected benefit and cost from all the positive cases, $p(TP)b(TP) + p(FP)c(FP)$, after weighing by the probability of positive cases occurring, $p(AP)$. The second part shows the expected profit from all the negative cases, $p(TN)b(TN) + p(FN)c(FN)$, after considering the probability of negative cases occurring, $p(AN)$.

TABLE 5.5 CALCULATED PROBABILITIES FOR THE EXAMPLE IN
TABLE 5.3

		Prediction		
		Yes	No	
Actual Class	Yes	p(TP)=.90	p(FN)=.10	p(AP)=.80
	No	p(FP)=.01	P(TN)=.99	p(AN)=.20

We now apply the expected profit equation to tables 5.4 and 5.5 to calculate the expected profit for this model, and then we can compare it with an alternative model to decide on an optimal classification scheme.

$$E(Profit) = p(AP)[p(TP)b(TP) + p(FN)c(FN)] + p(AN)[p(TN)b(TN) + p(FP)c(FP)]$$

$$= .8(.9 * 100{,}000 + .1 * 0) + .2(.01 * (-1{,}000) + .99 * 0)$$

$$= .8 * 90{,}000 - .2 * 10 = \$71{,}998$$

The expected value is $71,998 if we use this model and enroll the identified students in the remedial program. We expect to gain a benefit of approximately $72,000 per student.

CUMULATIVE RESPONSE CURVE AND LIFT CHART

A cumulative response curve graphically represents the percentage of positives correctly classified out of the total true positives in the population (TP rate × 100 as the y axis) as a function of the percentage of the test instances (x axis). It demonstrates the improvement in incorrectly identifying true positives compared to a random guess. The classifier ranks all the test cases of instances by listing those that are highly likely to be positive higher on the list than those less likely. As a result, when we start at the top of the list, the model will correctly identify a larger proportion of the true positives. The diagonal line y = x represents a random model whereby the model identifies the same percentage of positives when it analyzes a certain percentage of the test cases. For example, a random model will identify 60 percent of all the positives after processing 60 percent of the test cases. Classification models that provide cumulative response curves above the diagonal are stronger models than the random one, providing some advantage in prediction. Figure 5.1 shows cumulative response curves of three models: a random model, Model A, and Model B. Model B appears to be the best model because it provides a higher true positive rate for every percentage of test instances or cases.

A cumulative response curve can be converted into a lift curve. The lift of a classification model reflects the gain, or advantage, it provides in predicting positives over a random model. For example, if after we evaluate 60 percent of the test cases we have correctly identified 60 percent of the positives, then the lift score is 1. This is typically

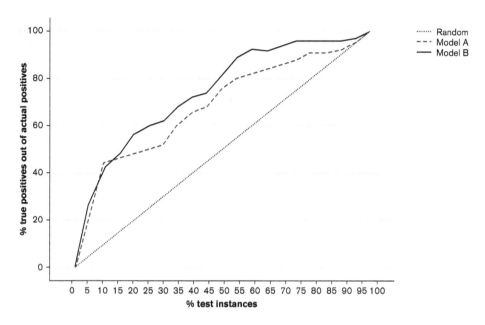

FIGURE 5.1
Cumulative Response Curves of Three Classification Models.

the performance of a random model. However, if a classifier offers some advantage and correctly identifies 90 percent of all the positives after processing 60 percent of the test cases, then its lift score is 1.5.

The lift curve is the value of the cumulative response curve at each point divided by the value of the diagonal line at that point. As result of this conversion, the diagonal line in the cumulative response curve becomes a flat line at y = 1 in a lift curve chart. By comparing the lift scores for different models and the change in lift scores across ranges of the test instances, we can determine which model performs more efficiently. Figure 5.2 shows lift curves of the same three models as in figure 5.1, with the random model having a lift score of 1 at all percentages of test instances. Models A and B have almost identical lift scores in the range of 14 to 20 percent of the test instances. Beyond this range, Model B consistently has higher lift scores until the models process around 90 percent of test instances, when both models converge.

RECEIVER OPERATING CHARACTERISTICS CURVE

The receiver operating characteristics (ROC) curve illustrates the entire space of performance possibilities (Swets, Dawes, and Monahan 2000; Fawcett 2006). It demonstrates the performance of classification models in a two-dimensional space, with the x axis representing the false positive rate and the y axis representing the true positive rate. By showing the trade-offs between true positives and false positives, an ROC plot assists in our decision about model selection.

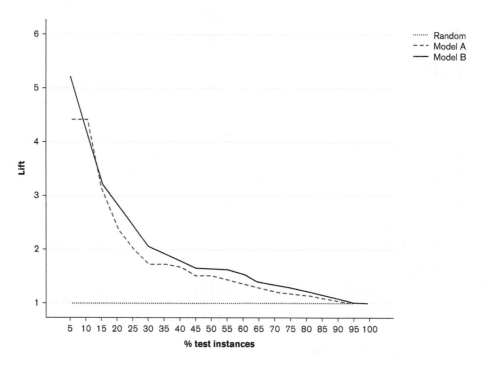

FIGURE 5.2
Lift Curves of Three Classification Models.

The ROC space represents characteristics of classification models. As shown in table 5.6, the lower left bottom of (0, 0) represents a model that does not identify any positives and thus has neither true nor false positives. The upper right corner of (1, 1) is the opposite, representing a model that unconditionally assigns all cases to the class. The lower right corner of (1, 0) represents the worst model, which identifies none of the true positives while all of the positives it classifies are false positives. The upper left corner of (0, 1) represents the best model, which successfully identifies all of the true positives without identifying any false positives. The best-performing models are those closest to the upper left corner, and the worst models are those closest to the lower right corner. The diagonal line connecting (0, 0) to (1, 1) represents random models that assign membership randomly to cases in proportion to the membership percentage in the population. Since the ROC curve measures models that improve over random models, it will be in the upper-left triangle area above the diagonal line.

We use the ROC curve to illustrate the performance of alternative models and make decisions about model selection. Based on the probabilities from the three models in table 5.7, we construct a ROC curve in figure 5.3. All three models, A, B, and C, are in the upper left triangle above the diagonal line, demonstrating that they all improve over models that randomly assign membership. Model A is the closest to the

TABLE 5.6 DEFINING ROC CURVE SPACE

		Prediction			
		Upper Left Corner		Upper Right Corner	
		Yes	No	Yes	No
Actual Class	Yes	p(TP)=1	p(FN)=0	p(TP)=1	p(FN)=0
	No	p(FP)=0	P(TN)=1	p(FP)=1	P(TN)=0
		Lower Left Corner		Lower Right Corner	
Actual Class	Yes	p(TP)=0	p(FN)=1	p(TP)=0	p(FN)=1
	No	p(FP)=0	P(TN)=1	p(FP)=1	P(TN)=0

TABLE 5.7 CALCULATED PROBABILITIES FOR THREE MODELS

		Prediction					
		Model A		Model B		Model C	
		Yes	No	Yes	No	Yes	No
Actual Class	Yes	p(TP)=.90	p(FN)=.10	p(TP)=.95	p(FN)=.05	p(TP)=.85	p(FN)=.15
	No	p(FP)=.01	P(TN)=.99	p(FP)=.10	P(TN)=.90	p(FP)=.05	P(TN)=.95

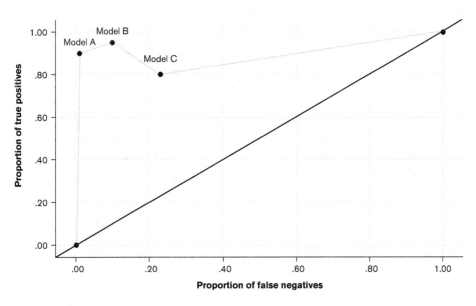

FIGURE 5.3
A ROC Curve for Three Models.

TABLE 5.8 **SAMPLE RECALL PRECISION MEASURES FOR THREE MODELS**

		Prediction					
		Model A		Model B		Model C	
		Yes	No	Yes	No	Yes	No
Actual Class	Yes	720	80	950	50	5,100	900
	No	2	198	100	900	700	13,300

upper left corner and is thus the strongest model, while Model C is the farthest away, making it the weakest among the three.

RECALL PRECISION CURVE

Another curve that is related to the lift chart and ROC curve is the recall precision curve (Burnham and Anderson 2003). It is concerned with building effective models that maximize the rate of retrieved documents that are relevant (TP) among all the documents that are relevant (TP+FN) and all documents that are retrieved (TP+FP), respectively. It is similar to the ROC curve in that it uses the same *y* axis of the true precision rate. In the field of information retrieval, this is called the *recall*, which is defined as the proportion of documents retrieved that are relevant (i.e., true positives, TP) out of all the documents that are relevant (actual positives, AP). The *x* axis is different from that of the ROC curve in that it is the *precision*, defined as the proportion of documents retrieved that are relevant (true positive, TP) out of all the documents that are retrieved (TP+FP, predicted positive PP). Table 5.8 presents confusion matrices for three models identical to those in table 5.7.

A recall precision curve space is defined by two axes. The lower left corner is (0, 0), representing the lowest recall and precision, with both at 0, and thus the weakest model. The upper right corner (1, 1) represents the strongest model with both recall and precision at the maximum, 1. The lower right corner of (1, 0) represent models with high precision but low recall, meaning that among the documents retrieved by the model, 100 percent are relevant (precision = 1), but the model failed to retrieve a large number of relevant documents (recall = 0). This indicates models that are highly conservative in retrieving documents, making sure that all the information retrieved is relevant while leaving large amounts of relevant information unretrieved. The upper left corner of (0, 1) indicates models with the opposite characteristics: low precision but high recall. These are models that retrieve all the information, but most of the retrieved documents are false positives. Models closest to the upper right corner are the most efficient models. Figure 5.4 shows recall precision curves for three models: A, B, C. Model A is plotted the closest to the upper right corner, so it appears to be the strongest model, with Precision = .90 and Recall = .997. Model B is a viable contender,

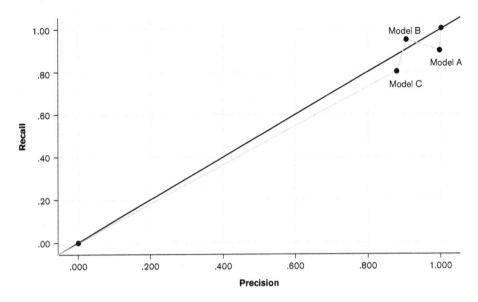

FIGURE 5.4
Recall Precision Curve for Three Models.

appearing similarly close to the corner of (1, 1) with Precision = .95 and Recall = .905. Model C performs worse than Models A and B.

To summarize, lift charts, ROC curves, and recall precision curves all use some measures from the confusion matrix to visualize model performance (Witten, Frank, and Hall 2011). These methods are preferred in different substantive fields. Lift charts along with cost-benefit analyses are more popular in business research and marketing. The ROC curve is more commonly used in the field of communication. Finally, the recall precision curve is widely used in information retrieval.

SUMMARY

In machine learning, we use a training data set to train the model and a test data set to evaluate the model. Sometimes a third data set is used to validate the model. These data sets are usually independent when there are sufficient data.

When the data are too small to afford independent samples, we can use two methods of cross-validation. The first is a holdout approach, which divides a single sample into two or sometimes three data sets of various sizes and carries out the training-testing cycle multiple times. When the data are divided into n parts, we carry out the training-testing sequence n times, each time holding out one nth of the data for testing and using $(n-1)$th data for training. The tenfold cross-validation is a standard way of finding a classification scheme. The second approach to cross-validation is called leave-one-out cross-validation. When n is the number of cases in the total data, we leave out one case each time for testing and use the remaining n-1 cases for training, repeating this process n times.

Bootstrapping is a procedure of sampling with replacement. Instead of splitting the total data into parts, bootstrapping draws training data and testing data from the total data set, allowing for the possibility that the same cases are used in both the training set and the testing set. The .632 bootstrap approach is a popular one, with the training set containing 63.2 percent of all the cases from the data and the testing set containings 36.8 percent of all the cases from the same data; this process is repeated several times.

When evaluating numerical prediction, we use mean squared error (MSE), root mean squared error (RMSE), and mean absolute error (MAE). They all provide some measurement of the error between the predicted value and the actual value. Akaike's information criterion (AIC) and Bayesian information criterion (BIC) provide methods to compare a series of statistical models that are not necessarily nested models. Both AIC and BIC rank all alternative models and provide a relative measure of model goodness-of-fit.

We use a number of measures calculated from a confusion table to evaluate model performance and select classification schemes. Accuracy measures the proportion of correct classifications out of all the cases processed. The error rate is the proportion of incorrect classifications across all cases. Sensitivity is the proportion of correctly identified positive cases that are actually members of the class. Specificity is the proportion of predicted false cases among all actual false cases. The product of sensitivity and specificity forms an overall measure of model performance. We also combine cost-benefit matrices with confusion tables to carry out profit calculations and evaluate model performance.

We can also derive a series of curves from the confusion table and cost-benefit matrix to aid in measuring model performance. A cumulative response curve graphically represents the percentage of true positives out of the total true positives in the population as a function of the percentage of the test instances. This curve can be converted into a lift chart, which reflects the improvement it provides in predicting positives over a random model. The ROC curve shows the performance of models in the trade-off between true positives and false positives. The recall precision curve shows the ratio between the precision rate and recall, which is the proportion of true positives out of all the actual positives.

PRACTICE QUESTIONS

1. What is a training set? What is a testing set? What roles do they play in machine learning? Under what circumstances can we use independent training and testing sets? If this condition is not satisfied, what do we do?

2. What is cross-validation? When is it used? What are the approaches for achieving representative data for both training and testing sets when data are limited?

3. Explain *n*-fold cross-validation. What is tenfold cross-validation? Describe the procedure.

4. What is leave-one-out cross-validation? Why is it also called *n*-fold cross-validation?

5. What is bootstrapping? How is it different from cross-validation? What is the most popular bootstrapping approach?

6. When we evaluate models with numerical outcome variables, what indices do we use to evaluate their performance?

7. Define mean squared error, root mean squared error, and mean absolute error.

8. What are AIC and BIC? In what ways are they similar and different?

9. What is accuracy? What is an error rate? What is sensitivity? What is specificity? What are false-positive rates and false-negative rates? What are proportions of true positives and proportions of false positives? What are proportions of true and false negatives? Calculate these terms using information from the following table. It shows the result from a classifier using a testing data set (10 percent of the total data) to predict donation to a political candidate.

TABLE P5.1 CONFUSION MATRIX OF A CLASSIFIER TO PREDICT DONATION TO A POLITICAL CANDIDATE

		Prediction		
		Donated	No Donation	
Actual Class	Donated	90	10	100
	No Donation	300	1600	1900
		390	1610	2000

10. Calculate expected profit based on the confusion matrix in Question 8 and the following cost-benefit matrix.

TABLE P5.2 COST-BENEFIT MATRIX OF A CLASSIFIER TO PREDICT DONATION TO A POLITICAL CANDIDATE

		Prediction	
		Donated	No Donation
Actual Class	Donated	$800	0
	No Donation	–$1	0

11. Compare the model in Question 9 with a different model with the following confusion table using expected profit. The testing data set is 20 percent of the total data.

TABLE P5.3   **ALTERNATIVE COST-BENEFIT MATRIX OF A
CLASSIFIER TO PREDICT DONATION TO A POLITICAL
CANDIDATE**

		Prediction		
		Donated	No Donation	
Actual Class	Donated	190	10	200
	No Donation	200	3600	3800
		390	3610	4000

12. Compare the two models in Questions 9 and 10, marking their cumulative response rates in a two-dimensional space using the same x and y axes for cumulative response curves: TP rate multiplied by 100 as the y axis and the percentage of the test instances as the x axis.

13. Using the same information in Question 11, mark the lift scores for these two models in a two-dimensional space using x and y axes for a lift curve. What can you conclude about the performance of these models?

14. Construct an ROC plot using the confusion tables from Questions 9 and 10. Which model is better?

15. Calculate and construct a recall precision curve for the two models in Questions 9 and 10. What can you conclude about these models?

REFERENCES

Akaike, Hirotugu. 1981. "Likelihood of a Model and Information Criteria." *Journal of Econometrics* 16: 3–14.

Burnham, Kenneth P., and David R. Anderson. 2003. *Model Selection and Multimodel Inference: A Practical Information-Theoretic Approach*. New York: Springer Science & Business Media.

———. 2004. "Multimodel Inference: Understanding AIC and BIC in Model Selection." *Sociological Methods and Research* 33 (2): 261–304.

Fawcett. Tom. 2006. "An Introduction to ROC Analysis." *Pattern Recognition Letters* 27 (8): 861–74.

Japkowicz, Nathalie, and Mohak Shah. 2011. *Evaluating Learning Algorithms: A Classification Perspective*. Cambridge: Cambridge University Press.

Sakamoto, Y., M. Ishiguro, and G. Kitagawa. 1986. *Akaike Information Criterion Statistics*. Dordrecht: D. Reidel.

Swets, John A., Robyn M. Dawes, and John Monahan. 2000. "Better Decisions through Science." *Scientific American* 283: 82–87.

Witten, Ian H., Eibe Frank, and Mark A. Hall. 2011. *Data Mining: Practical Machine Learning Tools and Techniques*. 3rd ed. Burlington, MA: Morgan Kaufmann.

## PART IV

DATA MINING: UNSUPERVISED LEARNING

Chapter 6

CLUSTER ANALYSIS

MACHINE LEARNING REFERS to the ability of computer systems to progressively improve their performance on data analytical tasks by using computer science and statistical techniques to learn from data (Samuel 1959). It builds models and algorithms by learning and improving from data. Machine learning is best for computing tasks in which it is difficult to design models with explicit structure and algorithms with good performance. In other words, the researchers do not have enough information beforehand to design explicit models to specify the relationships among variables or cases. They thus learn from the data to sort out the hidden patterns and structures and learn from these patterns and structures to build models.

SUPERVISED LEARNING AND UNSUPERVISED LEARNING

Supervised learning and unsupervised learning are the two main types of tasks in machine learning. The main difference between them is that supervised learning starts with knowledge of what the output values for our samples should be whereas unsupervised learning does not have explicit outputs to predict. The goal of supervised learning is to find and learn a computational function that best approximates the relationship between some attributes and the output, or outcome variable, in the data. The objective for unsupervised learning is to infer and reveal the hidden structure in data.

This chapter focuses on unsupervised learning. Supervised learning is discussed in part 5. The goal of unsupervised learning is to model the underlying structure from data when you have only input data and do not have corresponding outputs, or outcome variables. The process is called unsupervised learning because, in the absence of explicit outcomes to predict, no supervision or teaching takes place. Without feedback from data, algorithms learn on their own to discover interesting structures in the data.

Clustering and association are the two types of problems in unsupervised learning. Cluster analysis aims to discover the inherent groupings in the data, such as groupings of similar countries in the global system or groupings of students by their learning styles. Association, on the other hand, attempts to reveal rules that describe the data, such as if someone does A, they will also do B.

CLUSTER ANALYSIS

Cluster analysis separates people, organizations, products, behaviors, objects, or cities into relatively homogeneous subgroups, or clusters. A cluster is a collection of cases that are similar to each other and dissimilar to cases in other clusters. We assume that these clusters reflect some underlying mechanism that causes some cases to bear a stronger resemblance to each other than to the remaining cases, which belong to other clusters. Cluster analysis assigns cluster membership to cases by maximizing the similarity within the group while minimizing the similarity to observations outside the group. Cluster analysis classifies cases with precision and empirical support.

Cluster analysis is usually performed as a preliminary or preparatory step in a data mining process. The resulting clusters are used as inputs in subsequent analytical procedures. Because of the complex composition of traits that jointly shape groups of similar cases, it is useful to differentiate subjects into groups sharing similar traits to simultaneously analyze a package of characteristics. With an enormous amount of data, it is also beneficial to reduce the search space for the downstream algorithm. Another advantage of allocating subjects into different clusters first and carrying out analysis on these groups is to allow researchers to test theoretical ideas about these groups and observe heterogeneous outcomes. They thus are able to derive under what circumstance and to which group some theories hold while others do not.

WHEN TO USE CLUSTER ANALYSIS

In the social sciences, cluster analysis may be an effective method to separate cases into more homogeneous groups that have the potential to be explained by the same theory. Instead of mixing all cases together and applying theories indiscriminately to all cases, cluster analysis can effectively aid in the process of separating causal heterogeneity and informing theory development.

This practice is exemplified in Garip (2017, 207–11). Her research looks at attributes of immigrants before they migrate, including gender, education, occupation, and income level, and she considers different combinations of these attributes that might give rise to distinctive types of immigrants. Using this method allows her to identify groups, or clusters, of immigrants that have similar attributes. This unsupervised learning allows the clusters to emerge from the data rather than being forced on it using some prior theoretical models.

From the cluster analysis, Garip (2017) concludes that both the Mexican population and the composition of Mexican migrant groups in the United States have changed over time. Mexican immigrants can be grouped into four clusters. One group includes residents of rural, traditionally migrant-sending communities with limited employment opportunities. Another group includes economically secure individuals from urban communities who have access to more and better job opportunities in their communities of origin. Members of this group migrate to the United States when more desirable opportunities arise, or when they want to provide their middle-class family with a safety net in the face of economic depression.

Researchers usually apply existing theoretical models of immigration universally to all immigrants while disregarding the causal heterogeneity among them. The general theories and models derived from them can only describe and explain the behaviors of the average Mexican immigrant. They dismiss heterogeneity among immigrant motivations and fail to recognize and explain variation across cases. Thus the traditional approach constrains the models' ability to explain patterns and changes in migration flows that take place in response to different dynamics and motivations. For instance, most of the existing research uses neoclassical economic models that assume that higher wages in the destination country attract less-educated immigrants from poorer rural regions. Garip's unsupervised learning method of cluster analysis reveals a group of young, urban, and better-educated Mexican immigrants whose migration behaviors cannot be explained by neoclassical economic theory. Instead, Garip argues that results from the unsupervised learning support a new economic model that explains migration via a dual labor market structure in advanced capitalist societies. The economic uncertainty in the country of origin prompts individuals to migrate from households that face risks to their earnings and socioeconomic well-being. These immigrants are not from the most impoverished segment of the population but rather are members of the urban middle class. The immigrants undertake low-paying and labor-intensive work while natives occupy higher-paying jobs in the capital-intensive sectors. Employing cluster analysis enables Garip to arrive at significantly different conclusions compared to other scholars.

BASICS OF CLUSTER ANALYSIS

Cluster analysis is a form of unsupervised learning. It makes group assignments without obvious grouping information or visible decision rules. Thus it is often considered a form of exploratory analysis, in that the clusters emerge from the data. This approach is different from *classification* (see chap. 9), which is a supervised learning approach. Classification works with a target variable—a known group assignment—to search for decision rules to determine how the classification scheme will allocate cases into the known group structure. Researchers sometimes combine both cluster analysis and classification methods, first using cluster analysis to detect hidden structures of grouping (clusters) in the data and then using the outcome cluster as a target variable in classification to identify the decision rules to allocate cases into clusters to make the model interpretable, interesting, and meaningful.

STANDARDIZING NUMERICAL VARIABLES

Clustering algorithms require all variables used in the analysis to be normalized so that variables that take large values due to their measurement unit do not dominate the analysis. Distance is measured in this multidimensional space defined by all the variables used in the cluster analysis. The two methods that are most commonly used to normalize variables in preparation for cluster analysis are range normalization and Z-score standardization, discussed in chapter 3.

Range normalization is a scaling scheme that converts a variable into a proportion within its range between the minimum and maximum. It measures a variable as a proportion of the entire range of possible values, so the normalized variable is between $[0, 1]$.

$$N_{Range}(y) = \frac{y - \min(y)}{range(y)}$$

Z-score standardization takes the difference between the value y and the mean $\bar{y}$, and it converts this difference into the number of standard deviations from the mean, S_y or the Z-score.

$$Z = \frac{y - \bar{y}}{S_y}$$

MEASURING SIMILARITY AND DISTANCE

Cluster analysis divides the instance space into regions based on the closeness of cases in the instance space. This is a method for organizing the instance space so that cases near each other are treated similarly in the subsequent analysis. To accomplish this, we need to know the basic methods for measuring similarity and distance.

It is important to use a meaningful similarity measure with respect to the research questions at hand. There are a large number of similarity and distance measures. For

TABLE 6.1   A SAMPLE OF SOCIOECONOMIC ATTRIBUTES

Variables	Person A	Person B	Person C	Person D
Income	$40,000	$80,000	$160,000	$20,000
Occupational Prestige	36	64	78	22
Years of Education	12	16	22	10
Standardized Income	0.00	1.00	2.00	−.5
Standardized Occupational Prestige	0.00	2.00	3.00	−1.00
Standardized Years of Education	−.5	1.5	3	−2

example, Deza and Deza (2006) list several hundred ways to measure distance. For the purpose of data mining, a dozen of them are used regularly. These measures simplify a comparison of two complex cases with multiple attributes into a single number to indicate their difference, or distance. Variations in the type of data and the domain of application determine how variations in individual attributes should be combined into a single measure of distance. Table 6.1 presents a simple example of a three-variable space to differentiate people into socioeconomic groups based on their income, education, and occupational prestige scores.

EUCLIDEAN DISTANCE

These cases have multiple attributes, and there are many ways to measure the similarity and distance between them. One basic approach is to use basic geometry to measure distance. When the cases are differentiated on two attributes, such as income and occupational prestige, then the distance/similarity measures the distance in a two-dimensional space, as shown in figure 6.1. In the right triangle between the two persons A and B, the base width is the distance between income X_A–X_B, and the height is the distance between occupational prestige Y_B–Y_A. According to the Pythagorean theorem, the distance between A and B is the square root of the sum of squares of the lengths of the other two sides of the triangle. Thus the distance between two persons A and B is $Distance\ (A,\ B) = \sqrt{(x_B - x_A)^2 + (y_B - y_A)^2}$.

Since A is (0, 0) and B is (1, 2), C is (2, 3) and D is (−.5, −1),

$Distance\ (A,\ B) = \sqrt{(1 - 0)^2 + (2 - 0)^2} = \sqrt{5}.$

$Distance\ (A,\ C) = \sqrt{(2 - 0)^2 + (3 - 0)^2} = \sqrt{13},$

$Distance\ (A,\ D) = \sqrt{(-.5 - 0)^2 + (-1 - 0)^2} = \sqrt{1.25},$

$Distance\ (B,\ C) = \sqrt{(2 - 1)^2 + (3 - 2)^2} = \sqrt{2},$

$Distance\ (B,\ D) = \sqrt{(-.5 - 1)^2 + (-1 - 2)^2} = \sqrt{11.25},$

$Distance\ (C,\ D) = \sqrt{(-.5 - 2)^2 + (-1 - 3)^2} = \sqrt{22.25}.$

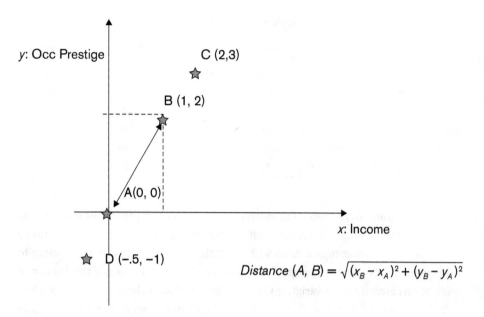

FIGURE 6.1

Euclidean Distance Based on Two Variables.

It appears that A and D are the closest, although B and C are also close.

Euclidian distance can be extended to multiple dimensions. When cases are characterized by n variables in n dimensions, the general equation is an extension of the Euclidean distance equations for two dimensions:

$$\text{Euclidean Distance } (A, B) = \sqrt{(x_B - x_A)^2 + (y_B - y_A)^2 + (z_B - z_A)^2 + \ldots}$$

Consider the three-variable space defined by income, occupational prestige, and years of education. Since A is (0, 0, -.5), B is (1, 2, 1.5), C is (2, 3, 3) and D is (-.5, -1, -2),

$$\text{Euclidean Distance } (A, B) = \sqrt{(1 - 0)^2 + (2 - 0)^2 + (1.5 + .5)^2} = \sqrt{9} = 3,$$

$$\text{Euclidean Distance } (A, C) = \sqrt{(2 - 0)^2 + (3 - 0)^2 + (3 + .5)^2} = \sqrt{25.25},$$

$$\text{Euclidean Distance } (A, D) = \sqrt{(-.5 - 0)^2 + (-1 - 0)^2 + (-2 + .5)^2} = \sqrt{7.5},$$

$$\text{Euclidean Distance } (B, C) = \sqrt{(2 - 1)^2 + (3 - 2)^2 + (3 - 1.5)^2} = \sqrt{4.25},$$

$$\text{Euclidean Distance } (B, D) = \sqrt{(-.5 - 1)^2 + (-1 - 2)^2 + (-2 - 1.5)^2} = \sqrt{23.5},$$

$$\text{Euclidean Distance } (C, D) = \sqrt{(-.5 - 2)^2 + (-1 - 3)^2 + (-2 - 3)^2} = \sqrt{47.25}.$$

Now B and C are the closest to each other, while A and D are the second closest.

MANHATTAN DISTANCE

The Manhattan distance treats the data points as if they were on the grid map of midtown Manhattan and measures the number of street blocks one needs to travel between two data points. This measure sums up the differences along all the dimensions between two cases A and B.

$$Manhattan\ Distance\ (A,\ B) = |x_B - x_A| + |y_B - y_A| + |z_B - z_A| + \ldots$$

These results are similar to those of the Euclidean distance, in that B and C are the closest to each other, while A and D are the second closest.

$Manhattan\ Distance\ (A,\ B) = |1 - 0| + |2 - 0| + |1.5 + .5| = 5,$

$Manhattan\ Distance\ (A,\ C) = |2 - 0| + |3 - 0| + |3 + .5| = 8.5,$

$Manhattan\ Distance\ (A,\ D) = |-.5 - 0| + |-1 - 0| + |-2 + .5| = 4,$

$Manhattan\ Distance\ (B,\ C) = |2 - 1| + |3 - 2| + |3 - 1.5| = 3.5,$

$Manhattan\ Distance\ (B,\ D) = |-.5 - 1| + |-1 - 2| + |-2 - 1.5| = 8,$

$Manhattan\ Distance\ (C,\ D) = |-.5 - 2| + |-1 - 3| + |-2 - 1.5| = 11.5.$

JACCARD DISTANCE

Jaccard distance measures the proportion of all the characteristics that are not shared by the two cases. It treats the cases as objects possessing sets of traits. This allows one to determine the size of the union of all the characteristics belonging to cases A and B, A∪B, as well as the size of the set of characteristics shared by the two cases, A∩B. This approach is appropriate when the possession of a common trait between two items is important. The Jaccard distance is expressed in a set notation:

$$Jaccard\ Distance\ (A,\ B) = 1 - \frac{A \cap B}{A \cup B}$$

The Jaccard distance is useful when the variables are categorical. For example, instead of using the numerical measures of SES attributes in table 6.1, we could treat the three measures as categorical measures, as shown in table 6.2.

$$Jaccard\ Distance\ (A,\ B) = 1 - \frac{A \cap B}{A \cup B} = 1 - \frac{0}{3} = 1$$

$$Jaccard\ Distance\ (A,\ C) = 1 - \frac{A \cap C}{A \cup C} = 1 - \frac{0}{3} = 1$$

$$Jaccard\ Distance\ (A,\ D) = 1 - \frac{A \cap D}{A \cup D} = 1 - \frac{1}{3} = \frac{2}{3}$$

$$Jaccard\ Distance\ (B,\ C) = 1 - \frac{A \cap B}{A \cup B} = 1 - \frac{2}{3} = \frac{1}{3}$$

TABLE 6.2 SOCIOECONOMIC TRAITS AS CATEGORICAL VARIABLES

	A	B	C	D
Income Group	Median	High	High	Low
Highest Degree	High School	College	Graduate	Less than HS
Occupational	Worker	Professional	Professional	Worker

$$Jaccard\ Distance\ (B, D) = 1 - \frac{B \cap D}{B \cup D} = 1 - \frac{0}{3} = 1$$

$$Jaccard\ Distance\ (C, D) = 1 - \frac{C \cap D}{C \cup D} = 1 - \frac{0}{3} = 1$$

Again with the new categorical measures, B and C have the smallest distance, and A and D have the next smallest difference.

COSINE DISTANCE

We often use cosine distance to measure the similarity between two documents. In classifications of a text, each word (or token) is a dimension of an attribute, and the number of occurrences of these words in the text represents the value of this dimension. It represents the differences as the proportion of occurrences of each of the word or token in a text regardless of the text length or word count. Cosine distance is the product of the two attribute vectors over the Euclidean length of each attribute vector. It ranges from 0 to 1, with 0 indicating no distance (or the highest similarity) and 1 the largest distance (minimal similarity).

$$Cosine\ Distance\ (A, B) = 1 - \frac{(x_A, y_A, z_A) * (x_B, y_B, z_B)}{\sqrt{(x_A)^2 + (y_A)^2 + (z_A)^2} * \sqrt{(x_B)^2 + (y_B)^2 + (z_B)^2}}$$

As shown in table 6.3, among the four applications for a job, the statements include words such as *intelligent, resilient,* and *multitask*. By analyzing similarities among these applications using words as their traits, we can find which ones are more similar to each other.

$$Cosine\ Distance\ (A, B) = 1 - \frac{(10, 1, 0) * (9, 6, 3)}{\sqrt{(10)^2 + (1)^2 + (0)^2} * \sqrt{(9)^2 + (6)^2 + (3)^2}}$$

$$= 1 - \frac{(10 * 9 + 1 * 6 + 0 * 3)}{\sqrt{100 + 1 + 0} * \sqrt{81 + 36 + 9}} = 1 - \frac{96}{\sqrt{12726}} \approx .15$$

$$Cosine\ Distance\ (A, C) = 1 - \frac{(10, 1, 0) * (0, 10, 6)}{\sqrt{(10)^2 + (1)^2 + (0)^2} * \sqrt{(0)^2 + (10)^2 + (6)^2}}$$

$$= 1 - \frac{(10 * 0 + 1 * 9 + 0 * 6)}{\sqrt{100 + 1 + 0} * \sqrt{0 + 100 + 36}} = 1 - \frac{9}{\sqrt{13736}} \approx .92$$

TABLE 6.3 **OCCURRENCE OF WORDS IN JOB APPLICATION STATEMENTS**

Variables	Text A	Text B	Text C	Text D
Intelligent	10	9	0	3
Resilient	1	6	10	2
Multitask	0	3	16	1

$$\textit{Cosine Distance } (A, C) = 1 - \frac{(10, 1, 0) * (3, 12, 8)}{\sqrt{(10)^2 + (1)^2 + (0)^2} * \sqrt{(3)^2 + (12)^2 + (8)^2}}$$

$$= 1 - \frac{(10 * 3 + 1 * 12 + 0 * 8)}{\sqrt{100 + 1 + 0} * \sqrt{9 + 144 + 64}} = 1 - \frac{42}{\sqrt{21917}} \approx 1.00$$

$$\textit{Cosine Distance } (B, D) = 1 - \frac{(9, 6, 3) * (3, 2, 1)}{\sqrt{(9)^2 + (6)^2 + (3)^2} * \sqrt{(3)^2 + (2)^2 + (1)^2}}$$

$$= 1 - \frac{(9 * 3 + 6 * 2 + 3 * 1)}{\sqrt{81 + 36 + 9} * \sqrt{9 + 4 + 1}} = 1 - \frac{42}{\sqrt{1764}} \approx 0$$

The cosine distance is very useful in situations where the difference in scales across cases can be ignored. It is efficient to evaluate, especially for sparse vectors, as only the non-zero dimensions need to be considered. In text classification, researchers can ignore the length of a document and concentrate instead on its content. For example, Text B and D have very different word counts on the three keywords, with B (9, 6, 3) and D (3, 2, 1), but the relative proportion of the frequency is the same. Therefore, the cosine distance (B, D) is 0, indicating that the two texts are very similar, with the same proportion of these words regardless of the length of the texts.

EDIT DISTANCE

Edit distance measures the number of edit operations required to convert one string or sequence so that it is identical to the other. Edit operations consist of inserting, deleting, or replacing a character (or element) in a string or sequence. Edit distance measures the difference between two cases when data consist of strings or sequences and the order is very important. It is commonly used in text analysis and biology, where it measures the genetic distance between strings of allelomorphs.

When comparing two words, the edit distance is the minimum number of edits (insertions, deletions, and replacements) one would need to convert one word into the other. For example, the edit between *evolution* and *involve* is 7. The edit script that transforms *evolution* into *involve* is the following:

1. evolution → ịevolution (add "i")
2. ievolution → in̲volution (replace "e" with "n")
3. involution → involv̲tion (replace "u" with "v")
4. involvtion → involveion (replace "t" with "e")
5. involveion → involve̲ion (delete "i")
6. involveon → involve̲on (delete "o")
7. involven → involve̶n̶ (delete "n")

METHODS TO DIVIDE CLUSTERS

The purpose of cluster analysis is to identify groups of cases such that the similarity within a group is maximized while the similarities to cases in other groups are minimized. That is to say, the algorithms maximize the between-cluster variance while minimizing the within-cluster variance. Figure 6.2 illustrates the distance between clusters and distance within clusters.

K-MEANS CLUSTER ANALYSIS

K-means cluster analysis is one of the most common clustering methods, and it defines each cluster using its centroid (MacKay 2003). The centroid is the geometric center of a group of cases assumed to be in the same cluster, based on a distance measure and all dimensions of attributes in a numerical instance space. There are a number of centroid-based clustering approaches, but K-means is the most frequently used in data science. K-means are calculated as the arithmetic average of the values along each dimension of traits for the cases in the cluster.

The K-means approach requires a desirable number of clusters so that it partitions the data into K groups. It then randomly chooses K records to be the starting centroid for each of the K clusters. It next assigns each case to the closest cluster center, usually based on the Euclidean distance. Then, for each cluster it finds the cluster centroid and updates cluster assignments for all cases based on the location of the new cluster center. Then it repeats the process of calculating a new centroid—updating cluster memberships until convergence, when some convergence criterion is met, or termination, when the centroids no longer change (Larose and Larose 2015).

The convergence criterion is usually defined as no significant shrinkage in the mean squared error (MSE): $MSE = \frac{SSE}{N-k}$, where SSE is the sum of squared error, N is the total sample size, and k is the number of clusters. This can be understood as an analysis of variance whereby the between-cluster variance is maximized while within-cluster variance is minimized. A pseudo-F test can be used in the same way as an ANOVA analysis: $F_{k-1,N-k} = \frac{MSB}{MSW} = \frac{SSB/k-1}{SSW/N-k}$, where MSB is the mean sum of squares between clusters, MSW is the mean sum of squares within clusters, SSB is the total sum of squares between clusters, and SSW is the total sum of squares within clusters, and k and N are

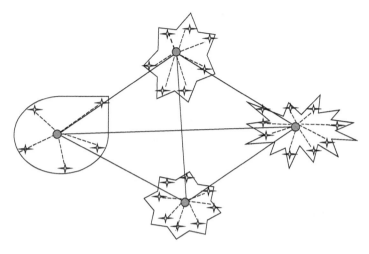

FIGURE 6.2
Distance between Clusters vs. Distance within Clusters.

the same as defined above. As the K-means algorithm improves the clusters, we expect that MSB will be maximized, MSW will be minimized, and F will increase.

HIERARCHICAL CLUSTER ANALYSIS

Hierarchical clustering is an approach whereby clusters are formed in hierarchical order by grouping cases by their similarity or distance from each other. In this scheme, the highest-level clustering is a single cluster containing all cases, while the lowest-level clustering contains as many clusters as the number of cases because each case is a separate cluster. The middle-level clustering groups adjacent cases into clusters in a hierarchical manner, with those closest at the lower level and those farther apart at the higher level, as indicated in figure 6.3.

There are two hierarchical clustering methods: *divisive* and *agglomerative*. The *divisive clustering method* creates a treelike cluster structure (expressed as a dendrogram, as in fig. 6.4) by recursive partitioning. This method begins with a single cluster containing all the cases, then splits off with the most dissimilar cases. This process is conducted recursively until each cluster contains only one case. The *agglomerative clustering method* starts with each case as a separate cluster, then aggregates the clusters that are closest to each other to form a new, combined cluster. This proceeds in a series of recursive steps, with each reducing the number of clusters by one until all cases are aggregated into a single final cluster.

Both divisive and agglomerative methods depend on the distance function between clusters, which is called the linkage function. There are three linkage functions: single linkage, complete linkage, and average linkage. The *single linkage* is the nearest neighbor approach. It is based on the minimum distance between any two cases in two clusters, respectively, so its length is determined by the two most similar cases from

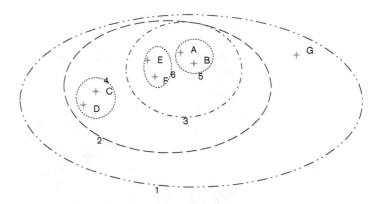

FIGURE 6.3

A Hierarchical Clustering Scheme of 7 Cases in 6 Clusters, by Distance.

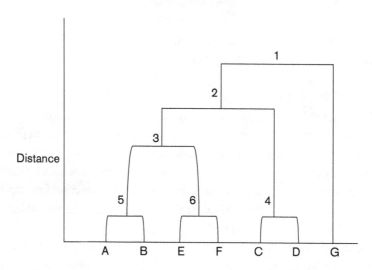

FIGURE 6.4

A Hierarchical Clustering Scheme in a Dendrogram.

two clusters. This approach tends to merge two clusters that have two or more cases that are close to each other, but other cases may be farther apart, resulting in clusters that are long and slender. This may mean that some heterogeneous cases may be clustered together. *Complete linkage* uses the farthest neighbor approach, which is based on the maximum distance between any two cases in the two clusters, respectively. It is thus determined by the similarity of the two least similar cases between the two clusters. This approach tends to result in compact and sphere-shaped clusters. *Average linkage* tries to avoid using extreme cases to measure the distance between two clusters. It is the average of all cases in one cluster from all the cases in another cluster. This forms clusters that tend to have approximately equal within-cluster variability.

One advantage of using hierarchical clustering it that it makes the structure of clustering schemes visible. This enables researchers to select classification schemes on the basis of the number of desired clusters. As shown in figure 6.4, if we decide on three clusters, we would move to the number 3 and see that cases A, B, E, and F are in one cluster (cluster 3), C and D are in another (cluster 2), and G is in a third (cluster 1).

CLUSTER QUALITY AND VALIDATION

After we complete one round of cluster analysis, we need to evaluate whether the model fits well with the data, whether the model corresponds to reality or to artifacts of the data, whether the optimal number of clusters have been identified, and whether the best-fitting set of clusters are used to characterize the data. Below I describe some frequently used methods to measure cluster quality (or goodness) as well as model validation.

Good measures of cluster quality should simultaneously evaluate cluster separation and cluster cohesion. Cluster separation indicates how far apart the clusters are from each other, while cluster cohesion indicates how closely located the cases are within each individual cluster. Good measures of cluster goodness should incorporate indicators of both characteristics. The pseudo-F statistic and the silhouette method are two approaches that account for both cluster separation and cluster cohesion.

OPTIMAL NUMBER OF CLUSTERS

The pseudo-F test measures the ratio of the separation between the clusters versus the spread of cases within the clusters. It is similar to an ANOVA test, in which all cases in the data are divided into K clusters or groups. The separation between clusters is represented by the mean squared distance between the cluster centers (or centroids) and the grand mean of all the data. The spread of data within clusters is represented by the mean squared distance between each case and the cluster centroid within groups.

$$F = \frac{MSB}{MSE} = \frac{SSB/(k-1)}{SSE/(N-1)}$$

The pseudo-F should not be used to test for the presence of clusters in the data because the null hypothesis is that there are no clusters, which is easily rejected using even a randomly generated data set (for an example, see Larose and Larose 2015, 591). However, this test is often used to find the optimal number of clusters using the following procedures:

1. Carry out multiple rounds of cluster analysis using multiple values of k, the number of clusters.
2. Calculate the pseudo-F statistic and associated p-value for each cluster solution.
3. Select the cluster solution with the smallest p-value as the optimal number of clusters.

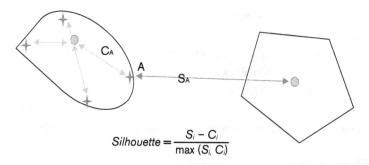

$$Silhouette = \frac{S_i - C_i}{\max(S_i,\ C_i)}$$

FIGURE 6.5
Silhouette Value Measures.

CLUSTER ASSIGNMENT

The silhouette value gauges the goodness of the cluster assignment for a particular case in the data. It considers both cluster cohesion and separation. It uses the distance between the case and its cluster center (C_i) to measure cluster cohesion and the distance between the case and the center of the next closest cluster (S_i) to estimate cluster separation. Figure 6.5 shows the relationship between these two measures.

A positive value indicates that the separation is larger than cohesion and is thus a good assignment. A higher value indicates a better assignment than a lower value. A negative silhouette value indicates that the separation is smaller than cohesion. Therefore the case is misclassified and it is a better fit with the next closest cluster than with its current assignment. A silhouette value close to zero indicates that the case could belong to either the current cluster or the next closest cluster. The average silhouette value of all cases in the cluster analysis yields a useful measure of the goodness of the cluster solution. In general, the size of the average silhouette value can be interpreted in the following way, although the substantive meaning of the clusters is also important in judging the quality of a cluster solution.

- $0.50 \leq$ Silhouette, solid evidence of clusters in the data.
- $0.25 \leq$ Silhouette < 0.50, some evidence of clusters in the data, and further support from the substantive field is needed to substantiate the cluster solution.
- Silhouette < 0.25, scant evidence of clusters in the data.

CLUSTER VALIDATION

Cluster validation safeguards from the possibility that the cluster solution results from random noise in the data set. We carry out cross-validation to ensure that the clusters are real. Cross-validation techniques are part of conventional approaches used to ensure good generalization and to avoid overfitting. The approach is to divide the data set into two subsets and to proceed in two steps: the training stage, which uses one subset of data as the training set while leaving the other subset out; and the testing stage, which evaluates the performance of the final model on the remaining subset, the testing data set. We can use simple statistical and graphic methods to compare the two cluster solutions based on these two data sets. The objective of cross-validation is to achieve a stable and confident estimate of the model performance.

1. Split the data into a training set and a testing set. For low-dimensional data sets, the most frequently used and often the most efficient selection method is simple random samples. For high-dimensional data sets, there are a variety of approaches (for a discussion, see Reitermanova 2010).
2. Carry out cluster analysis on the training set.
3. Carry out cluster analysis on the testing set.
4. Compare the two cluster solutions using statistics and graphs to confirm that the two solutions are highly similar.

SUMMARY

This chapter introduces machine learning as computer systems' ability to build models and algorithms to learn and improve with data. There are two types of machine learning: supervised and unsupervised. Supervised learning starts with a known outcome and searches for a computation function that best describes the relationship between this output and the input attributes. Unsupervised learning is the process of discovering a hidden structure in data without explicit output variables to provide supervision or teaching. There are two types of unsupervised learning: clustering and association.

Cluster analysis assigns cluster membership to cases by maximizing the similarity among the group and minimizing the similarity between groups. It sees clusters as reflecting some mechanism that causes some instances to resemble each other. It is a useful method to differentiate subjects into groups that have similar traits and enable researchers to simultaneously analyze a package of characteristics to account for causal heterogeneity.

Cluster analysis requires that all variables in the analysis be normalized so that distance can be measured appropriately. Range normalization and Z-score standardization are the most commonly used methods. Cluster analysis uses measures of similarity and distance to divide the instance space into regions based on the closeness of cases in the instance space.

There are at least five ways to measure such distances. Euclidean distance uses the Pythagorean theorem to calculate the distance between two points in a space. Manhattan distance sums the differences along all the dimensions between two cases. Jaccard distance measures the proportion of all the characteristics not shared by two cases. Cosine distance measures the similarity between two documents by representing the difference in the proportion of occurrence of each word in a text regardless of text length or word count. Edit distance measures the number of edit operations required to convert one string or sequence so that it is identical to the other.

To divide the instance space into clusters, we use the methods of K-means and hierarchical cluster analysis. The K-means approach focuses on the clusters by representing each cluster by its centroid, which is the geometric center of a group of cases assumed to be in the same cluster. Hierarchical clustering sees clusters as formed in hierarchical order by grouping cases based on their similarity to each other. Both methods of hierarchical clustering (divisive and agglomerative) are based on a choice of linkage functions to determine the distance between clusters: single linkage, complete linkage, or average linkage.

Frequently used methods to measure cluster goodness and model validation are the pseudo-F test, silhouette value, and cluster validation. The pseudo-F test measures the ratio of the separation between the clusters versus the spread of cases within the cluster. It is often used to find the optimal number of clusters. The silhouette value gauges the goodness of the cluster assignment for a particular case in the data after considering both cluster cohesion and separation. Cluster validation safeguards the analysis from random noise to ensure that the model has good generalization and avoids model overfitting.

PRACTICE PROBLEMS

1. What is machine learning? What are the two types of machine learning? What differentiates these two types of machine learning?
2. What does cluster analysis accomplish? When is cluster analysis useful in research?
3. Why is it important to normalize variables before cluster analysis? What are the most popular approaches to normalization?
4. Use range normalization and Z-score standardization to normalize the following countries using information on the variables in table P6.1 below.

TABLE P6.1   NORMALIZATION OF GDP PER CAPITA AND LIFE EXPECTANCY

	GDP per Capita	Life Expectancy
United States	$54,629	78.94
Spain	$29,722	83.08
Mexico	$10,326	76.72
Kenya	$1,358	61.58

Descriptive Statistics				
	Minimum	Maximum	Mean	Std. Deviation
Life expectancy at birth	48.93	83.98	71.4187	8.39310
GDP per capita	255	116613	14540.43	20799.778

5. Using the data in Question 4, calculate the Euclidean distances between these four countries. Which two countries are the closest?
6. Using the data in Question 4, calculate the Manhattan distance between these four countries. Which two are the closest? Is this conclusion the same or different from Question 5? Why or why not?
7. Using the information in table P6.2 for five organizations, calculate the Jaccard distance between them and determine which two organizations are closest to each other.

TABLE P6.2 **ORGANIZATION CHARACTERISTICS**

Organization	A	B	C	D	E
Change in size	Increased	Decreased	Decreased	Unchanged	Increased
Change in revenue	Increased	Unchanged	Unchanged	Increased	Unchanged
Organizational restructuring	No	No	Yes	Yes	No

8. We are interested in news reports on the 2018 midterm election and want to find out whether all the news agencies are similar or different in their reports. We tallied the occurrence of words by randomly picking one report in September 2018 from each news agency (table P6.3). Calculate the cosine distances between them and determine which two reports are the most similar.

TABLE P6.3 **NEWS REPORTS ON THE 2018 MIDTERM ELECTION**

	CNN	NYT	CNBC	FOX
Angry	5	10	5	4
Backfire	4	8	4	10
Economy	2	4	5	8
Support	6	12	4	1

9. Find the edit distance between the following pairs of terms. List each edit action in detail.
   sit → sat
   environment → environmental
   abcKdefg L8P → cdcKdekl L8PD
   green tea → ginger tea
   I am sipping a glass of wine → I am eating a box of chocolate
   It is raining dogs and cats → The house is full of dogs and cats
10. What is K-means cluster analysis? What parameter does the K-means method require before carrying out the analysis? What is the convergence criterion such that the algorithm decides to stop computation?

11. In what ways does hierarchical cluster analysis differ from the K-means approach? What are the two methods of hierarchical cluster analysis? What is linkage function? How many types of linkage functions are there? Describe each of the linkage functions.

12. What is the relationship between cluster quality, cluster separation, and cluster cohesion? How do we ensure cluster quality?

13. Define the pseudo-F test for cluster analysis. What do researchers use this test to achieve? What does the silhouette value measure? What do high, medium, and low Silhouette values indicate?

14. What do we aim to achieve with cluster validation? What are the steps in cluster validation?

15. With data from the 2016 General Social Survey (https://gss.norc.org/Get-The-Data), use the two variables measuring gender attitudes (genscale) and political attitudes (conserve) to carry out cluster analysis to classify the respondents.

    a. Use the K-means method to generate 3-, 4-, or 5-cluster solutions. Carry out a pseudo-F test to find out which of these clustering schemes fits best with the data.

    b. Use any type of hierarchical cluster analysis method to generate a hierarchical cluster analysis of Americans' attitudes. Compare this with the results from the K-means analysis. Discuss the differences between the two approaches.

    c. Split the data into two halves, treating one as a training set and the other as a testing set. Using the K-means approach with the choice of number of clusters from (a), carry out cluster analysis using the training set. Repeat by using the testing set. Compare the two cluster solutions using statistics and graphs. What do you find?

REFERENCES

Deza, Elena, and Michel-Marie Deza. 2006. *Dictionary of Distances.* Amsterdam: Elsevier Science. www .elsevier.com/books/dictionary-of-distances/deza/978-0-444-52087-6.

Garip, Filiz. 2017. *On the Move: The Changing Mechanisms of Mexico-U.S. Migration.* Princeton, NJ: Princeton University Press.

Larose, Daniel T., and Chantal D. Larose. 2015. *Data Mining and Predictive Analytics.* New York: Wiley.

MacKay, David J. C. 2003. *Information Theory, Inference and Learning Algorithms.* Cambridge: Cambridge University Press.

Reitermanova, Z. 2010. "Data Splitting." In *WDS 10 Proceedings of Contributed Papers*, pt. 1, 31–36. www.mff .cuni.cz/veda/konference/wds/proc/pdf10/WDS10_105_i1_Reitermanova.pdf.

Samuel, Arthur. 1959. "Some Studies in Machine Learning Using the Game of Checkers." *IBM Journal of Research and Development* 3 (3): 210–29.

Chapter 7

ASSOCIATIONS

———

UNSUPERVISED LEARNING includes two types of problems—cluster analysis and association. They are similar in that they both analyze connections within the data, but they differ in the type of connections on which they focus. Cluster analysis emphasizes the links among data instances and aims to discover inherent groupings of data cases. The clusters are groups of individuals or subjects sharing similar traits. Association, on the other hand, is interested in the association among attributes and attempts to reveal rules that describe relationships between variables in the data. Associations describe strong links or connections between traits or characteristics of the subjects in the data.

Association rule mining is a powerful exploratory tool for social science research in identifying causal relationship, particularly when analyzing large amounts of data with many candidate explanatory variables. In such a large space of combinations of attributes, association rules mine associations among variables to identify the combinations that are highly likely to affect some outcome. Association rule mining can help researchers discover which attributes and combinations of attributes occur most frequently with some outcomes. Association rules provide useful leads on the direction of the causal relationship between the antecedents and consequents. In combination with other methods, they are effective tools in suggesting fruitful directions in the search for causal relationships.

ASSOCIATION RULES

Association discovery, or co-occurrence grouping, is a method for finding associations between entities. The study of associations between characteristics is also called market basket analysis. It seeks to discover affinities among traits and find rules for quantifying the relationship between these traits. This approach is also called affinity analysis. It originated from marketing research on consumer behavior based on the theory that if consumers buy a certain group of items, they are more (or less) likely to buy another group of items. For example, data from supermarket purchases show that those who purchase diapers are also likely to buy beer. The set of items a customer buys is referred to as an itemset.

Association rules consist of three parts: a pair of antecedent and consequent events, a measure of the support, and a confidence associated with the rule. Purchasing diapers is the antecedent, and beer purchase is the consequent. The probability that a customer who buys diapers also purchases beer (i.e., when the antecedent is true, the consequent is also true) is referred to as the support for the rule, formally written as p(diapers, beer) or p(diapers ∩ beer). The conditional probability that a customer who has purchased diapers will also purchase beer is referred to as the confidence, written as p(beer|diapers). For example, hypothetical purchase data from a supermarket show that of 10,000 purchases made in a week, 200 purchases contained diapers and 300 contained beer. Among the 200 purchases containing diapers, 40 also contained beer.

The *support* for an association rule A→B is the proportion of transactions that contain both A and B out of all transactions. The support for the association rule that those who purchase diapers also buy beer is .004.

$$\text{Support} = p(A, B) = p(A \cap B) = \frac{\#\ transactions\ containing\ both\ A\ \&\ B}{\#\ of\ transactions}$$

$$\text{Support} = p(diapers \cap beer) = \frac{40}{10,000} = .004$$

The confidence of an association rule A→B measures the accuracy of the rule, as indicated by the proportion of transactions that contain both A and B of all transactions that contain A. The confidence for the association rule that those who purchase diapers also purchase beer is .20.

$$\text{Confidence} = p(B|A) = \frac{p(A \cap B)}{p(A)} = \frac{\#\ transactions\ containing\ both\ A\ \&\ B}{\#\ of\ transactions\ containing\ A}$$

$$Confidence = p(beer \backslash diapers) = \frac{p(diapers \cap beer)}{p(beer)} = \frac{40}{200} = .20$$

We may prefer rules that generate either high support or high confidence or both. We may also set minimum criteria for support and confidence when searching for strong rules that satisfy these conditions. Support measures the prevalence of the association rule in all purchases, while confidence indicates the strength of the association among the subset of purchases that contains the antecedent. For example, for a marketing analysis of items that are often purchased together online, we may set the minimum support level at .10 and the minimum confidence level higher, at .30. Since these transactions represent a high fraction of all transactions, a marketing promotion based on this analysis would be more effective than it would be for rarer types of transactions. On the other hand, if we are interested in medical insurance claims for very costly procedures, we may set a smaller support level at .01, as relatively few insurance claims are for very costly procedures.

GENERAL USES OF MARKET BASKET ANALYSIS

Market basket analysis was originally created for deciding the promotion and placement of goods inside a physical store. If, as has been observed, consumers who purchase diapers are more likely to buy beer, then beer might be placed near diapers. Market basket analysis provides clues as to which items consumers tend to purchase together, and it facilitates the promotional approach of placing these items together to make it convenient for consumers to make impulsive purchases.

An association rule can be local, limited only to certain stores but not to all other stores. Researchers therefore need to analyze the external conditions that might make these rules hold in some locations but not in others. These differences may arise from variations in clientele income, age, or other demographic characteristics, or they might arise in response to different store displays or staff behaviors. Differential market basket analysis can provide interesting results that are both new and valid, and it can eliminate the problem of trivial results that lose validity when external conditions change. Differential analysis compares association rules between different stores, between customers in different demographic groups, between different days of the week, different seasons of the year, and so on. Investigating such differences may yield useful insights into hidden influences on consumer behaviors.

Associations may also include a time lag between purchases. There is no requirement for all the items to be purchased simultaneously. The method can be adapted to analyze a sequence of events spread out over time. *Sequence analysis* (Blanchard, Bühlmann, and Gauthier 2014) is a variant of predictive market basket analysis that can be used to identify sets of events that generally occur in sequence.

Market basket analysis can be generalized to many other areas of application. In marketing research, a series of credit card purchases or online shopping purchases can be analyzed to find the association among these purchases. In health care research, a collection of prescription drugs taken by patients or a series of medical procedures received by patients can also be analyzed to reveal the associations among them. Facebook "Likes" can also be predicted using this approach. We can consider each of the Facebook users to have "a basket of Likes" by pooling together all of their "Likes." We then analyze if certain "Likes" tend to co-occur more often than we would expect by chance.

MEASURING ASSOCIATION

Data scientists use two measures to determine the magnitude of association. One is *lift*, which measures how much more frequently an association occurs than would be expected by chance. The lift of the co-occurrence of A and B is the ratio between two probabilities: the probability that two actually occur together and the probability that the two co-occur randomly. A lift larger than one means the observed association between A and B is larger than their random co-occurrence.

$$Lift = (A, B) = \frac{p(A, B)}{p(A)p(B)} = \frac{p(A \cap B)}{p(A)p(B)}$$

Let us use the same example from the supermarket purchase data. Of 10,000 purchases made in a week, 200 customers bought diapers and 300 bought beer. Among these 200 customers who bought diapers, 40 bought beer: p(diapers) = 200/10,000 = .02 and p(beer) = 300/10,000 = .03, and p(diapers, beer) = 40/10,000 = .004.

$$Lift\ (diapers, beer) = \frac{p(diapers, beer)}{p(diapers)p(beer)} = \frac{.004}{.02 * .04} = \frac{.004}{.0008} = 5$$

The lift is 5, indicating that the probability of these two items appearing in the same market basket is five times larger than would co-occur by chance. This provides support for an association between the purchase of diapers and beer.

An alternative measure is called *leverage*, which is the difference of these two probabilities: the probability that two events occur together and the probability that the two occur together by chance. A positive leverage value indicates that the association between A and B outnumbers the probability of them co-occurring randomly.

$$Leverage(A, B) = p(A, B) - p(A)p(B) = p(A \cap B) - p(A)p(B)$$

Using the same data from purchases of diapers and beer, we calculate the leverage as the following. Leverage is positive, again indicating that the probability of co-occurrence outnumbers the probability of random co-occurrence.

$$Leverage(diapers, beer) = p(diapers, beer) - p(diapers)p(beer) = .004 - .0008 = .0032$$

ASSOCIATION RULE ALGORITHMS

The algorithm we apply to mine association rules from data sets needs to deal with large numbers of potential association rules that grow exponentially with the number of attributes. If we consider k number of binary attributes and focus only on the positive cases (with the binary attribute present), the number of association rules will be in the order of $k*2^{(k-1)}$ (Hand, Mannila, and Smyth 2001). The complexities mainly arise from the huge number of searches and data entries. For example, a typical supermarket may have 10,000 or more items for sale, and the number of purchases made each day could be in the tens of thousands. Exploring association sets in the space of large potential sets can reach combinatorial explosions, at $10,000*2^{9999}$. Even a tiny vending machine with only 20 items can reach a total number of potential association rules in the order of 2^{20} or, to be precise, $20*2^{19} \approx 1.05\times10^7$, which is more than 10 million.

It is thus imperative to reduce the search space to a more manageable size. One method for achieving this is the *a priori algorithm*, which takes advantage of the structure within the association rules to trim unnecessary searches. This algorithm first finds all *itemsets* and documents their frequencies.

- An itemset is a set of items out of all items under consideration. K-itemset is an itemset containing k items. For example, {diaper, beer} is a 2-itemset, and {diaper, beer, chips} is a 3-itemset.
- Itemset frequency is the number of times a certain itemset appears in transactions.
- If an itemset appears a certain minimum number of times $f \geq \eta$, we then label it a frequent itemset. If we set $f \geq 8$, then itemsets that occur eight or more times are considered frequent itemsets.
- An a priori has the following property: If an itemset F is not frequent, then for any item I, F $\cup$ I will not be frequent. If an itemset F is not frequent, then adding another item I to the itemset will not make F more frequent.

For example, table 7.1 shows hypothetical course taking patterns of eight sociology classes regularly offered. We examine students' course taking patterns.

From these data, we first identify one-item itemsets. The frequency is listed in the bottom row of table 7.1. If we set $f \geq 8$, then itemsets occurring eight or more times are considered frequent itemsets, and Sociology of Education and Social Psychology do not make the cut. Thus, one-item itemsets F_1 consist of {Gender, Statistics, Race & Ethnicity, Theory, Inequality, Research Methods}.

We next identify frequent 2-item itemsets. To find F_2, the a priori algorithm first constructs a set of candidate 2-item itemsets C_2 by combining F_1 with itself. From the six items in F_1 = {Gender, Statistics, Race & Ethnicity, Theory, Inequality, Research Methods}, we get 15 2-itemsets, as listed in table 7.2.

TABLE 7.1   COURSE TAKING DATA FROM TWENTY STUDENTS

	Sociology of Gender	Statistics	Race & Ethnicity	Theory	Inequality	Research Methods	Sociology of Education	Social Psychology
A	1				1			
B	1		1		1			
C	1		1		1			
D	1	1		1	1	1		1
E	1	1	1	1	1	1		
F	1	1		1		1		1
G	1	1	1	1	1	1		
H		1	1	1		1	1	
I		1		1	1	1		1
J	1	1	1			1		
K	1		1	1		1	1	
L	1			1	1	1		
M	1	1	1	1	1			
N	1	1			1			
O		1	1			1		1
P		1	1		1	1		
Q		1	1	1	1	1	1	
R		1		1	1	1		
S	1	1	1	1				
T	1		1	1				
Total	**14**	**14**	**13**	**13**	**13**	**13**	**3**	**4**

TABLE 7.2   CANDIDATE ITEMSETS OF TWO ITEMS, C_2

Itemsets of Two	Count	Itemsets of Two	Count
Gender, Statistics	8	Statistics, Research Methods	11
Gender, Race & Ethnicity	8	Race & Ethnicity, Theory	8
Gender, Theory	9	Race & Ethnicity, Inequality	7
Gender, Inequality	9	Race & Ethnicity Research Methods	8
Gender, Research Methods	7	Theory, Inequality	8
Statistics, Race & Ethnicity	9	Theory, Research Methods	10
Statistics, Theory	10	Inequality, Research Methods	8
Statistics, Inequality	9		

TABLE 7.3   **FREQUENT ITEMSETS OF TWO, F₂**

TABLE 7.3   **FREQUENT ITEMSETS OF TWO, F_2**

Itemsets of Two	Count	Itemsets of Two	Count
Gender, Statistics	8	Statistics, Research Methods	11
Gender, Race & Ethnicity	8	Race & Ethnicity, Theory	8
Gender, Theory	9	Race & Ethnicity Research Methods	8
Gender, Inequality	9	Theory, Inequality	8
Statistics, Race & Ethnicity	9	Theory, Research Methods	10
Statistics, Theory	10	Inequality, Research Methods	8
Statistics, Inequality	9		

TABLE 7.4   **CANDIDATE ITEMSETS OF THREE ITEMS, C_3**

Frequent Itemsets of Three	Count
Gender, Statistics, Race & Ethnicity	5
Gender, Statistics, Theory	6
Gender, Statistics, Inequality	5
Gender, Race & Ethnicity, Theory	5
Gender, Race & Ethnicity, Inequality	5
Gender, Theory, Inequality	4
Statistics, Race & Ethnicity, Theory	6
Statistics, Race & Ethnicity, Inequality	4
Statistics, Race & Ethnicity, Research Methods	7
Statistics, Theory, Inequality	6
Statistics, Theory, Research Methods	8
Statistics, Inequality, Research Methods	7
Race & Ethnicity, Theory, Research Methods	5
Theory, Inequality, Research Methods	7

If we again apply the cutoff of $f \geq 8$, then itemsets occurring eight or more times are considered frequent itemsets. Table 7.3 contains all 13 of the frequent two-item itemsets.

We next use the frequent itemsets in F_2 to generate the candidate itemsets of three items, C_3. We combine F_2 with itself by joining itemsets if they have the first items in common. In table 7.3, {Gender, Theory} and {Gender, Inequality}, {Statistics, Race & Ethnicity} and {Statistics, Theory}, {Statistics, Inequality} and {Statistics, Research Methods}, {Statistics, Race & Ethnicity} and {Statistics, Inequality}, and {Statistics, Race & Ethnicity} and {Statistics, Research Methods} have the first item in common, so they are joined together to form candidate itemsets of three items C_3 = {{Gender,

TABLE 7.5 CANDIDATE ASSOCIATION RULES FOR ONE AND TWO ANTECEDENTS FOR ITEMSETS
OF THREE

Antecedent and Consequent	Support	Confidence
{Statistics, Theory}=>{Research Methods}	8/20=40%	(8/20)/(10/20)=8/10=80%
{Statistics, Research Methods}=>{Theory}	8/20=40%	(8/20)/(11/20)=8/11=73%
{Theory, Research Methods}=>{Statistics}	8/20=40%	(8/20)/(10/20)=8/10=80%
{Research Methods}=>{Statistics, Theory}	8/20=40%	(8/20)/(13/20)=8/13=62%
{Theory}=>{Statistics, Research Methods}	8/20=40%	(8/20)/(13/20)=8/13=62%
{Statistics}=>{Theory, Research Methods}	8/20=40%	(8/20)/(14/20)=8/14=57%

Theory, Inequality}, {Statistics, Race & Ethnicity, Theory}, {Statistics, Inequality, Research Methods}, {Statistics, Race & Ethnicity, Inequality}, {Statistics, Race & Ethnicity, Research Methods}}. Table 7.4 shows these three-item itemsets.

If we again apply the cutoff of $f \geq 8$, then itemsets occurring eight or more times are considered frequent. The only frequent itemset of 3 is {Statistics, Theory, Research Methods}. We prune the other itemsets with counts fewer than 8, and our search for candidate sets ends because we no longer have multiple itemsets to combine into itemsets of four. We now have a frequent itemset of one 3-item itemset F_3 = {Statistics, Theory, Research Methods}.

We can generate association rules using this frequent itemset. We first generate all subsets of the frequent item set, ss, by combining all items in F_3. We then consider the association rule: $ss => (s\text{-}ss)$, where $(s\text{-}ss)$ is the set s without ss. For the frequent set F_3, s = {Statistics, Theory, Research Methods}, and the subsets of s are {Statistics}, {Theory}, {Research Methods}, {Statistics, Theory}, {Statistics, Research Methods}, and {Theory, Research Methods}. Now we can generate candidate association rules for three itemsets with either one or two antecedents using the frequent itemset F_3. See table 7.5.

We can also generate candidate association rules for itemsets of two with one antecedent and one consequent using the frequent itemset F_2. See table 7.6.

From these candidate association rules, we can use an overall measure of usefulness, the product of support and confidence, to rank the rules based on their prevalence and confidence. Table 7.7 presents the final association rules after trimming them through a minimum confidence level of 70 percent. It shows that the top two strongest association rules are between {Research Methods}=>{Statistics} and{Statistics}=>{Research Methods}. However, the lift measure shows that the association rules of {Statistics, Theory}=>{Research Methods} and {Theory, Research Methods}=>{Statistics}are the strongest, even though they are not the most prevalent. Statistics and Theory may not be taken together very frequently, but students who do take both courses are highly likely to take Research Methods as well.

Antecedent and Consequent	Support	Confidence
{Statistics}=>{Theory}	10/20=50%	(10/20)/(14/20)=10/14=71%
{Theory}=>{Statistics}	10/20=50%	(10/20)/(13/20)=10/13=77%
{Statistics}=>{Research Methods}	11/20=55%	(11/20)/(14/20)=11/14=79%
{Research Methods}=>{Statistics}	11/20=55%	(11/20)/(13/20)=11/13=85%
{Theory}=>{Research Methods}	10/20=50%	(10/20)/(13/20)=10/13=77%
{Research Methods}=>{Theory}	10/20=50%	(10/20)/(13/20)=10/13=77%
{Gender}=>{Theory}	9/20=45%	(9/20)/(14/20)=9/14=64%
{Theory}=> {Gender}	9/20=45%	(9/20)/(13/20)=9/13=69%
{Gender}=>{Inequality}	9/20=45%	(9/20)/(14/20)=9/14=64%
{Inequality}=>{Gender}	9/20=45%	(9/20)/(13/20)=9/13=69%
{Statistics}=>{Race & Ethnicity}	9/20=45%	(9/20)/(14/20)=9/14=64%
{Race & Ethnicity}=>{Statistics}	9/20=45%	(9/20)/(13/20)=9/13=69%
{Statistics}=>{Inequality}	9/20=45%	(9/20)/(14/20)=9/14=64%
{Inequality}=>{Statistics}	9/20=45%	(9/20)/(13/20)=9/13=69%
{Gender}=>{Statistics}	8/20=40%	(8/20)/(14/20)=8/14=57%
{Statistics}=> {Gender}	8/20=40%	(8/20)/(14/20)=8/14=57%
{Race & Ethnicity}=>{Theory}	8/20=40%	(8/20)/(13/20)=8/13=61.5%
{Theory}=>{Race & Ethnicity}	8/20=40%	(8/20)/(13/20)=8/13=61.5%
{Race & Ethnicity}=>{Research Methods}	8/20=40%	(8/20)/(13/20)=8/13=61.5%
{Research Methods}=>{Race & Ethnicity}	8/20=40%	(8/20)/(13/20)=8/13=61.5%
{Theory}=>{Inequality}	8/20=40%	(8/20)/(13/20)=8/13=61.5%
{Inequality}=>{Theory}	8/20=40%	(8/20)/(13/20)=8/13=61.5%
{Inequality}=>{Research Methods}	8/20=40%	(8/20)/(13/20)=8/13=61.5%
{Research Methods}=>{Inequality}	8/20=40%	(8/20)/(13/20)=8/13=61.5%

APPLICATION OF ASSOCIATION RULES IN
SOCIAL RESEARCH

SELECTION OF ASSOCIATION RULES

Association rules can sometimes be deceptive. From table 7.7, we chose association rules such as {Theory}=>{Statistics}, and {Statistics}=>{Theory} as some of the final rules based on the measure of support × confidence. These are itemsets of antecedents and consequents that are highly like to appear when the antecedents are present.

However, when we evaluate the lift measures, the ratio between the co-occurrence of these itemsets and these items occurring randomly, we find that the lift measures are 1.10 for these three association rules, meaning that the application of these association rules, {Theory}=>{Statistics}, and {Statistics}=>{Theory}, only improves

TABLE 7.7 **FINAL ASSOCIATION RULES RANKED BY SUPPORT × CONFIDENCE, WITH A MINIMUM CONFIDENCE OF 70%**

Antecedent and Consequent	Support	Confidence	Lift	support × confidence
{Research Methods}=>{Statistics}	11/20=55%	(11/20)/(13/20)=11/13=85%	$\frac{\frac{11}{20}}{\frac{14}{20} \times \frac{13}{20}} = 1.21$	.468
{Statistics}=>{Research Methods}	11/20=55%	(11/20)/(14/20)=11/14=79%	$\frac{\frac{11}{20}}{\frac{14}{20} \times \frac{13}{20}} = 1.21$	.435
{Theory}=>{Statistics}	10/20=50%	(10/20)/(13/20)=10/13=77%	$\frac{\frac{10}{20}}{\frac{13}{20} \times \frac{14}{20}} = 1.10$	.385
{Theory}=>{Research Methods}	10/20=50%	(10/20)/(13/20)=10/13=77%	$\frac{\frac{10}{20}}{\frac{13}{20} \times \frac{13}{20}} = 1.18$	.385
{Research Methods}=>{Theory}	10/20=50%	(10/20)/(13/20)=10/13=77%	$\frac{\frac{10}{20}}{\frac{13}{20} \times \frac{13}{20}} = 1.18$	.385
{Statistics}=>{Theory}	10/20=50%	(10/20)/(14/20)=10/14=71%	$\frac{\frac{10}{20}}{\frac{13}{20} \times \frac{14}{20}} = 1.10$	.355
{Statistics, Theory}=>{Research Methods}	8/20=40%	(8/20)/(10/20)=8/10=80%	$\frac{\frac{8}{20}}{\frac{13}{20} \times \frac{13}{20} \times \frac{14}{20}} = 1.35$	.320
{Theory, Research Methods}=> {Statistics}	8/20=40%	(8/20)/(10/20)=8/10=80%	$\frac{\frac{8}{20}}{\frac{13}{20} \times \frac{13}{20} \times \frac{14}{20}} = 1.35$	.320
{Statistics, Research Methods}=> {Theory}	8/20=40%	(8/20)/(11/20)=8/11=73%	$\frac{\frac{8}{20}}{\frac{13}{20} \times \frac{13}{20} \times \frac{14}{20}} = 1.35$	.288

the probability of predicting the consequent by 10 percent over random chance. In other words, because 70 percent of the course taking contains taking Statistics, when we apply the association rule {Theory}=>{Statistics}, we obtain a confidence of 77 percent. This is a slight increase of 7 points, which is a 10 percent percent improvement in predicting the consequent of {Statistics}.

We can convert the lift measure to a confidence ratio, which is the proportion of the percent improvement of using the association rule over not using it. The confidence ratio for the association rules {Theory}=>{Statistics}, {Theory}=>{Research Methods}, and {Statistics}=>{Theory} is .09.

$$Confidence\ Ratio = 1 - \frac{1}{Lift} = 1 - \frac{p(B)}{p(B|A)}$$

Alternatively, we can calculate the confidence difference between the prior probability before the association rule and the confidence after applying the association rule. In the case of {Theory}=>{Statistics}, the confidence difference is .77-.7 = .07.

$$Confidence\ Difference = p(B|A) - p(B)$$

In this case, researchers need to consider the prior probability of the consequent before the association rule and compare it to the confidence. This example demonstrates the importance of context. If some events already have a high frequency of occurrence, the association rules of these events as a priori need to be much stronger.

CATEGORICAL AND NUMERICAL DATA

Association rules are not limited to the Boolean data type that indicates the presence of a trait or a product, as in the case of market basket analysis. The a priori algorithm can also be applied to categorical data more generally. Association rules cannot work with continuous variables as antecedents or consequents, however. Continuous variables must be converted into categorical variables before analyzing association rules.

Data mining association rules with categorical variables poses some difficulties, which can be avoided if they are first converted into dichotomous variables. We can divide categorical variables into a series of dichotomous variables to use in a priori algorithms to identify association rules. For example, if we are interested in determining the association rules for people who feel "very happy" and "somewhat happy" in a 3-category variable, where the third category is "not so happy," we can lump the first two categories into a Boolean variable of "happy." We also convert other categorical variables such as marital status, highest educational degree obtained, gender, and race into a series of Boolean variables.

Unlike in regression analysis, the dichotomous variables in association rule mining do not need to be mutually exclusive or exhaustive. These dichotomous variables will not generate effect parameters that must be interpreted relative to an omitted category or compared to the other categories. Rather, we may enter any dichotomous variable with any combination of attributes that may be interesting and relevant. For example, for a 5-category measure of marital status (single, married, separated, divorced, widowed), we may enter all five dummy variables for each status, or we may combine two dummy variables to create a new category for those who were once married but not are no longer married (separated or divorced and widowed) and leave other categories out. We might also convert all of those who have ever been married (married, separated or divorced, and widowed) into one dummy variable. We may use these newly created dichotomous variables that are not mutually exclusive in association rule mining.

ASSOCIATION MINING AS AN EXPLORATORY TOOL

Association rule mining is very good at identifying associations among combinations of attributes. Association rules are generated in the form of multivariate associations.

They therefore provide novel or unexpected combinations of prior conditions that co-occur before the outcomes or the target variables. Discovering such combinations, expected and unexpected, directs researchers to investigate interesting joint effects among explanatory variables.

IDENTIFYING OUTCOME VARIABLES

With association rule mining, instead of indiscriminately evaluating all associations among all attributes, it is more efficient to limit the search for associations with one or two (when interested in chain relationships) outcome variables of interest. This will substantially reduce the search space and the number of generated rules. Researchers can then focus on searching through many input variables to determine which ones tend to occur with the outcome variable(s).

ADVANTAGES OF ASSOCIATION RULES

Association rule mining has several advantages over correlation analysis. First, the rules are generated automatically and semiautomatically and can be ranked by any measure of the association strength. A correlation matrix is less effective because we need to manually inspect all of the associations in the order in which the variables were entered, not in the order of their association strength. Second, association rule mining is very good at identifying associations among combinations of attributes. Association rules are generated in the form of multivariate associations. They therefore provide novel or unexpected combinations of prior conditions that co-occur before the outcomes or the target variables. Discovering such combinations, expected and unexpected, directs researchers to investigate interesting joint effects among explanatory variables. Third, association rules do not require the assumptions of multivariate normality, homoscedasticity, and independent residuals as conventional multivariate models do. They are nonparametric statistics that are more flexible and can be widely used on a variety of data distributions.

DIFFERENCES BETWEEN ASSOCIATION RULES, CORRELATIONS, AND REGRESSION

It should also be noted that association rules are different from regressions in a few ways. First, although association rules are nonparametric statistics that make fewer assumptions about the sample data and thus its application is wider in scope than parametric statistics, this type of nonparametric statistics has a lower degree of confidence than do results from parametric statistics. We thus need methods to combine association rules with more rigorous statistical tests to generate robust results. Second, association rules do not impose statistical controls, so we need to interpret and understand the resulting rules carefully and in context. It is important to carry out further multivariate analysis, such as logistic regression, to take advantage of the new insights generated by association rule mining, on the one hand, and impose statistical controls to ensure true net effects, on the other. Third, association rules focus exclusively on the relationship between the antecedent group and the consequent outcome, and they do not pay attention to comparison groups. The association rules are therefore absolute, not relative to other groups as in regression where dummy variables include a reference group. As a result, it is important to pay attention to rules governing other groups to gauge the relative effects.

USING ASSOCIATION RULES ON DATA

Let me now demonstrate how we can use association rule mining in the social sciences to identify important combinations of attributes that are associated with an outcome. We use a data set on the fate of passengers on the *Titanic* that contains four variables: class on the ship (first, second, or third), gender (female or male), age (child or adult), and survival (yes or no). The data are available at http://www.rdatamining.com/data.

We first load the data set. The passengers were in four classes: first, second, third, and Crew. Among them, 470 were women and 1,731 were men, and 2,092 were adults and 109 were children. Only 711 people survived; 1,490 perished.

```
> load("C:/Users/.../titanic.raw.rdata")
> View(titanic.raw)
> summary(titanic.raw)
Class Sex Age Survived
1st :325 Female: 470 Adult: 2092 No:1490
2nd :285 Male :1731 Child: 109 Yes: 711
3rd :706
Crew:885
```

We then install the package "arules."

```
> install.packages("arules")
Installing package into 'C:/Users/xshu/Documents/R/win-library/3.5'
(as 'lib' is unspecified)
trying URL 'https://cran.rstudio.com/bin/windows/contrib/3.5/arules_1.6-1.zip'
Content type 'application/zip' length 2675943 bytes (2.6 MB)
downloaded 2.6 MB

package 'arules' successfully unpacked and MD5 sums checked
The downloaded binary packages are in C:\Users\xshu\AppData\Local\Temp\RtmpiUnbSj\
downloaded_packages
> library(arules)
Loading required package: Matrix

Attaching package: 'arules'

The following objects are masked from 'package:base':

abbreviate, write
```

We next generate all the association rules. Many of these rules are irrelevant and uninteresting.

```
> rules.all<-apriori(titanic.raw)
Apriori


Parameter specification:
confidence minval smax arem aval originalSupport maxtime support minlen maxlen
target ext
0.8 0.1 1 none FALSE TRUE 5 0.1 1 10 rules FALSE


Algorithmic control:
filter tree heap memopt load sort verbose
0.1 TRUE TRUE FALSE TRUE 2 TRUE


Absolute minimum support count: 220


set item appearances . . .[0 item(s)] done [0.00s].
set transactions . . .[10 item(s), 2201 transaction(s)] done [0.00s].
sorting and recoding items . . . [9 item(s)] done [0.00s].
creating transaction tree . . . done [0.00s].
checking subsets of size 1 2 3 4 done [0.00s].
writing . . . [27 rule(s)] done [0.00s].
creating S4 object . . . done [0.00s].
> quality(rules.all)<-round(quality(rules.all), digits=3)
> rules.all
set of 27 rules
> inspect(rules.all)
lhs rhs support confidence lift count
[1] {} => {Age=Adult} 0.950 0.950 1.000 2092
[2] {Class=2nd} => {Age=Adult} 0.119 0.916 0.964 261
[3] {Class=1st} => {Age=Adult} 0.145 0.982 1.033 319
[4] {Sex=Female} => {Age=Adult} 0.193 0.904 0.951 425
[5] {Class=3rd} => {Age=Adult} 0.285 0.888 0.934 627
[6] {Survived=Yes} => {Age=Adult} 0.297 0.920 0.968 654
[7] {Class=Crew} => {Sex=Male} 0.392 0.974 1.238 862
[8] {Class=Crew} => {Age=Adult} 0.402 1.000 1.052 885
[9] {Survived=No} => {Sex=Male} 0.620 0.915 1.164 1364
[10] {Survived=No} => {Age=Adult} 0.653 0.965 1.015 1438
[11] {Sex=Male} => {Age=Adult} 0.757 0.963 1.013 1667
[12] {Sex=Female,Survived=Yes} => {Age=Adult} 0.144 0.919 0.966 316
[13] {Class=3rd,Sex=Male} => {Survived=No} 0.192 0.827 1.222 422
[14] {Class=3rd,Survived=No} => {Age=Adult} 0.216 0.902 0.948 476
[15] {Class=3rd,Sex=Male} => {Age=Adult} 0.210 0.906 0.953 462
[16] {Sex=Male,Survived=Yes} => {Age=Adult} 0.154 0.921 0.969 338
[17] {Class=Crew,Survived=No} => {Sex=Male} 0.304 0.996 1.266 670
[18] {Class=Crew,Survived=No} => {Age=Adult} 0.306 1.000 1.052 673
[19] {Class=Crew,Sex=Male} => {Age=Adult} 0.392 1.000 1.052 862
[20] {Class=Crew,Age=Adult} => {Sex=Male} 0.392 0.974 1.238 862
[21] {Sex=Male,Survived=No} => {Age=Adult} 0.604 0.974 1.025 1329
[22] {Age=Adult,Survived=No} => {Sex=Male} 0.604 0.924 1.175 1329
[23] {Class=3rd,Sex=Male,Survived=No} => {Age=Adult} 0.176 0.917 0.965 387
[24] {Class=3rd,Age=Adult,Survived=No} => {Sex=Male} 0.176 0.813 1.034 387
[25] {Class=3rd,Sex=Male,Age=Adult} => {Survived=No} 0.176 0.838 1.237 387
```

```
[26] {Class=Crew,Sex=Male,Survived=No} => {Age=Adult} 0.304 1.000 1.052 670
[27] {Class=Crew,Age=Adult,Survived=No} => {Sex=Male} 0.304 0.996 1.266 670
```

We are interested only in rules with Survival as the consequent, so we make sure that only survivors will appear in the rules.

```
> rules<-apriori(titanic.raw, control = list(verbose=F), parameter=list(minlen=2,
supp=.005, conf=.8), appearance =list(rhs=c("Survived=No", "Survived=Yes"),
default="lhs"))
> quality(rules)<-round(quality(rules),digits = 2)
> rules.sorted<-sort(rules,by="lift")
> inspect(rules.sorted)
lhs rhs support confidence lift count
[1] {Class=2nd,Age=Child} => {Survived=Yes} 0.01 1.00 3.10 24
[2] {Class=2nd,Sex=Female,Age=Child} => {Survived=Yes} 0.01 1.00 3.10 13
[3] {Class=1st,Sex=Female} => {Survived=Yes} 0.06 0.97 3.01 141
[4] {Class=1st,Sex=Female,Age=Adult} => {Survived=Yes} 0.06 0.97 3.01 140
[5] {Class=2nd,Sex=Female} => {Survived=Yes} 0.04 0.88 2.72 93
[6] {Class=Crew,Sex=Female} => {Survived=Yes} 0.01 0.87 2.69 20
[7] {Class=Crew,Sex=Female,Age=Adult} => {Survived=Yes} 0.01 0.87 2.69 20
[8] {Class=2nd,Sex=Female,Age=Adult} => {Survived=Yes} 0.04 0.86 2.66 80
[9] {Class=2nd,Sex=Male,Age=Adult} => {Survived=No} 0.07 0.92 1.35 154
[10] {Class=2nd,Sex=Male} => {Survived=No} 0.07 0.86 1.27 154
[11] {Class=3rd,Sex=Male,Age=Adult} => {Survived=No} 0.18 0.84 1.24 387
[12] {Class=3rd,Sex=Male} => {Survived=No} 0.19 0.83 1.22 422
> subset.matrix<-is.subset(rules.sorted, rules.sorted)
> subset.matrix[lower.tri(subset.matrix,diag = T)]<-NA
```

Some of these rules are redundant, identifying the same rule without additional information. For example, children in second class who survived and female children in second class who survived have the same support, confidence, and lift, so they should be consolidated into a single rule, by not differentiating gender of the children.

```
> redundant<-colSums(subset.matrix,na.rm=T)>=1
> which(redundant)
{Class=2nd,Age=Child,Survived=Yes} {Class=2nd,Sex=Female,Age=Child,Survived=Yes}
1 2
{Class=1st,Sex=Female,Survived=Yes} {Class=1st,Sex=Female,Age=Adult,Survived=Yes}
3 4
{Class=2nd,Sex=Female,Survived=Yes} {Class=Crew,Sex=Female,Survived=Yes}
5 6
{Class=Crew,Sex=Female,Age=Adult,Survived=Yes} {Class=2nd,Sex=Female,Age=Adult,
Survived=Yes}
7 8
{Class=2nd,Sex=Male,Age=Adult,Survived=No} {Class=2nd,Sex=Male,Survived=No}
9 10
{Class=3rd,Sex=Male,Age=Adult,Survived=No} {Class=3rd,Sex=Male,Survived=No}
11 12
```

Since some of the generated rules provide little additional information relative to other rules, we prune redundant rules. We also classify all the people by class and age group (adult / child) to compare across these groups, as some of these groups have lower support than the cutoff and were not included. (Some events are rare; for example, few children were in first class, with a support of only .0027.) Results are sorted by lift.

```
> rules.pruned<-rules.sorted[!redundant]
> inspect(rules.pruned)
> subset.matrix[lower.tri(subset.matrix,diag=T)]<-NA
> inspect(rules.pruned)
> rules<-apriori(titanic.raw,parameter = list(minlen=3, supp=.002,conf=.02),
appearance = list(rhs=c("Survived=Yes"), lhs=c("Class=1st","Class=2nd",
"Class=3rd", "Age=Child","Age=Adult"), default="none"), control=list(verbose=F))
> rules.sorted<-sort(rules, by="confidence")
> inspect(rules.sorted)
lhs rhs support confidence lift count
[1] {Class=2nd,Age=Child} => {Survived=Yes} 0.010904134 1.0000000 3.0956399 24
[2] {Class=1st,Age=Child} => {Survived=Yes} 0.002726034 1.0000000 3.0956399 6
[3] {Class=1st,Age=Adult} => {Survived=Yes} 0.089504771 0.6175549 1.9117275 197
[4] {Class=2nd,Age=Adult} => {Survived=Yes} 0.042707860 0.3601533 1.1149048 94
[5] {Class=3rd,Age=Child} => {Survived=Yes} 0.012267151 0.3417722 1.0580035 27
[6] {Class=3rd,Age=Adult} => {Survived=Yes} 0.068605179 0.2408293 0.7455209 151
```

All children in first and second classes survived. Only six children were from the first class and were thus a rare occurrence. Adults in the first class have the third highest lift, with adults in second class trailing. Children in third class fared only slightly better than the group with the lowest survival rate, adults in third class.

For people who are interested in the mortality rates, we may specify the rules for this outcome.

```
rules<-apriori(titanic.raw,parameter = list(minlen=3, supp=.002,conf=.02), appear-
ance = list(rhs=c("Survived=No"), lhs=c("Class=1st","Class=2nd", "Class=3rd",
"Age=Child","Age=Adult", "Sex=Male", "Sex=Female"), default="none"),
control=list(verbose=F))
> rules.sorted<-sort(rules, by="confidence")
> inspect(rules.sorted)
lhs rhs support confidence lift count
[1] {Class=2nd,Sex=Male,Age=Adult} => {Survived=No} 0.069968196 0.9166667
    1.3540828 154
[2] {Class=2nd,Sex=Male} => {Survived=No} 0.069968196 0.8603352 1.2708710 154
[3] {Class=3rd,Sex=Male,Age=Adult} => {Survived=No} 0.175829169 0.8376623
    1.2373791 387
[4] {Class=3rd,Sex=Male} => {Survived=No} 0.191731031 0.8274510 1.2222950 422
[5] {Sex=Male,Age=Adult} => {Survived=No} 0.603816447 0.7972406 1.1776688 1329
[6] {Class=3rd,Age=Adult} => {Survived=No} 0.216265334 0.7591707 1.1214326 476
[7] {Class=3rd,Sex=Male,Age=Child} => {Survived=No} 0.015901863 0.7291667
    1.0771113 35
[8] {Class=1st,Sex=Male,Age=Adult} => {Survived=No} 0.053611995 0.6742857
    0.9960422 118
[9] {Class=3rd,Age=Child} => {Survived=No} 0.023625625 0.6582278 0.9723218 52
[10] {Class=1st,Sex=Male} => {Survived=No} 0.053611995 0.6555556 0.9683743 118
[11] {Class=2nd,Age=Adult} => {Survived=No} 0.075874602 0.6398467 0.9451696 167
[12] {Class=3rd,Sex=Female,Age=Child} => {Survived=No} 0.007723762 0.5483871
    0.8100671 17
```

```
[13] {Sex=Male,Age=Child} => {Survived=No} 0.015901863 0.5468750 0.8078335 35
[14] {Class=3rd,Sex=Female} => {Survived=No} 0.048159927 0.5408163 0.7988837 106
[15] {Class=3rd,Sex=Female,Age=Adult} => {Survived=No} 0.040436165 0.5393939
     0.7967826 89
[16] {Class=1st,Age=Adult} => {Survived=No} 0.055429350 0.3824451 0.5649408 122
[17] {Sex=Female,Age=Child} => {Survived=No} 0.007723762 0.3777778 0.5580462 17
[18] {Sex=Female,Age=Adult} => {Survived=No} 0.049522944 0.2564706 0.3788535 109
[19] {Class=2nd,Sex=Female,Age=Adult} => {Survived=No} 0.005906406 0.1397849
     0.2064877 13
[20] {Class=2nd,Sex=Female} => {Survived=No} 0.005906406 0.1226415 0.1811637 13
```

We inspect the rules that are redundant.

```
> redundant<-colSums(subset.matrix,na.rm=T)>=1
> which(redundant)
{Class=2nd,Age=Child,Survived=Yes} {Class=2nd,Sex=Female,Age=Child,Survived=Yes}
{Class=1st,Sex=Female,Survived=Yes}
1 2 3
{Class=1st,Sex=Female,Age=Adult,Survived=Yes} {Class=2nd,Sex=Female,Survived=Yes}
{Class=Crew,Sex=Female,Survived=Yes}
4 5 6
{Class=Crew,Sex=Female,Age=Adult,Survived=Yes} {Class=2nd,Sex=Female,Age=Adult,Sur
vived=Yes} {Class=2nd,Sex=Male,Age=Adult,Survived=No}
7 8 9
{Class=2nd,Sex=Male,Survived=No} {Class=3rd,Sex=Male,Age=Adult,Survived=No} {Class
=3rd,Sex=Male,Survived=No}
10 11 12
>
```

The Crew and adults in third class have the highest lift in not surviving, while children
in third class have the second highest lift, more than adults in second and first class,
respectively.

```
> rules<-apriori(titanic.raw,parameter = list(minlen=3, supp=.002,conf=.02),
appearance = list(rhs=c("Survived=No"), lhs=c("Class=1st","Class=2nd",
"Class=3rd", "Class=Crew", "Age=Child","Age=Adult"), default="none"),
control=list(verbose=F))
> rules.sorted<-sort(rules, by="confidence")
> inspect(rules.sorted)
lhs rhs support confidence lift count
[1] {Class=Crew,Age=Adult} => {Survived=No} 0.30577010 0.7604520 1.1233254 673
[2] {Class=3rd,Age=Adult} => {Survived=No} 0.21626533 0.7591707 1.1214326 476
[3] {Class=3rd,Age=Child} => {Survived=No} 0.02362562 0.6582278 0.9723218 52
[4] {Class=2nd,Age=Adult} => {Survived=No} 0.07587460 0.6398467 0.9451696 167
[5] {Class=1st,Age=Adult} => {Survived=No} 0.05542935 0.3824451 0.5649408 122
```

SUMMARY

Association rule mining measures the association among attributes, with the goal of
discovering rules that describe relationships between variables in the data. Association
rule mining originated in marketing research on consumer behaviors, called market
basket analysis.

Association rules have three parts: a pair of antecedent and consequent events, support, and confidence. The antecedent and consequent are two events or attributes that occur in sequence. The support is the proportion of times when both antecedent and consequent occur. The confidence is the proportion of times that both antecedent and consequent appear when the antecedent occurs.

Data scientists use two methods to measure the strength of association. Lift measures the frequency by which an association occurs compared to random chance. It is the ratio of the probability that both antecedent and consequent occur together versus the probability that they occur randomly together. Leverage is the difference between these two probabilities.

To handle a large number of potential rules, the association rule algorithm reduces the search space using an a priori algorithm. After we obtain the rules, we use an overall measure of usefulness, the product of support and confidence, to rank the rules according to their prevalence and confidence. To account for the prior probability, we compare the advantage of using the association rule over not using it by converting lift into a confidence ratio, the proportion of the improvement from using the association rule over not using it. We may also calculate the confidence difference, which is the difference between the proportion of improvement from using the association and that of not using it.

We need to convert continuous variables into categorical variables before analyzing association rules. We can divide categorical variables into a series of dichotomous variables and use them in a priori algorithms to identify association rules. Dichotomous variables in association rule mining do not need to be mutually exclusive or exhaustive. These dichotomous variables will not generate effect parameters that must be interpreted relative to the omitted category and compared to other categories.

Association rule mining can serve as a powerful exploratory tool for social science research. Researchers can use association rules to mine associations among variables in a large space of combinations of attributes to identify the combinations that are highly likely to affect some outcome. Association rules provide useful leads on the direction of the causal relationship between the antecedents and the consequents.

With association rule mining, it is efficient to limit the search for associations to those between one or two outcomes of interest and other attributes. This will substantially reduce the search space as well as the number of rules generated. Researchers can then focus on searching through many input variables to determine which ones tend to occur with the outcome variables.

Association rule mining has advantages over correlation analysis. The rules are generated automatically and semiautomatically and can be ranked by any measure of the strength of the association. Association rule mining is very good at identifying associations among combinations of attributes that are novel or unexpected conditions prior to the outcomes. Such discoveries direct researchers to investigate interesting joint effects among explanatory variables.

Association rules are different from regressions. Association rules are nonparametric statistics and do not impose statistical controls. In addition, association rules do not pay attention to comparison groups.

PRACTICE QUESTIONS

1. What is association rule mining? In what field did association rule mining originate?
2. What are the components of association rules? What is support? What is confidence?
3. In a high school graduating class of 1,000 students, 400 are from higher-income families and 400 are planning to attend college. Among those going to college, 300 are from higher-income families.
   a. Find the support for the association of Higher Income → College.
   b. Find the confidence for the association of Higher Income → College.
   c. Calculate the lift for the association of Higher Income → College. Explain its meaning.
   d. Calculate the leverage for the association of Higher Income → College. Explain its meaning.
4. What do we use to measure the strength of association? Explain each measure and how to calculate it.
5. What is an a priori algorithm? Why is it useful in association rule mining?
6. Use the data in table P7.1 and the association rule algorithm to find association rules.

TABLE P7.1   ASSOCIATION RULES AMONG EDUCATION, INCOME, SCHOOL PERFORMANCE, AND GENDER

	College	Higher Income	Higher School Performance	Female
A	1	1	1	1
B	0	1	1	0
C	1	1	1	0
D	0	0	0	0
E	0	0	0	1
F	0	0	0	1
G	1	0	1	1
H	0	0	0	0

a. If we set f ≥ 2, identify and list one-item itemsets.

b. Identify and list 2-item itemsets.

c. Identify and list 3-item itemsets.

d. Identify and list 4-item itemsets.

e. Generate all candidate association rules for itemsets of four, three, and two. Calculate support and confidence for each rule.

f. Prune association rules with college as a consequent. For the remaining rules, calculate their lift and the product of support by confidence.

g. Write a short conclusion based on the findings from f.

7. How do you measure the overall usefulness of an association rule?

8. What are confidence ratios and confidence differences? Why do we need to use these measures in searching for robust and valid association rules?

9. Can association rules be used on continuous data? If not, what can we do to enable association mining on such data?

10. What roles can association rule mining play in social science research?

11. In social science research, we tend to focus on one or two variables as outcomes. Can this feature be accommodated in association rule mining?

12. What advantages does association rule mining have over correlation analysis?

13. In what ways is association rule mining different from regression?

REFERENCES

Blanchard, Philippe, Felix Bühlmann, and Jacques-Antoine Gauthier, eds. 2014. *Advances in Sequence Analysis: Theory, Methods, Applications*. New York: Springer.

Hand, Davis J., Heikki Mannila, and Padhraic Smyth. 2001. *Principles of Data Mining*. Cambridge, MA: MIT Press.

## PART V

DATA MINING: SUPERVISED LEARNING

Chapter 8

GENERALIZED REGRESSION

―――――

SUPERVISED LEARNING

Supervised learning differs from unsupervised learning in that an algorithm learns from a training data set in a process similar to that of a teacher supervising a student's learning. In supervised learning, we have prior knowledge of the target variables—the correct answers—and the algorithm progressively makes predictions on the training data, compares them to the outcome variables (which act as the teacher), and makes corrections with feedback.

In supervised learning, we use a series of input variables to predict an output variable. We do so by using an algorithm to learn about the function by using the input variable x to produce an output variable y: $y = f(x)$. The goal is to identify the function f such that the function f can produce the outcome variables y using new input data x.

There are two general types of supervised learning problems: those predicting categorical output variables and those predicting continuous output variables. For categorical output variables, decision trees, logistic regressions, and neural networks build functions using input variables to estimate and predict categorical output variables, such as divorced versus married or survival versus death. For continuous output variables, regression models generate functions that link input variables to numerical output variables, such as income in dollars or time in hours.

PARAMETER LEARNING

Parameter learning is a form of supervised learning. This approach starts with models by specifying their structures but leaving unspecified their numerical parameters. Researchers then compute the best values for these parameters using data to train the model with feedback from the existing output variables. They specify the model structure as a parameterized mathematical function in the form of an equation with a set of numerical attributes as inputs x, a mathematical function f that reads the inputs and generates the output, and an output y: $y = f(x)$.

Researchers specify the inputs, the outputs, and the functional form while machine learning searches for the best-fitting parameters. Researchers choose input attributes based on their domain-specific knowledge, which is informed both by theories and by their accumulated knowledge about the subject matter. Researchers specify functional forms based on their prior knowledge about the mechanisms by which the inputs influence the output. The goal of data mining is to find and adjust the parameters to achieve the best-fitting model.

The mathematical functions linking inputs and outputs can take many forms, but most of them are a linear model structure that treats the outputs as the weighted, simple additive sum of all the input values. The magnitudes of the weights on the input attributes are unknown parameters to be fit by the data mining. This group of linear modeling methods includes linear regression for numerical outputs, logistic regression for categorical outputs, and linear discriminants such as support-vector machines for classification.

LINEAR REGRESSION

A linear regression model approximates the relationship between a continuous output variable and a set of input variables. The regression equation is expressed in the following form:

$$y = \hat{y} + \varepsilon = \beta_0 + \beta_1 x_1 + \beta_2 x_2 + \ldots + \beta_K x_K + \varepsilon$$

where y is an output (typically a continuous variable), $\hat{y}$ is the estimated value of the output based on the regression, ε is the error term to account for individual variations from the prediction, $x_1, x_2 \ldots x_K$ are k numbers of inputs (which may be continuous or categorical variables), β_0 is the y-intercept of the regression plane with the y axis (which is the expected value of y when all x's are zero), and $\beta_1, \beta_2 \ldots \beta_K$ are partial regression slopes after controlling for influences from all the other input variables.

Once the function is identified, the next task is to fit parameters $\beta_0, \beta_1, \beta_2 \ldots \beta_K$. The guiding principle is to identify a line that minimizes the population sum of squared errors. The equation for calculating the sum of squared errors is

$$SSE = \sum \varepsilon_i^2 = \sum (y_i - \hat{y}_i)^2$$

The error is the difference between the expected value for the output variable $\hat{y}_i$ and the actual value y_i. To avoid having negative values, we square the differences to obtain all positive values. Finally, we sum up all the squared errors. The best regression line is the one that obtains the smallest sum of squared errors (SSE) among all the infinite candidate regression lines. This is the least squares approach. Although there are alternative methods for obtaining a line that best describes the relationship among the input and output variables, the least squares method has remained the most common approach.

The least squares method provides estimates for the regression parameters. For regressions with one input variable, $y = \beta_0 + \beta_1 x_1 + \varepsilon$, which is called bivariate regression or simple regression, we can derive equations for calculating the model parameters (Larose and Larose 2015). To minimize equation $SSE = \sum \varepsilon_i^2 = \sum (y_i - \hat{y}_i)^2 = \sum [y_i - (\beta_0 + \beta_1 x_1)]^2$ and differential calculus, we can use these equations for the two regression parameters:

$$b_1 = \frac{\sum xy - \frac{\sum x \sum y}{n}}{\sum x_2 - \frac{\sum x^2}{n}}$$

$$b_0 = \bar{y} - b_1 \bar{x}$$

Applying these questions to the data set in table 3.2 from the United Nations on life expectancy at birth and GDP per capita, we obtain a regression line of $\hat{y} = 67.43 + .000246x$. The intercept b_0 is 67.43, indicating that for countries with zero GDP per capita, the expected life expectancy is 67.43 years. Since the lowest GDP per capita in the data set is above $500, the y-intercept does not exist in the data and the regression line does not extend to that range. The slope is .000246, so for each thousand-dollar increase in per capita GDP, life expectancy increases by 0.246 year. Figure 8.1 shows this regression line and the distribution of countries relative to this regression line.

Mean of Life Expectancy = 71.42, Standard Deviation of Life Expectancy = 8.39

We use this regression line to evaluate two cases. For the United States, which has a GDP per capita of $54,629, we calculate the expected life expectancy as 80.87 years: $\hat{y} = 67.43 + .000246x$. $\hat{y} = 80.87$. The observed y is 78.94. For the United States, then, the error $\varepsilon = 78.94 - 80.87 = -1.93$. This is consistent with what is illustrated in figure 8.1, that is, the observed data point (the orange dot) for the United States falls below the regression line. For Hong Kong, which has a GDP per capita of $40,170, the expected

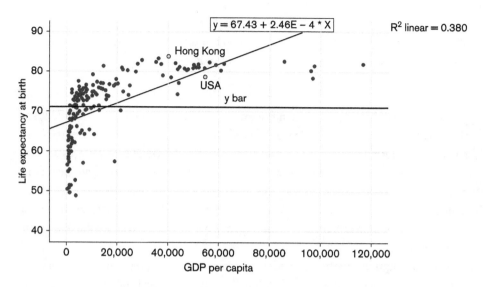

FIGURE 8.1

Scatter Plot of Life Expectancy at Birth vs. GDP per Capita for Countries.

life expectancy is 77.31 years. The observed life expectancy in Hong Kong is 83.98. This is again consistent with the illustration in figure 8.1, where the data point (the green dot) for Hong Kong is well above the regression line.

MEASURING MODEL PERFORMANCE

Although the least squares method provides a regression line that best approximates the relationship between input and output variables, we have no information on how well the regression performs in predicting outcome variables. For this we need measures of regression goodness-of-fit with the data.

COEFFICIENT OF DETERMINATION

To measure the model's goodness-of-fit, we calculate the coefficient of determination. This is a measure of the improvement we gain from using the regression line to predict the output variable relative to the situation without the regression line. Without the regression line, our best prediction for the output variable for each case is the mean, or average, of this variable.

Let us consider the case of Hong Kong in figure 8.1. The average for life expectancy at birth for all the countries is $\bar{y}$ = 71.42, as indicated by the horizontal line over y (the "y bar"). The difference between the dot representing Hong Kong and the horizontal line is the total deviation from the mean $(y_i - \bar{y})$ = 83.98 – 71.42 = 12.56. This is the total amount of error we have when we do not use the regression line. The total distance from the mean $\bar{y}$ to the dot can be separated into two parts: the top portion is the difference between the dot and the regression line $\hat{y}$, which is $(y_i - \hat{y})$ = 83.98 – 77.31 = 6.67,

TABLE 8.1 **ANALYSIS OF VARIANCE (ANOVA) TABLE FOR LIFE EXPECTANCY AND GDP PER CAPITA REGRESSION MODEL**

Model		Sum of Squares	df	Mean Square	F	Sig.
1	Regression	4925.212	1	4925.212	112.641	.000[b]
	Residual	8045.402	184	43.725		
	Total	12970.614	185			

a. Dependent Variable: life expectancy at birth

b. Predictors: (Constant), GDP per capita

and the bottom portion is the difference between the regression line and the mean $\bar{y}$, which is $(\hat{y} - \bar{y}) = 71.42 - 72.42 = 5.89$. The total amount of error we would have without the regression line is 12.56. By using the regression line, we reduce the error to only 6.67. In this way, using the regression line improves the prediction by 5.89.

If we square all three quantities and sum them up for all data points, we have three corresponding sums of squares. The total sum of squares (TSS) is the total amount of variability in the output variables. The sum of squares regression (SSR) is the total amount of variability accounted for or reduced by the regression line. The SSE is the remaining residuals that the regression model fails to explain:

$$TSS = SSR + SSE$$

where $TSS = Total\ Sum\ of\ Squares = \Sigma(y_i - \bar{y}_i)^2$, $SSR = Sum\ of\ Squares\ Regression = \Sigma\ (\hat{y} - \bar{y})^2$, and $SSE = Sum\ of\ Squared\ Errors = \Sigma\ (y_i - \hat{y})^2$.

The coefficient of determination measures the proportion of variability in the output variable accounted for in the regression model $r^2 = \frac{SSR}{TSS}$. Table 8.1 shows the TSS, SSR, and SSE. We can calculate the coefficient of determination as

$$r^2 = \frac{SSR}{TSS} = \frac{4925.21}{12970.61} = .38$$

The regression model of a linear relationship between GDP per capita and life expectancy at birth accounts for 38 percent of the variability in life expectancy over using the mean as a predictor.

The r^2 ranges from 0 to 1. When $r^2 = 0$, the regression model does not improve over the mean. In this case, the regression model is identical to the mean. When $r^2 = 1$, the regression accounts for all the variability in the output variable. The regression line passes through all data points and perfectly accounts for all variation. In the social sciences, models with $r^2 \geq .6$ are generally considered strong models. When $.3 \leq r^2 < .6$, models are considered moderately strong. It is not unusual to find models with $r^2 < .3$ in the social sciences, and these models are nevertheless considered acceptable because of large between-person variability uncaptured by input variables.

STANDARD ERROR OF THE ESTIMATE

Another measure of the accuracy of the regression model is the standard error of the estimate. It is the statistical average amount of error unaccounted for by the regression line. It is the typical distance between the predicted output according to the regression line and the actual value of the output variable. The smaller the value of the standard error of the estimate, the better the regression model fits with the data:

$$s = \sqrt{\frac{SSE}{n-p-1}}$$

where n is the total number of cases in the data, p is the number of input variables in the regression, and SSE is the sum of squared error.

We apply this equation to table 8.1 to calculate the standard error.

$$s = \sqrt{\frac{SSE}{n-p-1}} = \sqrt{\frac{8045.402}{186-1-1}} = 6.61$$

Compare this standard error of 6.61 with the standard deviation of the output variable of 8.39. The standard error is substantially smaller than the standard deviation.

ASSUMPTIONS FOR REGRESSION MODELS

Regression models are based on the following assumptions, which must be validated so that parameter inferences and model building are possible:

1. Normality: The outcome variable y is a normally distributed random variable.
2. Independence: For any set of values for all the independent variables $x_1, x_2, x_3. . ., x_m$, the values of y are also independent.
3. Homoscedasticity: For any set of values for all the independent variables $x_1, x_2, x_3. . ., x_m$, the variance of the y's is always constant.

ANOVA OR F TEST

A more accurate method to test if the regression model effectively accounts for the variation in the output variable is to carry out an ANOVA test, also called an F test. An ANOVA table, for example, table 8.2, succinctly summarizes the features of a regression model. The last step of an ANOVA test is to calculate the F score, which is the ratio between the mean squares regression and the mean squares error. Based on the calculated F score, the degrees of freedom (for MSR, df = p = number of input variables; for SSE, df = n-p-1), and the F table, we can find the probability P.

NULL AND ALTERNATIVE HYPOTHESES

H_0: The output is statistically independent of all the input variables in the regression.

H_a: The output is not statistically independent of all the input variables in the regression.

TABLE 8.2 **COMPONENTS OF AN ANOVA TABLE**

Model	Sum of Squares	df	Mean Square	F	Sig.
Regression	SSR	P	$MSR = \frac{SSR}{P}$	$F = \frac{MSR}{MSE}$	P
Error/Residual	SSE	n-p-1	$MSE = \frac{SSE}{N-P-1}$		
Total	TSS	n-1			

After choosing an α level (usually at $\alpha = .001$ or $\alpha = .01$ or $\alpha = .05$), we are ready to make a decision regarding the model.

When $P < \alpha$, we reject the null hypothesis that the output variable is statistically independent of all the input variables in the regression. We conclude that it is plausible that the output is not statistically independent of the input variables in the regression model.

When $P \geq \alpha$, we fail to reject the null hypothesis that the output variable is statistically independent of all the input variables in the regression. We cannot accept the alternative hypothesis that the output is not statistically independent of the input variables in the regression model.

Now let us calculate the F score for the question in table 8.1. The F score is 112.64 with $df_1 = 1$ and $df_2 = 184$. Using an F calculator (http://onlinestatbook.com/2/calculators/F_dist.html), we find the probability $P < .001$. Since $P < \alpha = .001$, we reject the null hypothesis that life expectancy at birth is statistically independent of GDP per capita. We conclude that it is plausible that life expectancy is not statistically independent of GDP per capita.

We now conduct another F test using a multiple regression model. Table 8.3 shows information from an ANOVA test for a model with two inputs, GDP per capita and child mortality rate, with life expectancy as the output. $F = 54.925$, with $df_1 = 2$ and $df_2 = 165$. The P value = .000. We again reject the null hypothesis that life expectancy is statistically independent of both GDP per capita and the child mortality rate. We conclude that it is plausible that life expectancy is statistically associated with GDP per capita and child mortality.

T TESTS AND CONFIDENCE INTERVALS FOR THE REGRESSION SLOPE

Once we have obtained estimates of regression coefficients from a sample, we wonder whether such a relationship also holds in the population. To gain information about the population parameter, we carry out t tests on regression slopes.

The hypotheses for a t test in multiple regression are the null hypothesis:

$H_0: \beta_i = 0$ after controlling for all the other independent variables in the regression; and the alternative hypothesis, which can be specified in three ways:

TABLE 8.3 **ANALYSIS OF VARIANCE (ANOVA) TABLE FOR LIFE EXPECTANCY AS OUTPUT GDP PER CAPITA AND CHILD MORTALITY RATE (AGES 0–5) AS INPUTS IN A REGRESSION MODEL**

Model		Sum of Squares	Df	Mean Square	F	Sig.
1	Regression	4609.514	2	2304.757	54.925	.000[b]
	Residual	6923.670	165	41.962		
	Total	11533.184	167			

a. Dependent Variable: life expectancy at birth

b. Predictors: (Constant), mortality rate (ages 0–5), GDP per capita

$H_a: \beta_i = 0$ (two-tailed test) after controlling for all the other independent variables in the regression, or

$H_a: \beta_i > 0$ (one-tailed test) after controlling for all the other independent variables in the regression, or

$H_a: \beta_i < 0$ (one-tailed test) after controlling for all the other independent variables in the regression

The t test equation is

$$t = \frac{b_i - 0}{s_{b_i}}$$

where b_i is the estimated regression slope from the sample, s_{b_i} is the estimated standard error for the corresponding regression slope b_i, and the t score is from a distribution with degrees of freedom of $df = n - p - 1$ with p number of independent variables in the model. We then use the t table to find the corresponding probability.

When $P < \alpha$, we reject the null hypothesis that the input variable of interest is statistically independent of the outcome variable, after controlling for all the other independent variables in the regression. We conclude that it is plausible that the input variable of interest is statistically associated with the output variable, after controlling for all the other independent variables in the regression.

When $P \geq \alpha$, we fail to reject the null hypothesis that the input variable of interest is statistically independent of the outcome variable, after controlling for all the other independent variables in the regression. We do not accept the alternative hypothesis that the input variable of interest is statistically associated with the output variable, after controlling for all the other independent variables in the regression.

For the regression using GDP per capita and child mortality as inputs and life expectancy at birth as the output, we test if child mortality is positively associated with life expectancy. Table 8.4 provides information on the regression coefficients, their standard errors, t scores, and significance levels. We choose $\alpha = .05$.

Model	Unstandardized Coefficients		Standardized Coefficients	
	B	Std. Error	Beta	T
1 (Constant)	68.594	.822		83.479
GDP per capita ($ thousand)	.249	.025	.600	9.861
Mortality rate, 0–5	−.035	.016	−.138	−2.263

a. Dependent Variable: life expectancy at birth

Hypotheses:

H_0: $\beta_{child\ mortality}$ = 0 after controlling for GDP per capita

H_α: $\beta_{child\ mortality}$ < 0 (one-tailed test) after controlling for GDP per capita

t test:

$t = \frac{b_i - 0}{s_{b_i}}$ = −2.263 with df = 165 (the same as df_2 in Table 8.3)

P-Value:

Using the t table, we find .01 < P < .025

Conclusion:

$P < \alpha = .05$, so we reject the null hypothesis that child mortality rate is statistically independent of life expectancy, after controlling for GDP per capita. The data suggest that the child mortality rate is statistically negatively associated with life expectancy, after controlling for GDP per capita.

TRANSFORMING VARIABLES TO ACHIEVE LINEARITY

Regression models assume multivariate linear relationships between the independent variables and the dependent variable. We can visually inspect whether this is true using various plots, including scatter plots and residual plots. If there are no discernible concerns about this violation, linear regression models may be a good approach for the research question at hand. However, if the graphs indicate some pattern of nonlinear relationship, we may consider methods of variable transformation to achieve linearity. For example, figure 8.1 shows that the linear regression line generally fits well with the data, but increases in life expectancy are much greater at lower levels of GDP per capita than at higher levels. We may therefore consider transforming GDP per capita to its natural log, Ln(GDP per capita). Figure 8.2 shows the new regression

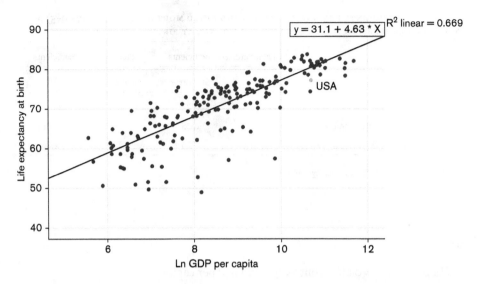

FIGURE 8.2
Scatter Plot of Life Expectancy at Birth vs. LN GDP Per Capita for Countries.

TABLE 8.5 ANALYSIS OF VARIANCE (ANOVA) TABLE FOR LIFE EXPECTANCY AS OUTPUT LN GDP
PER CAPITA AS INPUTS IN A REGRESSION MODEL

Model	Sum of Squares	df	Mean Square	F	Sig.
1 Regression	8673.251	1	8673.251	371.362	.000[b]
Residual	4297.363	184	23.355		
Total	12970.614	185			

a. Dependent Variable: life expectancy at birth
b. Predictors: (Constant), Ln (GDP per capita)

line connecting Ln (GDP per capita) and life expectancy. The line appears to fit with
the data points much better than the line in figure 8.1 that uses untransformed GDP
per capita.

We use information from this new model to test if it has better goodness-of-fit
with the data. We use information from table 8.5 to calculate the coefficient of
determination:

$$r^2 = \frac{SSR}{TSS} = \frac{8673.25}{12970.61} = .669$$

This is a substantial improvement over the model using the untransformed GDP per
capita, which has a r^2 of .38.

The Box-Cox transformation is another general approach of variable transformation. It uses the following equation to transform variable x:

$$f(BC) \begin{cases} \dfrac{(x^\alpha - 1)^2}{\alpha}, for\ \alpha \neq 0 \\ \ln x, for\ \alpha = 0 \end{cases}$$

We may choose a range of values for α to identify the best-fitting transformation. For example, we could use $\alpha = 1$, then $f(BC) = (x - 1)^2$, or $\alpha = 2$, then $f(BC) = \dfrac{(x^2 - 1)^2}{2}$, or $= 1.5$, then $f(BC) = \dfrac{(x^{1.5} - 1)^2}{1.5}$, and so on. We use the method of maximum likelihood to find the optimal value of α. The procedure is summarized in the following steps (Draper and Smith 1998):

1. Identify a series of candidate values for α;
2. Use each value of α to transform the variable;
3. For each of the transformed variables x, estimate a regression model;
4. Find model SSE_α for each of the regression models;
5. Plot all the values of SSE_α versus α;
6. Find the lowest point of this curve, which is the maximum likelihood estimate of α.

LOGISTIC REGRESSION

Logistic regressions model the relationship between a categorical outcome and a set of independent variables. For dichotomous outcome variables, the error term can take on only two values. This is different from the assumption for linear regression models that the error term is normally distributed, with mean zero and constant variance. The binary outcome variable ranges only from 0 to 1, is not continuous, and is not linearly related to the independent variables. In order to convert the binary dependent variable so that it is linearly related with the independent variables on a continuous line that spans from negative to positive values, we transform the outcome variable to *ln* odds ratios:

$$\ln\left(\frac{p(y)}{1 - p(y)}\right) = \beta_0 + \beta_1 x_1 + \beta_2 x_2 + \dots + \beta_m x_m \qquad \text{Equation 8.1}$$

where the left-hand side of the equation is the *ln* odds ratio between p(y), the probability of the outcome being 1 (the outcome is positive), and 1 − p(y), the probability of the outcome being 0 (the outcome is negative). This equation can be converted in the form of

$$\frac{p(y)}{1 - p(y)} = e^{\beta_0 + \beta_1 x_1 + \beta_2 x_2 + \dots + \beta_m x_m} \qquad \text{Equation 8.2}$$

We will need to carry out extra steps to achieve valid interpretations of logistic regression coefficients. Table 8.6 shows estimations of logistic regression coefficients using the age of the respondent, gender, and education to predict whether the respondent supports allowing anti-religionists to teach.

TABLE 8.6 **LOGISTIC REGRESSION ON YES TO ALLOW ANTI-RELIGIONISTS TO TEACH**

VARIABLES IN THE EQUATION

	B	S.E.	Wald	Df	Sig.	Exp(B)
Step 1[a] age of respondent	−.016	.003	28.497	1	.000	.984
Male	.187	.104	3.213	1	.073	1.206
highest year of school completed	.161	.018	79.652	1	.000	1.175
Constant	−.759	.299	6.466	1	.011	.468

a. Variable(s) entered on step 1: age of respondent, Male, highest year of school completed.

We use these estimated coefficients to construct the prediction equation:

$$\ln\left(\frac{\widehat{p(y)}}{1 - \widehat{p(y)}}\right) = -.759 - .016 * Age + .187 * Male + .161 * Educ \qquad \text{Equation 8.3}$$

Compared to women having the same attributes, a man's likelihood of supporting anti-religionists increases by $\ln\left(\frac{\widehat{p(y)}}{1 - \widehat{p(y)}}\right) = .187$.

ODDS, ODDS RATIOS, AND EXPECTED PROBABILITY

Odds. Odds are the ratio between the probability that an event occurs and the probability that the event does not occur. When the odds > 1, the event is more likely than not to occur; when the odds < 1, the event is less likely than not to occur; when the odds = 1, the event is just as likely to occur as not to occur.

When working with binary input variables, the odds that the outcome is 1 for $x_1 = 1$ and $x_1 = 0$ are the following, respectively:

$$\frac{p(y:x_1 = 1)}{1 - p(y)} = e^{\beta_0 + \beta_1 x_1 + \beta_2 x_2 + \ldots + \beta_m x_m} \qquad \text{Equation 8.4}$$

$$\frac{p(y:x_1 = 0)}{1 - p(y)} = e^{\beta_0 + \beta_2 x_2 + \ldots + \beta_m x_m} \qquad \text{Equation 8.5}$$

Odds Ratio. The odds ratio is the ratio of the odds that the outcome variable is positive (y = 1) for $x_1 = 1$ divided by the odds that the outcome variable is positive for $x_1 = 0$, which is the ratio between Equations 8.4 and 8.5.

$$\frac{\frac{p(y:x_1 = 1)}{1 - p(y)}}{\frac{p(y:x_1 = 0)}{1 - p(y)}} = \frac{e^{\beta_0 + \beta_1 x_1 + \beta_2 x_2 + \ldots + \beta_m x_m}}{e^{\beta_0 + \beta_2 x_2 + \ldots + \beta_m x_m}} = e^{\beta_1 x_1} \qquad \text{Equation 8.6}$$

Because the regression slope for logistic regression is the change in *ln* odds for each unit increase in the input variable of interest, after controlling for the effects of other input variables, we can convert the regression slope into odds ratios. The odds ratio has been widely used in the social sciences, and software programs routinely convert logistic regression slopes into odds ratios to take advantages of the simple relationship between the regression slope and *ln* odds.

Probability. Probability is the proportion of times that y occurs out of all occurrences. We can transform Equation 8.2 into an equation for the probability for $y = 1$:

$$p(y) = \frac{e^{\beta_0 + \beta_1 x_1 + \beta_2 x_2 + \ldots + \beta_m x_m}}{1 + e^{\beta_0 + \beta_1 x_1 + \beta_2 x_2 + \ldots + \beta_m x_m}} \qquad \text{Equation 8.7}$$

CALCULATING PROBABILITY, ODDS, AND ODDS RATIOS

Odds. In order to calculate the odds, we can convert Equation 8.3 into the following:

$$\frac{\widehat{p(y)}}{1 - \widehat{p(y)}} = e^{-.759 - .016 * Age + .187 * Male + .161 * Educ} \qquad \text{Equation 8.8}$$

For a forty-year-old woman with a college education (17 years of education: K-12 and 4-year college), the expected odds of support versus nonsupport for allowing antireligionists to teach is

$$\frac{\widehat{p(y)}}{1 - \widehat{p(y)}} = e^{-.759 - .016 * 40 + .187 * 0 + .161 * 17} = 3.81 \qquad \text{Equation 8.9}$$

For a forty-year-old woman with a high school education (13 years of education: K–12), the expected probability of support for allowing anti-religionists to teach is

$$\frac{\widehat{p(y)}}{1 - \widehat{p(y)}} = e^{-.759 - .016 * 40 + .187 * 0 + .161 * 13} = 2.00 \qquad \text{Equation 8.10}$$

Odds Ratio. The odds ratio is $e^{\beta_1 x_1}$, so we only need to calculate the exponential of the regression coefficient. Each additional year of education increases the odds by $e^{.161} = 1.21$. Accordingly, four years of additional education increases the odds by $e^{.161*4} = 1.90$. This is precisely the ratio between the odds of 3.81 for a college-educated woman in Equation 8.9 versus the odds of 2.00 for a high school-educated woman in Equation 8.10, $\frac{3.81}{2.00} = 1.90$.

Probability. To convert the results into estimated probability, we use the following equation:

$$\widehat{p(y)} = \frac{e^{-.759 - .016 * Age + .187 * Male + .161 * Educ}}{1 + e^{-.759 - .016 * Age + .187 * Male + .161 * Educ}}$$

For a forty-year-old woman with a college education, the expected probability of support for allowing anti-religionists to teach is

$$\widehat{p(y)} = \frac{e^{-.759 - .016 * Age + .187 * Male + .161 * Educ}}{1 + e^{-.759 - .016 * Age + .187 * Male + .161 * Educ}} = \frac{e^{-.759 - .016 * 40 + .187 * 0 + .161 * 17}}{1 + e^{-.759 - .016 * 40 + .187 * 0 + .161 * 17}} = \frac{3.81}{1 + 3.81} = .79$$

For a forty-year-old woman with a high school education, the expected probability of support for allowing anti-religionists to teach is

$$\widehat{p(y)} = \frac{e^{-.759-.016*Age+.187*Male+.161*Educ}}{1+e^{-.759-.016*Age+.187*Male+.161*Educ}} = \frac{e^{-.759-.016*40+.187*0+.161*13}}{1+e^{-.759-.016*40+.187*0+.161*17}} = \frac{2.00}{1+2.00} = .67$$

TESTING LOGISTIC REGRESSIONS

For logistic regression models, we use maximum likelihood estimation to find estimates for regression coefficients that maximize the likelihood of observing the existing data. Because there is no close-formed solution for the optimal values of the logistic regression coefficient, we must use maximum likelihood estimation.

We use maximum likelihood estimation to test whether a logistic regression model is significant in improving estimation of the output variable compared with a model omitting the input variables. We do so by examining the deviance, which is a measure derived from a ratio of two likelihoods. One is from a saturated model that contains as many parameters as there are data points and predicts the response variable perfectly without any error. The other is the maximum likelihood from the estimated model. We carry out a likelihood-ratio test by calculating the deviance, which compares the values predicted by the model to those predicted by the saturated model:

$$Deviance = -2\ln\left(\frac{\max likelihood\ of\ estimated\ model}{\max likelihood\ of\ saturated\ model}\right)$$

The deviance is the unaccounted-for error in the model after the model estimates the effects of the input variables.

To compare two nested models, we can also calculate the difference in their deviance:

$$\Delta D = D_0 - D_1 = -2\ln\left(\frac{\max likelihood\ of\ model\ 0}{\max likelihood\ of\ model\ 1}\right)$$

ΔD has a chi-squared distribution with k degree of freedom (i.e., differences in the number of regression coefficients between these two models). The null hypothesis for this chi-squared test is that the two models account for the same amount of variance in the outcome variable. The alternative hypothesis is that Model 1 accounts for more variance in the outcome variable and thus has a better goodness-of-fit with the data.

VALIDATING REGRESSION MODELS

We can cross-validate regression models by dividing the sample into a training set and a testing set. We then use these two data sets to generate two sets of estimates with identical regression models. We first evaluate all of the regression parameters to see if pairs of the same regression coefficients from the two data sets are consistently statistically significant or not. We then compare the values of these coefficients to see if their values are similar. We next use data from a specific respondent in the two equations to see if they generate similar predicted values for the outcome variable. These procedures of cross-validation safeguard us from overfitting the model and ensure the model's generalizability.

SUMMARY

Supervised learning occurs when a computer system learns from a training data set and validates it through a testing data set. The learning is supervised because we have prior knowledge of the target variable and can thus make improvements through learning. The algorithm learns about the function such that it can reproduce the outcome variables using new data.

One form of supervised learning is parameter learning. This method starts with models with known structures and computes the best values for the model parameters using data to train the model with feedback from the target variable. The most common mathematical function of such models is the linear model.

A linear regression model describes the relationship between a continuous output variable and a set of input variables. The output is seen as a weighted sum of the inputs. The purpose of a good model is to minimize the sum of squared errors, which is the difference between the expected value for the output variable and its actual value. The least squares method is the most common approach for obtaining a line that best approximates the relationship between the output and the inputs.

The coefficient of determination measures the improvement we gain from the regression line in predicting the output variable over using the mean of the output. The coefficient of determination is the proportion of variability in the output variable accounted for by the regression model. It is the ratio between sum of squares regression and total sum of squares.

The standard error is the statistical average of errors unaccounted for by the regression line. By comparing the standard error with the standard deviation of the output variable, we can see whether the model is effective in substantially reducing the error if the standard error is much smaller than the standard deviation.

Linear regression models assume normality, independence, and homoscedasticity. When these conditions are satisfied, we can carry out a series of statistical tests, including ANOVA tests (also called F tests) and t tests.

An ANOVA test is a method for evaluating whether the regression model effectively accounts for the variability in the output variable. A t test allows us to evaluate whether a regression coefficient or slope indicates a statistical relationship between the input variable and output variable.

The Box-Cox transformation is a general approach to variable transformation. We use the method of maximum likelihood to find the optimal form of variable transformation.

Logistic regressions model the relationship between a categorical outcome variable and a set of input variables. The outcome variable in a logistic regression is transformed into *ln* odds ratio, so the interpretation of logistic regression is more complicated than for a linear regression. The odds are the ratio between the probability that an event occurs and the probability that the event does not occur. The odds ratio is the odds that an event occurs when an input is present divided by the odds that an event occurs when an input is absent. The probability is the proportion of times an event occurs out of the total number of occurrences.

For logistic regression models, we use maximum likelihood estimation to find estimates for regression coefficients for which the likelihood of observing the existing data is maximized. We use the maximum likelihood to test whether a logistic regression model is significant in improving estimation of the output response variable compared with a model not using the input variables. We do so by using the deviance, which is a measure derived from a ratio of two likelihoods: a saturated model that predicts the response variable perfectly and the estimated model. We can compare two models using differences between the deviance using a chi-squared distribution.

We can cross-validate regression models by dividing the sample into a training set and a testing set. We generate two sets of estimates with identical regression models and compare model parameters, significance levels, and estimated values to safeguard us from over-fitting the models and ensure the model's generalizability.

PRACTICE PROBLEMS

1. What is supervised learning? In what ways is supervised learning different from unsupervised learning?

2. What is parameter learning? Is it supervised or unsupervised learning? What is the most common functional form linking inputs and output in parameter learning?

3. What is a linear regression? Write a regression equation and explain the terms. What is the sum of squared errors? How do you calculate it? In what ways does it assist in the search for the best-fitting model?

4. Use the following information in table P8.1 to calculate errors for the two models A and B.
   a. Find the squared errors for both models.
   b. Calculate the mean for y and the squared deviations.
   c. Sum up the squared errors for both Model A and Model B to find the sum of errors.
   d. Sum up all the squared deviations to find the total sum of squares.

5. Researchers have estimated a regression model using data from 600 county hospitals: $\hat{y} = 1809.2 + 120 * x_1 + 380 * x_2 + 200 * x_3$

   y is the average charges (in dollars) per patient per hospital stay,

   x_1 is the percentage of county funding in the total budget,

Data Instances	Model A $\hat{y}_i$	Model B $\hat{y}_i$	Actual y_i	Error Model A $y_i - \hat{y}_i$	Error Model B $y_i - \hat{y}_i$	Squared Error Model A $(y_i - \hat{y}_i)^2$	Squared Error Model B $(y_i - \hat{y}_i)^2$	Squared Deviation $(y_i - \bar{y}_i)^2$
A	100.5	98.6	89.5					
B	88.0	87.6	86.0					
C	99.9	99.8	99.0					
D	76.2	77.0	77.6					
E	38.2	39.4	39.9					
F	65.8	89.9	70.8					
G	48.6	49.3	50.6					
		Total						

x_2 is the percentage of insurance company payments in the total budget,

x_3 is the percentage of patient payments in the total budget.
   a. Interpret the y intercept and all the slopes.
   b. For a hospital with the following budget composition—county 10 percent, insurance 80 percent, and patient 10 percent, what is its expected average charge per patient? Compare that with another hospital with this budget composition: county 20 percent, insurance 60 percent, and patient 20 percent.

6. What is the least squares method? Apply the least squares method to Question 4 to identify the line that minimizes the sum of squared errors.

7. Using information from Question 4, calculate the coefficient of determination for Models A and B. Explain what they mean for each model. Which model is a better-fitting model?

8. Using information from Question 4, calculate the standard error for Models A and B. Both models have one independent variable. Calculate the standard deviation of y. Compare the standard error with the standard deviation. Which model fits better with the data?

9. A multiple regression model has 5 independent variables with $n = 1000$. The SSE = 800 and the TSS = 2000.
   a. Construct an ANOVA table.
   b. Carry out an F test to see if this model is effective in accounting for variation in the outcome variable.

10. From Question 5 we have the following information in table P8.2 on the regression coefficients. For each of the independent variables, calculate the t score and find the significance level. Test the research hypotheses that these input variables are correlated with the outcome variable.

Model		Unstandardized Coefficients		T score	significance
		B	Std. Error		
1	(Constant)	1809.2	398.2		
	County funding (%)	120	60		
	Insurance payment (%)	380	120		
	Patient payment (%)	200	120		

a. Dependent Variable: Average charge to patient per hospital stay

11. What is a Box-Cox transformation? Describe how you can use the maximum likelihood approach to find the best Box-Cox transformation for a variable to achieve linearity.

12. Describe the differences between a logistic regression and a linear regression. What is the left-hand side of a logistic regression?

13. We are interested in who is more likely to support gun permits (support for gun permits = 1; no support = 0). Based on the 2016 General Social Survey data in the computer output in table P8.3, answer the following questions:

    a. Write the estimation equation.

    b. What are the odds for a thirty-year-old woman with 12 years of education to support gun permits? What are the odds for a thirty-year-old woman with 16 years of education to support gun permits? What are the odds for a thirty-year-old man with 12 years of education to support gun permits?

    c. What is the odds ratio between a man and a woman in favor of gun permits?

    d. What is the probability for a thirty-year-old woman with 12 years of education to support gun permits? What is the probability for a thirty-year-old woman with 16 years of education to support gun permits? What is the probability for a thirty-year-old man with 12 years of education to support gun permits?

TABLE P8.3   **SUPPORT FOR GUN PERMIT (2016 GSS)**

VARIABLES IN THE EQUATION

		B	S.E.	Wald	df	Sig.	Exp(B)
Step 1[a]	age of respondent	.009	.002	16.184	1	.000	1.009
	Male	−.239	.076	9.840	1	.002	.787
	highest year of school completed	.039	.013	9.324	1	.002	1.040
	Constant	−1.001	.216	21.465	1	.000	.368

a. Variable(s) entered on step 1: Age of respondent, Male, Highest year of school completed

14. We are interested in who is more likely to support allowing anti-religionists to teach (allow = 1; not allow = 0). As shown in table P8.4, we estimated a model A with age, education, and gender (male = 1, female = 0) as inputs. We also estimated another model B with two additional inputs measuring race (white, black, and others as the omitted category). We used data from the 2016 General Social Survey. Compare the two models and conclude which model has a better fit with the data.

TABLE P8.4 **COMPARISON OF TWO MODELS**

MODEL A SUMMARY

Step	-2 Log likelihood	Cox & Snell R Square	Nagelkerke R Square				
1	3893.821[a]	.014	.019				
		B	S.E.	Wald	df	Sig.	Exp(B)
Step 1[a]	age of respondent	.008	.002	14.983	1	.000	1.008
	rs highest degree	.118	.031	14.430	1	.000	1.125
	Male	−.239	.076	9.846	1	.002	.787
	Constant	−.643	.129	24.842	1	.000	.526

a. Variable(s) entered on step 1: age of respondent, rs highest degree, Male.

MODEL B SUMMARY

Step	-2 Log likelihood	Cox & Snell R Square	Nagelkerke R Square				
1	3885.538[a]	.017	.023				
		B	S.E.	Wald	df	Sig.	Exp(B)
Step 1[a]	age of respondent	.009	.002	18.312	1	.000	1.009
	rs highest degree	.127	.031	16.531	1	.000	1.135
	Male	−.233	.076	9.263	1	.002	.793
	white	−.322	.131	6.025	1	.014	.725
	black	−.127	.152	.695	1	.405	.881
	Constant	−.454	.165	7.615	1	.006	.635

a. Variable(s) entered on step 1: Age of respondent, rs highest degree, Male, White, Black

a. Carry out a maximum likelihood test to see if Model B has improved over Model A using $\alpha = .05$.
b. Are the inputs White and Black statistically associated with attitudes to allowing anti-religionists to teach at $\alpha = .05$?
c. Are the conclusions from a. and b. consistent with each other? Why or why not?

REFERENCES

Draper, Norman, and Harry Smith. 1998. *Applied Regression Analysis*. 3rd ed. New York: Wiley. https://onlinelibrary.wiley.com/doi/book/10.1002/9781118625590.

Larose, Daniel T., and Chantal D. Larose. 2015. *Data Mining and Predictive Analytics*. 2nd ed. New York: Wiley.

Chapter 9

CLASSIFICATION AND DECISION TREES

SUPERVISED DATA CLASSIFICATION

Supervised data classification segments data into groups that differ with respect to some attributes of interest. This process involves identifying informative attributes to segment the cases and then classifying data by progressively classifying cases based on these attributes. The purpose of this method is to differentiate the population with respect to some outcome that we would like to predict. The classification and decision tree approach predicts discrete outcomes. Target outcomes might be negative consequences we aim to avoid, such as patient deaths, student dropouts, employee dismissals, dissolution of businesses, or credit card fraud. Target outcomes may also be positive, such as getting into college, receiving a promotion, or curing diseases. Most research focuses on target outcomes that are socially significant to individuals and the broader society, such as different income levels, housing neighborhoods, sentencing outcomes, marital status, or fertility outcomes. Supervised classification plays an important role in informing theory development, policy design and implementation, and applied practice in businesses and government alike.

DECISION TREES

Decision tree algorithms are a form of supervised learning. A decision tree is a classification method with a target variable indicating group membership. It provides information on how to make decisions at critical nodes to classify data cases into the known groups, or classes. A decision tree starts with the *root* node, extends to *branches* that connect a collection of nodes, and ends in *leaf* nodes. The analysis begins at the root node that includes all data points, tests the decision nodes by assigning each possible outcome in a branch, and decides whether each branch leads to another decision node or terminates in a leaf node. It uses input characteristics to create a model to sort cases into categories of different values on a target variable.

The target or outcome attribute representing preclassification must be discrete. The discrete nature of the outcome class clearly classifies data points as either belonging to a particular class or not. When working with continuous outcome variables, researchers need to decide how to convert them into discrete classes to facilitate decision tree classification. For example, a continuous income measure may be recoded into High, Middle, and Low levels of income or above or below the federal poverty line.

Decision tree algorithms, as a form of supervised learning, require a training set. The training set should contain large variations, providing rich and varied data for the decision tree algorithm to learn. When the training set is limited or systematically lacking, decision trees trained using this data set may be unable to handle a wider variety of data when predicting outcomes, and the decision rules generated will be problematic or erroneous.

Decision trees have been a very popular data mining method. They are easy to use, straightforward to understand, quick to implement, and inexpensive to compute. Tree induction research started as early as the 1950s and 1960s. Researchers developed popular software programs for decision trees that include CHAID (Chi-squared Automatic Interaction Detection) (Kass 1980), CART (Classification and Regression Trees) (Breiman et al. 1984); tree procedure in IBM SPSS using four established tree growing algorithms including CHAID, Exhaustive CHAID, Classification and Regression trees (CART); and QUEST (IBM 2018) and the rpart package in R (Therneau and Atkinson 2018). C4.5 and C5.0 are also very popular tree induction algorithms (Quinlan 1986, 1994), and a reimplementation of C4.5 in the Weka package is called J48 (Witten, Frank, and Hall 2011).

IMPORTANT TERMINOLOGY

Before we present decision tree algorithms, let us introduce some important terms. As shown in figure 9.1, the *root node* represents the entire sample. It is divided into at least two homogeneous sets. We call the process of dividing a node into subnodes *splitting*.

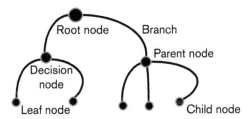

FIGURE 9.1
Tree Terminology.

When a subnode splits into further subnodes, then it is called a *decision node*. A node that does not split into further subnodes is called a *leaf node* or *terminal node*. A node that is divided into subnodes is called a *parent node* of subnodes. Subnodes are the *child nodes* of the parent node. A subsection of the entire tree is called a *branch* or *subtree*. When we remove subnodes of a decision node, this process is called *pruning*, which is an opposite process to splitting.

DECISION TREE ADVANTAGES AND DISADVANTAGES

The decision tree approach has several advantages. Decision trees are one of the fastest ways to explore data and quickly identify the most significant explanatory variables and the relations between predictor and outcome variables. When we are working on a problem involving hundreds of variables, decision trees can help us quickly identify the most significant variables.

First, a decision tree tends to produce better-fitting models than general regression models. Decision trees focus on predicting the outcome variable rather than estimating parameters of the relationship between explanatory and outcome variables. Decision trees therefore tend to produce more accurate predictions than do more conventional statistical methods, such as regressions. Decision trees often generate better-fitting models than conventional regressions.

Second, decision trees construct a complex, treelike set of classification decisions based on specific characteristics of different segments of the data. They pay attention to relationship heterogeneity by identifying and building interaction and nonlinear relations to maximize accuracy in prediction. Decision trees generate interactions and differential relations automatically.

Third, decision trees allow us to create new variables that have better power to predict target variables. For example, because decision trees can identify combinations of characteristics that are powerful predictors, researchers can construct new explanatory variables based on these features of interactive effects among variables and incorporate them into regression models.

Fourth, decision tree analytical results are straightforward and easy to understand even for people with no background in data analytics. Decision trees require little statistical knowledge to interpret. In addition, graphic representations of decision trees are intuitive to interpret, so users with little data science knowledge can easily relate their field knowledge to the output.

Fifth, decision trees are considered a nonparametric method. This means that decision trees have no assumptions about the space distribution and the classifier structure. They are thus more flexible and can be widely used on a variety of data distributions.

Sixth and finally, decision trees are not constrained by missing data or data types. Decision trees require less data cleaning compared to other modeling techniques because they are largely uninfluenced by outliers or missing data. Decision trees can also handle both numerical and categorical variables, although they lose some information by converting continuous variables into discrete ones.

Decision trees are not perfect. They also suffer from some weaknesses. Model overfitting is one of the most practical difficulties that researchers encounter when using decision trees and other predictive approaches. Overfitting happens when the learning algorithm continues to develop rules that reduce error in the training set at the cost of increased error in the testing set or the model's ability to generalize to other data. Researchers can resolve these issues by setting constraints on model parameters and pruning unnecessary branches that tend to overfit with the training data.

Decision trees might produce accurate predictions by building complex and flexible models. These powerful models might suffer from a lack of simplicity and transparency. This is especially true when a model is based on a large number of variables, a complex combination of features measured by many variables, and a huge data set with many branches. This type of complicated decision tree has a vast number of branches with decision nodes based on complex combinations of variables, so interpretation of the rules can be difficult.

DECISION TREE ALGORITHM

To illustrate the process of decision tree induction, let us use an example of visual data. In this data set, people have different head and body shapes. We know that they belong to two different classes of people, those who survived a virus attack and those who died. We use S and D to represent their target class. We are interested in discovering which traits determine their class.

The tree induction approach is elegant and attractive because the divide-and-conquer method allows us to reduce the large data into smaller sets and recursively apply the same method to partition the subsets. As shown in figure 9.2, after the first partition, the two subgroups are smaller versions of the same classification. We then take each data subset and apply attribute selection recursively to find the best attribute to partition these subsets.

In summary, decision tree classification is a recursive procedure of divide and conquer. The goal of each step is to select an attribute that can partition the current group into subgroups that are as pure as possible with respect to the target variable. This partition is performed recursively, splitting again and again until we classify all cases

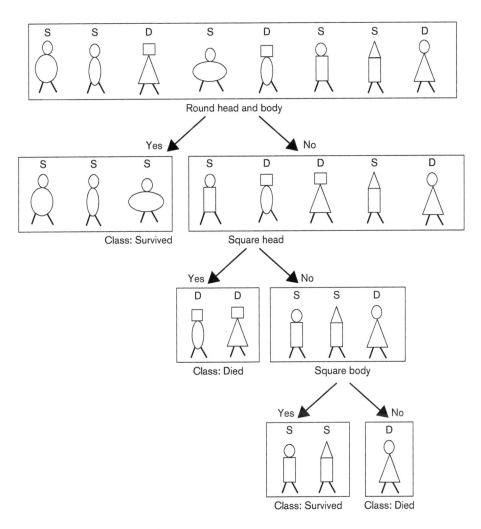

FIGURE 9.2

Decision Tree on Survival Based on Head and Body Types.

into classes. We choose the splitting attributes by testing all of them and selecting whichever ones yield the purest subgroups. We stop when the nodes are pure or when we run out of variables to split. We may also decide to stop earlier.

The tree structure model, or tree induction, is the most popular method for supervised segmentation from a data set because tree models are easy to understand and the induction procedures are elegant (simple to describe) and easy to use. They are robust to many common data problems and are relatively efficient. Most data mining packages include some type of tree induction technique.

The goal of the tree is to provide a supervised segmentation, or partition, of the instances based on their attributes into subgroups that have similar values for their

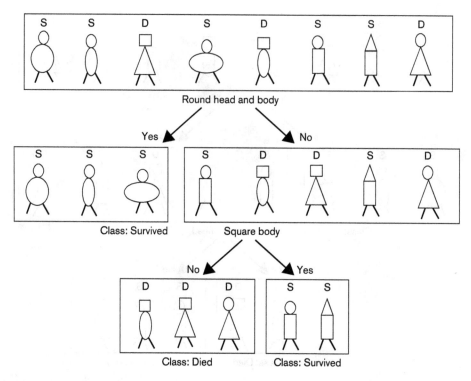

FIGURE 9.3

Decision Tree on Survival Based on Head and Body Types.

target variables. Our goal is for each leaf segment to contain instances that tend to belong to the same class.

Decision trees take a divide-and-conquer approach, starting with the whole data set and applying variable selection to try to create the purest possible subgroups using the attributes. Figure 9.2 first separates those with round heads and round bodies, who have all survived. In the next step, it divides those with square heads, who all died. The last step separates those with square bodies, who all survived. As shown in figure 9.3, the second split can be further improved by first separating those with square bodies. This results in two pure groups of those who survived and those who died.

TREES AS SETS OF RULES

The classification rules for decision trees can be interpreted in the form of logical statements. In figure 9.3, we classify a new unseen instance by starting at the root node and following the attribute tests downward until we reach a leaf node, which specifies the predicted class of the instance. When we trace down a single path from the root node to a leaf, collecting the conditions as we go, we generate a rule. Each rule consists of all the attribute tests along the path, connected with "AND" to indicate conjunctive conditions.

Children	Not Divorced	Divorced		Income	Not Divorce	Divorced	
No Children	2	8	10	Low Income	6	8	14
Children	13	7	20	High Income	9	7	16
	15	15			15	15	

IF (Round head and body = Yes) THEN Class = Survived

IF (Round head and body = No) AND (Square body = Yes) THEN Class = Survived

IF (Round head and body = No) AND (Square body = No) THEN Class = Died

This set of classification rules can be used to represent the decision tree. In fact, every decision tree can be expressed as a set of rules. When the model is large, people may prefer the rule set as a more intelligible way to express the model.

HOW TO DECIDE WHERE TO SPLIT

Decision trees use multiple algorithms to decide how to split a decision node into two or more subnodes. These subnodes contain instances with higher purity than their parent nodes with respect to the target variable. Constructing these subnodes thus increases homogeneity as we move downstream from parent nodes to child nodes. Decision trees split the nodes on all available variables and then select the splits that result in the most homogeneous subnodes. There are four most commonly used algorithms in decision trees: Chi-squared, variance reduction, Gini index, and information gain.

To demonstrate these algorithms, let us use an example. We want to construct a decision tree to divide a data set of 30 people to predict whether they divorce or not. We use two variables to classify them: whether they have children and whether the family income is high. Table 9.1 shows the distribution of data with regard to the predictor variables, Income and Children, and the outcome target variable, Divorce.

Figure 9.4 demonstrates two different schemes to split the data: one based on whether they have children and another on income. Triangles indicate people who are divorced; squares indicate people who remain married.

CHI-SQUARED

Chi-squared is an algorithm that finds the statistical significance of the differences between subnodes and parent nodes. We measure it by the sum of squares of standardized differences between the observed and expected frequencies of the target variable. It generates a tree called CHAID (Chi-squared Automatic Interaction Detector).

The chi-squared algorithm works with categorical target variables. It can perform two or more splits. The higher the value of chi-squared, the higher the statistical

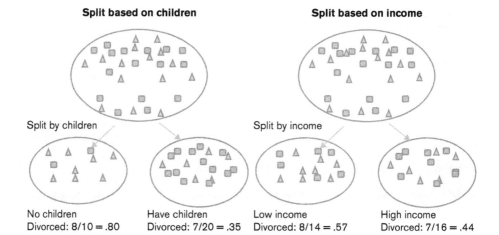

Split based on children   **Split based on income**

Split by children   Split by income

No children   Have children   Low income   High income
Divorced: 8/10 = .80   Divorced: 7/20 = .35   Divorced: 8/14 = .57   Divorced: 7/16 = .44

FIGURE 9.4

Decision Tree Split Based on Children and Based on Income to Predict Divorce.

significance of the differences between subnodes and parent nodes. The chi-squared of each node is calculated using this formula, where Of_{ij} is the observed number of cases in class i, Ef_{ij} is the expected number of cases in class i if the target variable is independent of the predictor variable, t is the number of categories in the target variable, and p is the number of categories in the predictor variable:

$$\chi^2 = \sum_{\substack{all\ classes\ i \\ children\ j}} \frac{(Of_{ij} - Ef_{ij})^2}{Ef_{ij}}, df = (t-1)(p-1)$$

Based on information from table 9.2 listing lists the expected distributions for divorce if independent of income and children, respectively, we can calculate their chi-squared values. If the decision tree splits the data based on whether they have children, the chi-squared value is 5.4.

$$\chi^2 = \sum_{\substack{all\ classes\ i \\ children\ j}} \frac{(Of_{ij} - Ef_{ij})^2}{Ef_{ij}} = \frac{(2-5)^2}{5} + \frac{(13-10)^2}{10} + \frac{(8-5)^2}{5} + \frac{(7-10)^2}{10} = 5.4$$

When the df = 1, the probability is < .025.

If the decision tree splits based on income, the chi-squared value is .43.

$$\chi^2 = \sum_{\substack{all\ classes\ i \\ children\ j}} \frac{(Of_{ij} - Ef_{ij})^2}{Ef_{ij}} = \frac{(6-7)^2}{7} + \frac{(9-8)^2}{8} + \frac{(8-7)^2}{7} + \frac{(7-8)^2}{8} = .43$$

The probability is >.25. We can conclude that the chi-squared test identifies that using children to split the sample is significant while using income to do so is not statistically significant.

Children	Not Divorced	Divorced		Income	Not Divorce	Divorced	
No Children	5	5	10	Low Income	7	7	14
Children	10	10	20	High Income	8	8	16
	15	15			15	15	

GINI INDEX

The Gini index says that if a population is pure and we select two items from this population at random, the probability for these two items belonging to the same class should be 1. The Gini index works only with binary target variables, such as Survival vs. Demise, Success vs. Failure, or Yes vs. No. The higher the value of the Gini index, the greater the homogeneity in the class that results from the split. CART (Classification and Regression Tree) uses the Gini method to create binary splits:

$$Gini = \frac{\sum n_j (p_j^2 - q_j^2)}{N}$$

where n_j is the number of cases in a class j using the split scheme, p_j^2 is the square of probability for the target variable to be 1 (or success) for all the cases in the class of j, and q_j^2 is the square of probability for the target variable to be 0 (or failure) in the j class.

Again, using information from table 9.1 and figure 9.4, when we split the cases by the presence of children, the Gini index is .59.

$$Gini = \frac{\sum n_j p_j^2 q_j^2}{N} = \frac{10(.2^2 + .8^2) + 20(.35^2 + .65^2)}{30} = .59$$

When we split the cases by income group, the Gini index is .51.

$$Gini = \frac{\sum n_j p_j^2 q_j^2}{N} = \frac{14(.43^2 + .57^2) + 16(.56^2 + .44^2)}{30} = .51$$

Because the Gini score for *Split on Children* is higher than *Split on Income*, the decision node will split based on children rather than income.

INFORMATION GAIN

Information theory uses entropy as a measure to define the degree of disorganization in a system. Purer nodes require less information to describe them, while more impure nodes require more information. When the sample is completely homogeneous, the entropy is zero; if the sample is equally divided (50% – 50%), it has an entropy of one. Entropy is also used with categorical target variables. The split with the lowest entropy is the optimal split for a decision node. From this we can derive that information gain from entropy is 1- **Entropy:**

$$Entropy = \frac{\Sigma\, n_j(-p_j\, log_2\, p_j - q_j\, log_2\, q_j)}{N}$$

where n_j is the number of cases in a class j using the split scheme, p_j is the probability for the target variable to be 1 (or success) for all the cases in the class of j, and q_j is the probability for the target variable to be 0 (or failure) in the j class.

If we split on children, the entropy is .86, and the information gain is 1–.86 = .14.

$$Entropy = \frac{10(-.2\, log_2(.2) - .8\, log_2(.8)) + 20(-.65\, log_2(.65) - .35\, log_2(.35))}{30} = .86$$

If we split on income, the entropy is .99, and the information gain is 1–.99 = .01.

$$Entropy = \frac{14(-.43\, log_2(.43) - .57\, log_2(.57)) + 16(-.56\, log_2(.56) - .44\, log_2(.44))}{30} = .99$$

We can derive that entropy for *Split on Children* is lower than that for *Split on Income*, and the information gain from *Split on Children* is higher. As a result, we will split the tree on children.

VARIANCE REDUCTION

Variance reduction is an algorithm used for continuous target variables (regression problems). It uses the standard formula of analysis of variance to decide on the best variable for the split. The split with the lowest variance is selected:

$$Variance = \frac{\Sigma(y_{ij} - \hat{y}_j)}{N}$$

where y_{ij} is an actual case, $\hat{y}_j$ is the class mean for class j after using a split scheme, and N is the number of cases used.

Using data from table 9.1 and figure 9.4 and treating the target variable as if it were continuous, when the decision tree splits based on children, the variance is .205.

$$Variance = \frac{\Sigma(y_{ij} - \hat{y}_j)^2}{N} = \frac{2(0 - .8)^2 + 8(1 - .8)^2 + 7(1 - .35)^2 + 13(0 - .35)^2}{30} = .205$$

When the decision splits based on income, the variance is .275.

$$Variance = \frac{\Sigma(y_{ij} - \hat{y}_j)^2}{N} = \frac{8(1 - .56)^2 + 6(0 - .56)^2 + 7(1 - .43)^2 + 9(0 - .43)^2}{30} = .275$$

Splitting on children has lower variance compared to splitting on income, so we would prefer to split on children to reduce the unaccounted-for variance.

AVOIDING OVERFITTING

When carrying out decision tree analysis, overfitting is a major challenge. Overfitting happens when the learning algorithm continues to split nodes that reduce the error for the training data but increase error for the testing data as well as for the general population. If we impose no limit on the size of a decision tree, it will generate a tree that precisely classifies all cases by building one leaf for each observation. It is thus critical to prevent overfitting when building decision tree models. There are two ways to achieve this: constraining tree size and tree pruning.

PRE-PRUNING

Pre-pruning, also called constraining tree size, stops the tree before it grows so large that it perfectly classifies the training set but loses predictability for the testing set. It can be done by using various parameters that define a correct final tree size. There are several ways to define a tree size, including the minimum number of cases required for a node split, the minimum number of cases for a terminal node or leaf, maximum tree depth, maximum tree width (number of terminal nodes), and maximum number of features or traits used.

Researchers may define the minimum number of observations required in a node to be considered for splitting. Higher values for the minimum number of observations prevent a model from depending too heavily on relations that might be highly specific to the data used to generate the tree. However, when the number is too high, it may lead to underfitting, when the model stops its algorithm too early. Researchers can also define the minimum number of observations required for a terminal node or leaf. Generally speaking, higher values safeguard overfitting the decision tree. However, when working with imbalanced classes, we may need to reduce the values of this requirement to allow for the minority class to be detected as the regions in which they become the dominant group are very small. Researchers may limit the maximum depth of a decision tree to control overfitting because taller trees allow the model to learn very specific relations between the features splitting the nodes and the particular data set. Researchers can limit the maximum number of terminal nodes or leaves to avoid overfitting, which controls the width of the resulting tree. When the number of leaves is large, observations are classified into larger numbers of classes that may result from the relationships between the traits used for splitting and the particular data set. As discussed earlier, the technique of setting constraints is a greedy approach. In other words, it will check for the best split instantaneously and move forward until one of the specified stopping conditions is reached. These pre-pruning approaches are not as successful as the next method introduced, post-pruning, because it is not easy to correctly estimate the best time to stop a growing tree without seeing the costs and benefits of further building the tree.

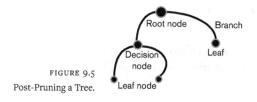

FIGURE 9.5
Post-Pruning a Tree.

POST-PRUNING

Post-pruning is another strategy to avoid overfitting. It first grows a full tree, then prunes it based on information about the fully grown tree and a testing data set as shown in figure 9.5. This approach tends to be more successful than pre-pruning, as we have information of the tree structure as well as the costs and benefits of modifying the tree by pruning some branches or leaves.

One pruning strategy—reduced error pruning—starts at the bottom and removes leaves that are not effectively reducing errors relative to their parent nodes. We propagate the errors from the leaves upward to the parent nodes and replace the subtree rooted at the node with a single leaf node. By labeling this new leaf node as predicting the majority class, we can calculate the reduction in validation error for every node in the tree. The subtrees rooted at the node with error reduction can be pruned and replaced by a leaf node. R has the *rpart* library that provides a function to prune.

Another method is rule-based post-pruning. In rule-based pruning, we first convert a decision tree into a set of rules. We generate a separate rule for each path (root to leaf) in the decision tree. For example, we can specify one path in figure 9.3 as the following rule:

IF (Round head and body = No) AND (Square body = Yes) THEN Class = Survived

The pruning strategy is then to refine each rule by removing any preconditions or antecedents. We now convert the rule above into the following rules:

IF (Round head and body = No)   THEN Class = Survived
IF (Square body = Yes)   THEN Class = Survived

We then calculate if any of these reduced rules have a lower error than the original rule. If they do, we replace the original rule with the new pruned rule. The pruning process will recurse over the new and shorter rules and stop when all the pruned rules fail to provide lower errors than their unpruned versions. At the end of this post-pruning procedure, the algorithm will have sorted all the rules based on their accuracy.

ADVANCED TOPICS

To overcome the deficiency of a single tree, Random Forest uses an ensemble approach that grows multiple trees to classify new objects based on attributes, with each tree giving a different classification. Based on the number of tree "votes" for that class, the forest chooses the classification having the most votes in the forest. This way, a powerful model is formed by combining a group of weak models.

Random Forest is considered an all-around tool for data science problems. It is a versatile machine learning method capable of performing classification tasks, conducting dimensional reductions, and treating missing values, outlier values, and many other essential tasks of data exploration. The Random Forest algorithm is capable of handling large data sets with higher dimensionality. It can identify the most significant variables from thousands of input variables. It is considered one of the more effective dimensionality reduction methods. It is also an effective method for estimating missing data, and it maintains model accuracy when missing data are highly prevalent in the data set. In addition, Random Forest contains methods for balancing errors in data sets where classes are imbalanced.

Random Forest pays a price for its versatile abilities by building models that are large, complex, and hard to interpret. Researchers have little control over what the model does other than specifying different parameters.

Random Forests have commonly known implementations in R packages using library (randomForest) (https://cran.r-project.org/web/packages/randomForest /randomForest.pdf) and Python scikit-learn (http://scikit-learn.org/stable/modules /ensemble.html#forest).

SUMMARY

Supervised data classification identifies data attributes to segment data instances and decides on the best way to differentiate them with respect to an outcome that we would like to predict. The decision tree is one method of supervised data classification. Decision trees start with a target variable indicating class membership, and they work to find information on how to make decisions at critical points to divide data into known groups.

Decision tree analysis classifies data in a treelike manner. It starts with the root node with all data points, assigns each possible outcome to a branch, and decides whether each branch leads to another decision node or to a terminating leaf node.

Decision trees have advantages and disadvantages. Decision trees tend to produce better-fitting models than do regression models. They pay attention to relationship heterogeneity by identifying and building interactions and nonlinear relations to maximize prediction accuracy. They allow us to create new variables that have better power to predict the target variable. Decision trees also generate results that are straightforward and easy to understand. As a nonparametric method, it is flexible and can be applied to a wide variety of data. It is also not constrained by missing data or data types. However, decision trees pay a price for high accuracy in prediction: they tend to overfit data, often producing models that are large and complex.

A decision tree uses a recursive divide-and-conquer procedure. It starts with the whole data set and applies variable selection to create the purest possible subgroups using the available attributes. It uses logical statements as classification rules, and the entire tree can be expressed as a set of rules.

Decision tree analysis uses algorithms that are based on chi-squared, Gini index, information gain, and variance reduction to decide how to split a node into two or more subnode. The chi-squared method uses the sum of squares of standardized differences between the observed and expected frequencies of the target variable. The Gini index approach assigns cases into the class to achieve the highest class purity. The information gain method uses entropy to define degree of disorganization in a decision tree system. Finally, the variance reduction method is for continuous target variables and uses the analysis of variance to decide on the best variable to use for the split.

To prevent tree overfitting, we use the approaches of pre-pruning and post-pruning. Pre-pruning, also called constraining tree size, stops growing the tree before it gets too large by using various parameters to define a criterion for a correct final tree size. Post-pruning first grows a tree, then prunes it either by reduced-error pruning or rule-based pruning.

Random Forest is an ensemble approach that grows multiple trees to classify data instances, with each tree providing a vote, and the classification is based on the collective strength of all the trees. These relatively weak trees form a forest of a powerful model.

PRACTICE PROBLEMS

1. What does a decision tree accomplish? Compare decision trees with cluster analysis. In what ways are they similar or different?

2. Describe the structure of a decision tree. Draw a tree diagram and mark the root node, branch(es), decision node(s), parent node(s), leaf node(s), and child node(s) on the tree.

3. What advantage does a decision tree have over regression models? In what ways can we use decision trees to help improve regression models?

4. Besides using a tree diagram to represent a decision tree, what is another way to represent a decision tree?

5. Explain the following algorithms: chi-squared, Gini index, information gain, and variance reduction.

6. Based on the data in table P9.1 below on student dropout from an after-school Chinese language program, decide which variable would be better to use to split in a decision tree. Make your decision by calculating the chi-squared, Gini index, information gain, and variance reduction.

TABLE P9.1 **STUDENT DROPOUT FROM AN AFTER-SCHOOL CHINESE-LANGUAGE PROGRAM**

Bilingual in Other Languages	Age at Program Entry	Dropout
1	≤12	0
0	>12	1
1	≤12	0
1	>12	0
0	>12	1
0	≤12	1
0	>12	1
0	≤12	1
0	≤12	0
1	>12	0

a. Construct a cross table showing the relationship between bilingualism and dropping out.

TABLE P9.2 **RELATIONSHIP BETWEEN BILINGUALISM AND DROPOUT**

	Dropout	Not Dropout
Bilingual		
Not Bilingual		

b. Calculate the expected distribution for dropout if it is independent of bilingualism.

TABLE P9.3 **EXPECTED DISTRIBUTION FOR DROPOUT WHEN INDEPENDENT OF BILINGUALISM**

	Dropout	Not Dropout
Bilingual		
Not Bilingual		

c. Construct a cross table showing the relationship between age at program entry and dropout.

TABLE P9.4 **RELATIONSHIP BETWEEN AGE AT PROGRAM ENTRY AND DROPOUT**

	Dropout	Not Dropout
≤12		
>12		

d. Calculate the expected distribution for dropout if it is independent of age at program entry.

TABLE P9.5 **EXPECTED DISTRIBUTION OF DROPOUT WHEN INDEPENDENT OF AGE AT PROGRAM ENTRY**

	Dropout	Not Dropout
≤12		
>12		

e. Calculate chi-squares for splits by bilingualism and age, respectively. Find their probabilities and determine which variable is a better candidate for splitting the data.
f. Calculate the Gini index. Does the Gini index provide the same information on which variable to use to split the data?
g. Calculate the entropy for the two candidate split variables. Explain which variable provides a better division.

REFERENCES

Breiman, Leo, Jerome H. Friedman, R. A. Olshen, and Charles J. Stone. 1984. *Classification and Regression Trees*. Belmont, CA: Wadsworth International Group.

IBM 2018. IBM SPSS Decision Trees 25. http://public.dhe.ibm.com/software/analytics/spss/documentation /statistics/25.0/en/client/Manuals/IBM_SPSS_Decision_Trees.pdf.

Kass, Gordon V. 1980. "An Exploratory Technique for Investigating Large Quantities of Categorical Data." *Applied Statistics* 29 (2): 119–27.

Quinlan, J. Ross. 1986. "Induction of Decision Trees." *Machine Learning* 1 (1): 81–106.

———. 1994. *C4.5: Programs for Machine Learning*. Burlington, MA: Morgan Kaufmann Publishers.

Therneau, Terry M., and Elizabeth J. Atkinson. 2018. "An Introduction to Recursive Partitioning Using the RPART Routines." February 23. https://cran.r-project.org/web/packages/rpart/vignettes/longintro.pdf.

Witten, Ian H., Eibe Frank, and Mark A Hall. *Data Mining: Practical Machine Learning Tools and Techniques*. 3rd ed. Burlington, MA: Morgan Kaufmann Publishers.

Chapter 10

ARTIFICIAL NEURAL NETWORKS

ARTIFICIAL NEURAL NETWORKS ARE A TYPE of machine learning that imitates the complex learning systems in animal brains, which are made up of closely interconnected sets of neurons. One particular neuron may be relatively simple in structure, but dense networks of interconnected neurons can perform complex learning tasks such as pattern recognition and classification.

Neurons in animal brains form complex networks to learn from past experiences. Neurons use dendrites to gather and combine input information from other neurons. When some threshold is reached, the neuron generates a nonlinear response by "firing," or sending information to another neuron. In this way, the neuron transfers information to other neurons. Vast numbers of neurons form complex networks, communicating and processing information, and they are capable of learning based on previous errors. The human brain contains approximately 10^{11} neurons, each of which is connected to 10^4 other neurons, making a total of 10^{15} synaptic connections. At a very basic level, artificial neural

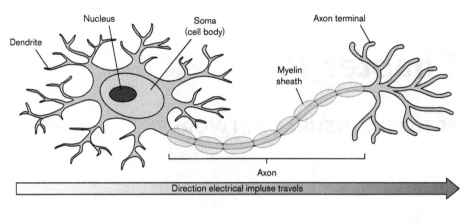

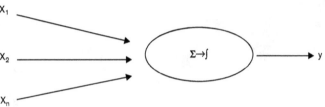

FIGURE 10.1
Artificial Neural Networks Imitate the Real Neuron.

networks imitate the type of learning that occurs in biological networks of neurons. The top part of figure 10.1 illustrates how a neuron uses its dendrites to gather input from upstream neurons, combines the inputs to reach a threshold, and fires signals to downstream neurons. The bottom part of figure 10.1 illustrates an artificial neuron model used in neural networks. The model collects information from the data set in the form of inputs (x_i), combines them in a function Σ, and then sends this result to an activation function, $\int$, to produce an output response, y. It then sends this output to neurons downstream (Larose and Larose 2016).

STRUCTURE OF ARTIFICIAL NEURAL NETWORKS

Neural networks consist of input nodes, hidden layers, and output layers. Figure 10.2 illustrates the structure of an artificial neural network. The leftmost nodes are the input nodes in the input layer that contains the predictor variables. In the middle, the round nodes represent two hidden layers that process and transform (sum, weigh, etc.) information from the input layer. On the right is the output layer that predicts the outcome.

Neural networks are networks of layered, feedforward, and weighted connections of nodes or neurons. The neural network generally consists of three or more layers of inputs, hidden layer(s), and an output layer. The input layer takes inputs from the data and passes information to the hidden layer. The number of input nodes is determined

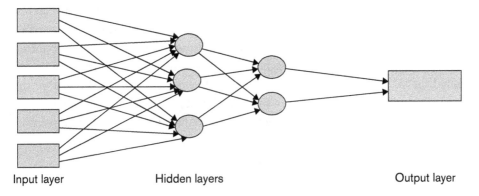

Input layer   Hidden layers   Output layer

FIGURE 10.2
A Four-Layer Neural Network.

by the number and type of attributes in the data. Researchers configure the number of hidden layers and the number of nodes in each hidden layer. When a hidden layer contains more nodes, it increases the power and flexibility of the network to identify complex patterns. However, an overly large hidden layer with vast numbers of nodes may lead to overfitting, shifting to the training set at the cost of generalizability. Researchers adjust the number of hidden nodes based on the performance of the neural network, increasing them when the training accuracy is unacceptably low and decreasing them when there is overfitting. The hidden layer may be composed of more than one layer. The output layer may have more than one node, depending on the classification task at hand. It is feedforward: it flows forward in a single direction and does not allow backward loops or cycling. Every node in every layer is connected to every node in the next layer, making neural networks completely connected. Each connection between nodes of different layers is weighted to reflect the size and nature of the associations between the nodes.

A simple neural network is equivalent to a logistic regression. However, neural networks usually perform much better than logistic regressions because they incorporate complexity through multiple hidden layers. Each input node in a neural network is a single variable. As each input node passes its values to the hidden layer, the values are assigned a weight that is similar to a regression coefficient. Neural networks then add these weighted values and use a specified mathematical function to transform the result and produce an output.

LEARNING BY NEURAL NETWORKS

A neural network learns in several steps. The first step involves randomly choosing initial weights for the input values. The model then iteratively adjusts these weights as it processes the data in order to correct for prediction errors. This process is repeated for each hidden node that randomly assigns a weight to each input variable and then is adjusted progressively based on new information to correct for prediction mistakes. Then each of the hidden nodes in the model predicts a value of the outcome variable in each hidden layer. The algorithm then randomly assigns weights to these predicted values and again adjusts these weights iteratively. When the best-fitting values are found for all of the weights, the final weighted values are combined based on the mathematical function to produce a single predicted probability for the outcome.

The most common activation function in the hidden layer is the *sigmoid function*, which can be expressed as the following:

$$f(x) = \frac{1}{1 - e^{-x}}$$

where *e* is base of natural logarithm and *x* is the input variable.

Another popular function is the hyperbolic tangent of an angle x. It is the ratio of the hyperbolic sine and hyperbolic cosine:

$$f(x) = \tanh(x) = \frac{\sinh(x)}{\cosh(x)} = \frac{e^{2x} - 1}{e^{2x} + 1}$$

Both the hyperbolic tangent function and the sigmoid function are versatile in describing a variety of functions, including nearly linear behavior, curvilinear behavior, and nearly constant behavior, depending on the values of the input variable *x*. Figure 10.3 illustrates the sigmoid function $f(x) = \frac{1}{1 + e^{-x}}$ and the hyperbolic tangent function $f(x) = \frac{e^{2x} - 1}{e^{2x} + 1}$ for $x \subset$ [-10, 10], although the function can theoretically take any real-number inputs from the data. For both functions, when the function approaches extreme values, $f(x)$ reaches upper and lower ceilings and becomes almost constant. However, in the center of this distribution, at approximately $x \subset$ [-1, 1], both functions appear to behave linearly. As *x* moves away from the center of the distribution at approximately $x \subset$ [-5, -1] and $x \subset$ [1, 5] for the sigmoid function and at approximately $x \subset$ [-2.5, -1] and $x \subset$ [1, 2.5] for the hyperbolic function, $f(x)$ becomes curvilinear. For the range of x < -5 and x > 5 for the sigmoid function, and the range of x < -2.5 and x >2.5 for the hyperbolic tangent function, both functions become constant.

The sigmoid function is also called a squashing function because it always produces outputs bounded between 0 and 1, $f(x) \subset$ [0, 1], after inputting real-number variables from the input layer. On the other hand, the hyperbolic tangent function always produces outputs bounded between -1 and 1, f(x) $\subset$ [-1, 1]. As a result, for both functions, the relationship between the input and output varies in different ranges of the input *x*. In the center of the distribution, $f(x)$ responds to increases in *x* proportionally and in a linear fashion. Farther away from the center, changes in *x* produce varied changes in $f(x)$, accelerating in values of $f(x)$ (on the left side) or attrition (on the right side). Near the extremes, changes in *x* produce almost no variation in the value of $f(x)$.

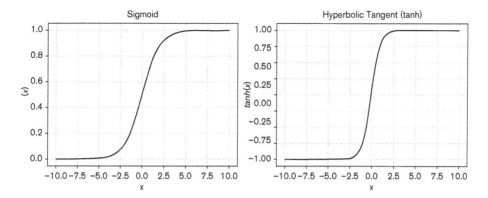

Sigmoid

Hyperbolic Tangent (tanh)

FIGURE 10.3

Sigmoid Function $f(x) = \dfrac{1}{1 + e^{-x}}$, hyperbolic tangent function $f(x) = \dfrac{e^{2x}-1}{e^{2x}+1}$ for $x \subset [-10, 10]$.

Because the hyperbolic tangent function produces outputs that are zero centered as it ranges between -1 to 1, optimization is *easier* in this method. This property of zero-centered output aids the back-propagation process. As a result, some argue that the tangent function is the preferred function for multilayer neural networks as it gives better training performance (Neal 1992). With a bound of [0, 1], the sigmoid function is good at approximating functions that map into probability spaces. A number of software programs (e.g., nnet in R and SPSS Neural Networks) thus use the sigmoid as the default activation function.

NEURAL NETWORK LEARNING: BACK-PROPAGATION

Neural networks use a supervised learning approach by employing a large, high-quality training set along with the target outcome variable. The neural network processes each case from the training set by reading the predictor variables in the input nodes, analyzing these variables in the hidden layers, and producing an output value in the output node. After comparing the output value calculated by the neural network to the actual outcome value in the training set, the error between the estimated output Y and the actual target variable is calculated as the squared errors summed over all the output nodes and all the observations in the training set in the form of $SSE = \Sigma\Sigma(y - \hat{y})^2$.

Similar to the least squares approach in regression, neural networks aim to construct a set of model weights that minimize the SSE. However, unlike the regression approach that uses the least squares method to search and find an optimal set of regression coefficients, there is no closed-form solution of weights to minimize SSE in a neural network due to the extensive nonlinear nature of the sigmoid function. As a result, the optimization method of gradient descent is used to locate the weights that will minimize SSE. The gradient-descent method provides the direction toward which we should adjust the weights to reduce prediction error.

The back-propagation algorithm works backward from the prediction error and divides it across the various connections in the neural network. Once the SSE is calculated using random weights, the back-propagation algorithm traverses back through the entire network to assign partitioned responsibility for the error. It does so by adjusting the weights on these connections to decrease the error using gradient descent.

DEEP-LEARNING NEURAL NETWORKS

When the number of nodes layer is large and the neural network is deep, it can achieve powerful deep learning. Earlier versions of neural networks were composed of one input and one output layer and at most one hidden layer in between. More than three layers (including input and output) qualifies as "deep" learning. Modern deep-learning networks are distinguished by their depth, that is, the number of layers through which data must pass in a multistep process of learning. In deep-learning networks, each layer of nodes trains on a distinct set of features based on the previous layer's output. The deeper the data advance into the neural net, the more complex the features the nodes can recognize, since they aggregate and recombine features from the previous layers. These deep neural nets are capable of discovering latent structures within unlabeled, unstructured, and complex data, including pictures, texts, and video and audio recordings.

Deep learning is the best approach for processing and grouping such raw, messy, and multidimensional data. Deep learning can take tens of thousands of images and categorize them according to their similarities. For example, in the 2012 ImageNet Large Scale Visual Recognition Challenge (ILSVRC), in which research teams evaluate their algorithms on a data set of tens of thousands of images and compete to achieve higher accuracy on several visual recognition tasks, a deep convolutional neural net (CNN) named AlexNet achieved 16 percent. By 2015, researchers at Microsoft reported that their CNNs exceeded human ability at these ILSVRC tasks. In 2017, 29 of the 38 competing teams achieved greater than 95 percent accuracy using a training data set, the ImageNet database that contains more than 14 million images classified into 17,000 categories, as well as the testing and validation data sets that contain several hundred thousand images in up to a thousand categories (https://www.scnsoft.com/blog/imagenet-challenge-2017-expectations).

Deep learning can also be applied to other types of data for a variety of usages. Deep neural networks can cluster raw text such as emails, news articles, and voice messages as messaging filters. It can use time series data to cluster around normal behaviors and anomalous behaviors, such as health and illness. It has been used for facial recognition, identifying people in images, recognizing facial expressions, identifying objects in images, recognizing gestures in video, detecting voices, identifying speakers, transcribing speech to text, recognizing sentiment in voices, classifying text as spam emails or fraudulent insurance claims, and recognizing sentiment in text.

ADVANTAGES AND DISADVANTAGES OF NEURAL NETWORKS

Neural networks have several advantages and disadvantages over other approaches. One advantage is that neural networks are quite robust with respect to noisy data. Networks contain many artificial neurons, with weights assigned to each connection, so the network can learn to work around uninformative or even erroneous examples in the data set.

Neural networks also have superior predictive capacity compared to regression models and sometimes even decision trees. With the help of multilevel hidden nodes, neural networks handle nonlinear relationships more efficiently and accurately than do regressions (Attewell and Monaghan 2015). They do so by modeling without the researcher's explicit input about the nature and type of nonlinear function (i.e., by manually creating nonlinear terms such as quadratic, exponential, or logarithm forms). However, researchers still need to try multiple times with different model choices and adjust through errors.

Despite these advantages, neural networks generate models that are relatively opaque to human interpretation. Often referred to as a "black-box" approach, neural networks differ from decision trees, which produce intuitive rules that are understandable even to nonspecialists. In addition, the large varieties of nonlinear behaviors in the hidden nodes, which provide wonderful flexibility in neural networks, constrain our ability to interpret the models in an easy and straightforward manner. Neural networks produce weights from iterations for a larger number of interactive parameters, the meaning of which is often difficult to interpret.

Although far from remedying this shortcoming, sensitivity analysis allows researchers to gauge the relative influence of each variable on the output target variable. It finds which variables or attributes have a greater effect on the outcome variable by varying these predictor variables between their minimum and maximum. When the network outcome is more sensitive to variations in a certain variable, we can conclude that this predictor is more important in predicting the outcome than other predictors.

Neural networks have other vulnerabilities that require our attention. First, neural networks can be expensive in computing time, usually requiring long training times, extending to several hours. Second, neural networks tend to overfit data as the complex hidden layers may construct models specific to particular patterns in the training data. It is thus important to use validation procedures to simplify and generalize a neural network to fit better with the testing data set. Finally, neural networks may generate different models even when using identical training data sets, variables, settings, and validation data sets due to their iterative learning procedures that are based on initial random values for the weights. To some extent, researchers may mitigate this inconsistency in model estimation by using large data sets and simpler models.

SUPERVISED LEARNING: NEURAL NETWORKS, LOGISTIC REGRESSION, AND DECISION TREES

To compare the performance of neural networks, decision trees, and logistic regression, we conducted an analysis using all three approaches. We used data from the 2016

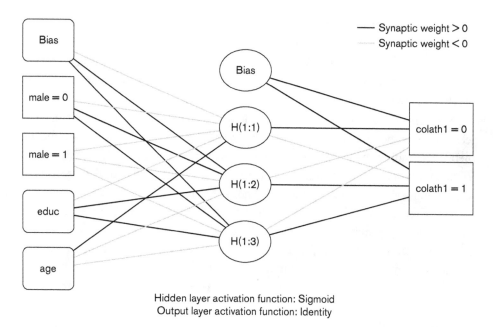

FIGURE 10.4

Neural Network Diagram on Allowing Anti-Religionists to Teach.

General Social Survey on attitudes to allowing anti-religionists to teach. The total number of cases is 2,867. First, we used a two-layer neural network with the sigmoid function in the hidden layer and the identity function in the output layer with inputs of age, education, and male gender (male = 1, female = 0). We used a cross-validation approach with 70 percent of the sample as the training set and 30 percent as the testing set. Figure 10.4 shows the network diagram of the input layer, the hidden layer, and the output layer. The synaptic weights are indicated by different colors for directions of influence (gray indicates a positive weight, and blue indicates a negative weight) and different thickness for the strength of influence (thicker lines indicate larger effects).

Table 10.1 displays the weights from the input layer to the hidden layer and the weights from the hidden layer to the output layer.

The classification table in table 10.2 shows the estimated outcomes and actual outcomes. This model has an accuracy rate of 67.9 percent for the training set and 68.6 percent for the testing set, and the error rates are 33.1 percent and 31.4 percent, respectively. For a simple model with only three input variables, this is a reasonably good model.

In order to determine the relative importance of inputs, we run sensitivity tests that compare models with and without each input. Figure 10.5 shows the normalized relative importance of inputs. Education is by far the most important input and is twice as important as the second most important input, age, and more than five times as important as the third most important input, male.

Predictor		Predicted				
		Hidden Layer 1			Output Layer	
		H(1:1)	H(1:2)	H(1:3)	[colath1=0]	[colath1=1]
Input Layer	(Bias)	−.425	.309	.307		
	[male=0]	−.012	.404	.102		
	[male=1]	−.500	−.289	−.007		
	Education	−.257	.256	.504		
	Age	.257	−.150	−.491		
Hidden Layer 1	(Bias)				.440	.408
	H(1:1)				.709	−.323
	H(1:2)				−.357	.164
	H(1:3)				−.254	.479

TABLE 10.2   CONFUSION MATRIX FOR ACCURACY AND ERROR RATE

CLASSIFICATION

Sample	Observed	Predicted		Percent Correct
		No	Yes	
Training	No	68	366	15.7
	Yes	49	809	94.3
	Overall Percent	9.1	90.9	67.9
Testing	No	25	145	14.7
	Yes	23	342	93.7
	Overall Percent	9.0	91.0	68.6

Dependent Variable: Allow Anti-Religionist to Teach

Now let us compare this neural network with a logistic regression with the same inputs and output variable. Table 10.3 shows the classification of observed and estimated cases from this model. The accuracy rate of the logistic regression is 67.7 percent, slightly lower than the neural network's performance for both the training and the testing sets.

The regression coefficients in table 10.4 show that for each one-year increase in age, the odds ratio of supporting versus opposing allowing anti-religionists to teach declines by 2 percent. This odds ratio is 20 percent higher for men, compared to women. However, the probability for the coefficient of gender is .073, so it is only marginally significant. This is consistent with the neural network's assessment that

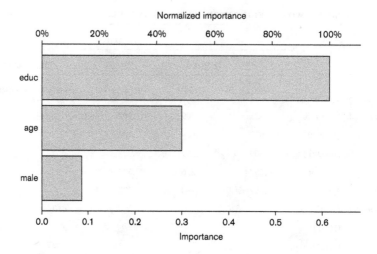

FIGURE 10.5
Normalized Relative Importance of Inputs.

TABLE 10.3   **CONFUSION MATRIX FROM LOGISTIC REGRESSION**

CLASSIFICATION TABLE[a]

			Predicted		
			Allow Anti-Religionist to Teach		
	Observed		No	Yes	Percentage Correct
Step 1	Allow Anti-Religionist to Teach	No	93	511	15.4
		Yes	80	1143	93.5
	Overall Percentage				67.7

a. The cut value is .500.

TABLE 10.4   **LOGISTIC REGRESSION COEFFICIENTS**

VARIABLES IN THE EQUATION

		B	S.E.	Wald	df	Sig.	Exp(B)
Step 1[a]	Age of respondent	−.016	.003	28.497	1	.000	.984
	Male	.187	.104	3.213	1	.073	1.206
	Highest year of school completed	.161	.018	79.652	1	.000	1.175
	Constant	−.759	.299	6.466	1	.011	.468

a. Variable(s) entered on step 1: Age of respondent, Male, Highest year of school completed

TABLE 10.5   **CONFUSION MATRIX FROM DECISION TREE**

Observed	Predicted		
	No	Yes	Percent Correct
No	107	503	17.5
Yes	70	1160	94.3
Overall Percentage	9.6	90.4	68.9

Growing Method: CHAID
Dependent Variable: Allow Anti-Religionist to Teach

the importance of being male (gender) is the lowest among all three inputs. The largest influence comes from education by far; for each year increase in education, the odds ratio increases by 17.5 percent.

Finally, we construct a decision tree to predict support for allowing anti-religionists to teach. This decision tree is based on a pair of split training and testing sets (50 percent in each) and the CHAID method. Table 10.5 displays the confusion matrix for the resulting decision tree. The decision tree has an accuracy rate of 68.9 percent, which is on par with the neural network and slightly stronger than the logistic regression in tables 10.3 and 10.4.

Compared to the neural network diagram, the decision tree in figure 10.6 appears more transparent and straightforward on the joint effects of inputs. The decision tree also identifies interactions and nonlinear relations. For example, it identified that those with more than 17 years of education (postgraduate), men with 14 to 17 years of education (college), and those younger than 32 and with 12 to 14 (some college) years of education are the most supportive of allowing anti-religionists to teach. Meanwhile, those older than 66 with 12 years or less of education (high school and less) are the least supportive, followed by people older than 55 with 12 to 14 years of education (some college) and those ages 55 to 66 with less than 12 years of education (less than high school). Based on this finding, researchers who want to move forward with logistic regressions may consider adding interaction terms between education and age to improve the model fit.

SUMMARY

Artificial neural networks imitate learning that occurs in the complex systems of animal brains consisting of closely interconnected sets of neurons. An artificial neural model collects information from a data set, combines it in a mathematical function, inputs the result into an activation function to produce an output response, and sends this output to neurons downstream.

A neural network consists of three types of layers: input layers, hidden layers, and output layers. The input nodes in the input layer take the predictor variables. The

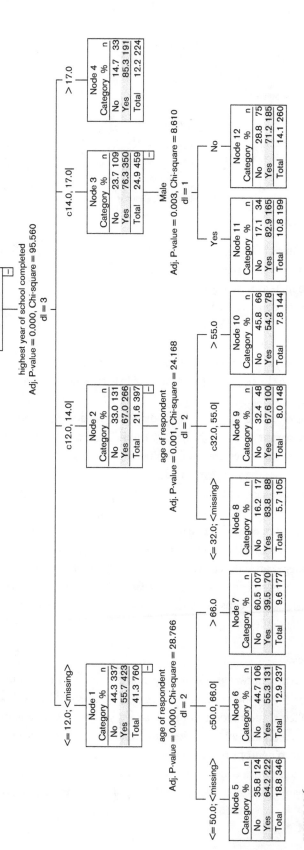

FIGURE 10.6

Decision Tree Diagram.

hidden layers process and transform information from the input layer. The output layer produces the outcome.

A simple neural network is equivalent to a logistic regression but generally outperforms it. Neural networks incorporate complexity through multiple hidden layers. The hidden layers take the input variables, assign weights, combine these weighted values, transform them using a specified mathematical function, and produce an output.

Neural networks learn in several steps. For each of the layers, random weights are initially assigned. The algorithm adjusts these weights iteratively using generated information. After repeating this learning process until the best-fitting values are found for all weights, the values are then combined to produce an outcome.

The most common activation functions in the hidden layer are the hyperbolic tangent function and the sigmoid function. They are both versatile in describing a variety of functions, including nearly linear, curvilinear, and nearly constant behaviors. The sigmoid function is also called a squashing function because it always produces outputs bounded between 0 and 1. The hyperbolic tangent function always produces outputs bounded between -1 and 1 and are zero centered; optimization is easier in the hyperbolic tangent function.

Neural networks use a back-propagation algorithm to achieve learning. After comparing the initial predicted value produced by the network to the actual outcome value in the training set by calculating squared errors, the algorithm uses a gradient-descent optimization method to locate the weights that will minimize the errors. The back-propagation then works backward from the prediction error and divides it across the various connections in the neural network.

Neural networks have advantages and disadvantages compared to other approaches. They are robust to noisy data containing uninformative or erroneous instances. They also have superior predictive capacity over regression models and even decision trees. However, the models generated by neural networks are relatively difficult to interpret as a result of the large number of nonlinear behaviors in the hidden nodes. Sensitivity analysis provides one approach to mitigating this shortcoming by determining the relative importance of each of the input variables on the output target variable.

Neural networks suffer from other vulnerabilities. They can be computationally greedy and thus expensive in computing time. They tend to overfit with data. They are also unstable and may generate different models with identical training data, variables, settings, and validation data.

PRACTICE PROBLEMS

1. What type of machine learning is artificial neural networks?
2. Describe how neurons in a human brain work. In what ways do artificial neural networks imitate the human brain?

3. How many layers does a neural network contain? What are the functions of each of these layers? How do these layers work together?
4. Compare and contrast a neural network with a logistic regression.
5. How does a neural network learn?
6. How do researchers set up a neural network? What do they do when the performance accuracy is too low?
7. How do we decide on the size of the hidden layers?
8. What is the sigmoid function? How does it behave? What advantages does it offer to a neural network?
9. What is the hyperbolic tangent function? How does it behave? Why is it used in neural networks? Compare the hyperbolic tangent function with the sigmoid function.
10. What is the method of back-propagation? How does the back-propagation approach minimize the squared errors?
11. What are the advantages and disadvantages of using a neural network?
12. Using data from the 2016 General Social Survey. Use the variable Yvote12 "Did you vote in the 2012 election?" (1 = Yes, 2 = No) as the output variable. Use three inputs: Educ (number of years of education), Male (male = 1), and Age (years). Use a Multilayer Perceptron with 70 percent of the data in the training set and 30 percent in the testing set. Set the number of hidden layers as 1, the number of units in the hidden layer as Automatic, the function in the hidden layer as Sigmoid, and the function in the output layer as Identity. Generate the neural diagram, weights, and lift chart.
   Hint: the IBM SPSS codes

```
MLP Yvote12 (MLEVEL=N) BY male WITH educ age
/RESCALE COVARIATE=STANDARDIZED
/PARTITION TRAINING=7 TESTING=3 HOLDOUT=0
/ARCHITECTURE AUTOMATIC=NO HIDDENLAYERS=1 (NUMUNITS=AUTO)
HIDDENFUNCTION=SIGMOID
OUTPUTFUNCTION=IDENTITY
/CRITERIA TRAINING=BATCH OPTIMIZATION=SCALEDCONJUGATE
LAMBDAINITIAL=0.0000005
SIGMAINITIAL=0.00005 INTERVALCENTER=0 INTERVALOFFSET=0.5 MEMSIZE=1000
/PRINT CPS NETWORKINFO SUMMARY CLASSIFICATION SOLUTION IMPORTANCE
/PLOT NETWORK ROC GAIN LIFT PREDICTED
/STOPPINGRULES ERRORSTEPS= 1 (DATA=AUTO) TRAININGTIMER=ON (MAXTIME=15)
MAXEPOCHS=AUTO
ERRORCHANGE=1.0E-4 ERRORRATIO=0.001
/MISSING USERMISSING=EXCLUDE.
```

13. Using the same input and output variables in Question 11, generate a logistic regression model. Compare the output to the neural network. What do you conclude?
14. Using the same input and output variables in Question 11, conduct a decision tree analysis. Compare the output to the neural network.

15. Based on all of the outputs in Questions 11, 12, and 13, compare the three methods, neural networks, decision trees, and logistic regression. Discuss their similarities and differences.

SOFTWARE PROGRAMS

Package "nnet" in R.
https://cran.r-project.org/web/packages/nnet/nnet.pdf. The major advantage of using the nnet package is that it is well designed and easy to use. However, the nnet package does not have much flexibility. nnet uses the logistic sigmoid function for hidden layer activation only and cannot use the hyperbolic tangent function. And nnet uses the BFGS algorithm for training rather than the back-propagation algorithm.

IBM SPSS Neural Networks.
https://public.dhe.ibm.com/common/ssi/ecm/yt/en/ytd03119usen/analytics-analytics-tools-yt-data-sheet-ytd03119usen-20180122.pdf. This procedure uses nonlinear data modeling to discover complex relationships among variables, constructing multilayer perceptron (MLP) or radial basis function (RBF) procedures. Users do not need to do any programming but can either set the conditions (i.e., controlling the training stopping rules, influencing weighting of variables, specifying network architecture, and selecting the type of model) or let the procedure choose.

MATLAB Neural Net Toolbox.
https://www.mathworks.com/products/deep-learning.html. A comprehensive environment for neural network research, design, and simulation within MATLAB. MATLAB Deep Learning Toolbox provides a framework for designing and implementing deep neural networks with algorithms, pretrained models, and apps. Users can use convolutional neural networks and long short-term memory networks to perform classification and regression on image, time-series, and text data. Users can use apps and plots to visualize activations, edit network architectures, and monitor training progress.

ADDITIONAL READING

Garson, David G. 1998. *Neural Networks: An Introductory Guide for Social Scientists.* Thousand Oaks, CA: Sage. Includes an introduction to the vocabulary and framework of neural networks, a history of neural network methods, a literature review, applications in the social sciences, model varieties, and examples.

Rashid, Tariq. 2016. *Make Your Own Neural Network: A Gentle Journey through the Mathematics of Neural Networks, and Making Your Own Using the Python Computer Language.* Scotts Valley, CA: CreateSpace. For ambitious readers who have knowledge of matrices and calculus and want to learn to code in Python and make their own neural network. It introduces the mathematical ideas, coding in Python, and improving performance of neural networks.

Haykin, Simon O. 2009. *Neural Networks and Learning Machines.* 3rd ed. New York: Pearson Education. Provides a complete introduction to neural networks with information on supervised learning with neural networks and unsupervised learning as well as nonlinear dynamic systems. It is for advanced undergraduate and graduate students who want to have a deep understanding of neural networks. It is mathematically rigorous. Matlab codes used for the computer experiments in the text are available for downloading at https://cours.etsmtl.ca/sys843/REFS/Books/ebook_Haykin09.pdf.

REFERENCES

Attewell, Paul, and David B. Monaghan. 2015. *Data Mining for the Social Sciences*. Berkeley: University of California Press.

Larose, Daniel T., and Chantal D. Larose. 2015. *Data Mining and Predictive Analysis*. New York: Wiley.

Neal, Radford M. 1992. "Connectionist Learning of Belief Networks." *Artificial Intelligence* 56 (1): 71–113. https://doi.org/10.1016/0004-3702(92)90065-6.

DATA MINING: TEXT DATA AND NETWORK DATA

PART VI

DATA MINING: TEXT DATA AND
NETWORK DATA

Chapter 11

WEB MINING AND TEXT MINING

THE WORLD WIDE WEB has become a major source for data mining. Because web content is often in the format of text, accessing and processing text data have become important in data mining. The astronomical rise of data on websites such as Facebook, WhatsApp, Twitter, and WeChat has opened new avenues for investigating social interactions (see, e.g., Takhteyev, Gruzd, and Wellman 2011). One example is the analysis of the infamous *New York Times* anonymous op-ed about the resistance inside the Trump White House written by "a senior official in the Trump administration" (Kearney 2018). To investigate the identity of the author, 3,200 Tweets from each member of the cabinet were mined to compare with the op-ed text on 107 numerical features. These text attributes include "capitalization, punctuation (commas, periods, exclamation points, etc.), use of white space, word length, sentence length, use of 'to be' verbs, and numerous thesaurus-like representations of word dimensions." To gauge the similarity between the op-ed and the Tweets, these numerical features by Twitter authors were calculated and then used to estimate the correlations between the op-ed text. These correlations were posted in ranked order from the highest to the lowest, including the president, the vice president, and the secretary of state, among others.

WEB MINING

Web mining involves collecting data from the web and applying data mining techniques to discover patterns. Researchers use automated methods to "mine the web," or extract data from web servers and generate reports on data patterns. To gather the enormous amount of web data, researchers first use crawlers or scrapers. They then engage in one or more of the three types of web mining: content mining, usage mining, and structure mining.

WEB CRAWLERS AND WEB SCRAPERS

Crawlers, scrapers, and browser automation are data extraction tools for collecting information from websites. When the size of data is very large and the data content is less complex, crawlers are suitable for large-volume, low-complexity content extraction. Scrapers are the opposite: they are best for smaller amounts of data with high complexity.

A web crawler is an automated program that methodically "crawls" through web pages to create an index of the data. There are various uses for web crawlers, but essentially they are used to collect huge amounts of data from the internet. Crawlers follow links from web pages and download pages.

Crawlers are scalable machines capable of downloading an enormous number of web pages. They are also called ants, automatic indexers, bots, web spiders, web robots, and web scutters. To increase scalability and volume, web crawlers can be distributed across many machines to download tens of thousands of web pages. Some of the most commonly used crawlers are Heritrix, Nutch, and Grub Next Generation. Heritrix is an open-source, extensible, web-scale, archival-quality web crawler from the Open Internet Archive (http://crawler.archive.org/articles/user_manual/intro .html). Nutch is a highly extensible and highly scalable web crawler from Apache (http://nutch.apache.org/). Grub Next Generation is a distributed client/server web crawling system that helps build and maintain indices of the web (http://freshmeat .sourceforge.net/projects/grubng). Both Hritrix and Nutch are in Java, while Grub Next Generation is implemented in Perl, C, C+, C++, and Python. Researchers can use web crawlers to gather current data on population trends. Many web search engines use crawlers as a tool to update information and provide insights into new patterns on the internet.

Web scrapers focus on extracting content (such as numeric and metadata information) from the web pages they download. Scrapers are typically less scalable and more hand-tuned than crawlers and focus on extracting content rather than data indices. When you need to extract structured data from web pages based on presentation structure, a scraper may be the best tool. When the web content is structured on the web page (e.g., using HTML tagging or JSON structures), scrapers are able to extract structured content. Scrapers require more work and programming than crawlers, but scrapers also generate output that is more structured and potentially more useful. There are a number of widely available scrapers. Scrapy is an open source and collaborative framework for extracting data from websites in a fast, simple, and extensible manner (https://scrapy.org/). It is a Python-based scraper and also has a hosted Cloud-based version and a graphic tool to help create scrapers (Portia). Octoparse is an MS-Windows scraper with visual tools that can quickly turn Web pages into a structured spreadsheet of data without coding (https://www.octoparse.com/). Apifier is a Cloud-based JavaScript scraper (https://www.apify.com/). Content Grabber is a screen scraper that automatically determines the action type and builds an agent for you based on the content elements selected. It saves the data locally in a structured database format and can export extracted web data in various database types, including CSV, Excel, XML, SQL Server, MySQL, Oracle and OleDB (http://unbouncepages.com /content-grabber-data-extraction-software/).

WEB CONTENT MINING

There are three types of web mining: content mining, structure mining, and usage mining. Web content mining is the process of data extraction, information mining, and knowledge integration from web page content. Much of the rapidly expanding web content is heterogeneous and lacks structure. This makes automated discovery, organization, and searching and indexing of web information challenging. We need effective tools to extract structural information from websites and to categorize, filter, and interpret online texts.

In response to these needs, researchers have developed intelligent tools for information retrieval. These include intelligent web agents, database extensions, and data mining techniques that provide a higher level of organization for semistructured web data. Intelligent web agents are sophisticated AI systems that can act autonomously or semiautonomously to discover and organize web-based information.

Once web data are retrieved, organized, and formulated, most researchers use a bag-of-words approach to process unstructured texts and treat single words found in the document collection (or corpus) as features. This method is introduced later in this chapter. When working with semistructured data, researchers take advantage of the HTML structure inside the documents and the hyperlink structure between documents for representation. Database approaches infer the structure of a website to transform it into a database to facilitate information management and querying on the web. The general algorithm evaluates words, or sets of words, as document features. Unsupervised and supervised learning techniques are used to conduct classification and pattern analysis in text data mining, methods similar to other data mining techniques (for more information, see Welbers, Atteveldt, and Benoit 2017).

WEB STRUCTURE MINING

Web structure mining generates structural summaries about websites and web pages. Web structure mining tries to discover the link structure of the hyperlinks at the interdocument level. Based on the topology of the hyperlinks, structure mining categorizes web pages and generates information on the relationship between different websites. Structure mining can also determine the structure of web documents, making it possible to investigate web page schemes for comparison, integration, and information access facilitated by a reference schema.

Structure mining involves gathering data from different pages linked by hyperlinks to discover a pattern. For example, to gather data from a person's public profile (blog, Facebook, Twitter, Instagram, LinkedIn, Google Scholar, or any other web pages), we extract data from all the linked and nested pages through the hyperlinks associated with each page.

WEB USAGE MINING

Web usage mining is the application of data mining techniques to discover interesting usage patterns from web data. Usage data captures the identity of web users along with their browsing behavior at a website. Web usage mining can be classified on the kind of usage data considered. For example, *web server data mining* collects user logs, including IP addresses, page references, and access times. *Application server data mining* tracks various kinds of business events and logs them in application server logs to enable e-commerce applications to be built. Application level data mining generates records of events in applications and maintains histories of various events in applications.

Web usage mining has many applications in and advantages as well as disadvantages for society. E-commerce companies use this technology to conduct personalized marketing. For example, Facebook, Amazon, and Google use members' web browsing histories to serve advertisements of products of interest to the current pages they visit. Companies also use this method to help improve customer relations by understanding and reacting to customers' needs better and faster. Government agencies use this technology to classify threats to their pages and fight against hacking. This method can also be used to identify fake Facebook accounts that have been used to shift public opinion in attempts to influence the U.S. presidential election (https://www.wired.com/story/facebook-uncovers-new-fake-accounts-ahead-of-midterm-elections/). This application can also benefit law enforcement by identifying and tracking criminal activities ranging from fraud detection, violent crime, traffic violation, and sexual assault and cyber crimes (for a review, see Prabakaran and Mitra 2018). For social scientists who track the social, cultural, and political pulse of the population, this approach provides important data on the popularity of various websites, as well as the individuals and organizations connected with them (https://www.smartinsights.com/social-media-marketing/social-media-strategy/new-global-social-media-research/).

TEXT MINING

Text mining is different from most other data mining methods. Texts are natural data that require extra effort in data collection, access, and preparation before conducting data mining. Researchers must either prepare text data to match with the existing data mining tools at our disposal or build new tools specifically for text data. Before we gained these capacities to analyze texts, text data used to fall into the realm of qualitative data analysis. Researchers either analyzed data manually or used teams of coders to carefully read and recode texts into numerical data for statistical analyses.

Text is an important form of data and is the most common medium for information exchange. Vast amounts of communications between people, for example, in newspaper reports, magazine articles, journal publications, books, historical and institutional documents, personnel dossiers, medical records, application statements, and reference letters, are all in text format. They represent a large amount of untapped data that was once beyond human processing capacity. The internet dramatically accelerated the amount of such data. Vast amounts of texts are hosted on the internet in the form of web pages, emails, Facebook posts, Twitter feeds, Amazon product reviews, blogs, forums, WeChat moments, and so on. Search engines such as Google, Bing, Yahoo, and Baidu are based on data mining of massive amount of texts.

Text is unstructured data. Unlike numerical data that we routinely process, texts do not have the nice features we expect for other data such as fixed structure of data records with linked vectors of variables. Rather, texts consist of words with varying lengths or text fields with a varying number of words having orders that may or may not matter. These words might be misspelled, written ungrammatically, abbreviated in different manners, or punctuated unexpectedly. There are also terms and jargon that vary between different fields or subgroups. Synonyms and homographs also make word records difficult to process. Furthermore, the understanding of a particular word must be conducted in the textual context of both the adjacent words and the larger textual background.

Although texts are another form of data in general and text mining is a special case of data summarization and representation, handling text data requires dedicated data retrieval and preprocessing steps as well as special expertise from research scientists. As a result of these difficulties, researchers need to handle several complexities with text data.

In order to analyze texts, the first task involves text representation. We convert texts into a data format organized in similar ways to the vector-based format we use for numerical data. To do so, we define several units of analysis. Text analysis is carried out as an examination of collections of texts called documents. A document can be of varying length, as short as one sentence or comment, as long as a book of several hundred pages, or of medium length in the format of a few paragraphs of news reports or Facebook entries. A document consists of words and other symbols that are called tokens or terms. A collection of documents forms a corpus. Because documents consist of a sequence of tokens (mostly words) that are relatively free-form, researchers need to transfer them into a fixed-form vector of "clean" data representation. One approach is to use the bag-of-words concept to treat each document as a collection of individual words and ignore other features in the document such as word order and other symbols such as punctuation, grammar, and sentence structure. In this way, the bag-of-words method focuses on every single word as the most important characteristic of the texts. This approach makes text representation simple, straightforward, and efficient. It works well for many tasks and objectives. However, word and sentence order and contextual effects are sometimes strong features of a document. Sometimes words are not the most basic unit of analysis, as common phrases consisting of a series of words should be interpreted together as a single unit. Individual words sometimes no longer carry their original meaning when analyzed out of context. The n-gram sequences approach is a frequently used alternative method to the bag of words that considers word order as an important feature in analyzing texts.

BAG OF WORDS

The bag-of-words approach treats words as the basic feature of a document, in the same way that variables are the basic target of analysis for numerical data. The value for each feature (word) in this case can also take on various values such as dichotomous or count values. A dichotomous value might represent the presence or absence of a word in a document. A count value might be the number of times a word appears in a document, as researchers sometimes use the frequency of a word to represent its prominence. Sometimes, term or word frequency is considered in relation to document length. Longer documents have more words so are more likely to dominate a comparison of documents by word occurrence because they are allowed more consideration proportional to the number of words contained in the document. To address this issue, the term or word frequency count might be weighted by the length of the document to normalize.

After these treatments, we can tally the number of times a word (in any form) is used, assuming that the importance of a term in a document is proportional to the frequency of its appearance. This approach is called *term frequency representation*. To demonstrate this approach, let us consider the following sentences. In this case, each sentence is considered a separate document. The bag-of-words approach converts these three documents into a collection of words or tokens, without particular order, and represents them with a table of term counts. Table 11.1 shows how the following three sentences can be converted into a table with term counts.

S1. Text mining is different from most data mining methods.

S2. Text is an important form of data.

S3. Text is unstructured data.

TABLE 11.1 **TERM FREQUENCY REPRESENTATION**

	Text	mining	is	different	from	most	data	methods	an	important	form	of	unstructured
S1	1	2	1	1	1	1	1	1	0	0	0	0	0
S2	1	0	1	0	0	0	1	0	1	1	1	1	0
S3	1	0	1	0	0	0	1	0	0	0	0	0	1

TABLE 11.2 **TERM FREQUENCY REPRESENTATIONS AFTER STOPWORD REMOVAL AND NORMALIZATION**

	text	mine	different	data	method	important	form	unstructured
Raw Term Frequency								
S1	1	2	1	1	1	0	0	0
S2	1	0	0	1	0	1	1	0
S3	1	0	0	1	0	0	0	1
Normalized Term Frequency								
S1	1/9	2/9	1/9	1/9	1/9	0	0	0
S2	1/7	0	0	1/7	0	1/7	1/7	0
S3	1/4	0	0	1/4	0	0	0	1/4

To create a word-based data representation, the bag-of-words approach also takes steps to handle data complexity. First, symbols that are considered unimportant or irrelevant are removed. Many common words in a language (e.g., *and, of, on, the,* in English) are defined as "stopwords" and are typically removed. Second, every word is normalized into lowercase. When all the words are changed into lowercase, words of the same spelling but in different cases are considered identical. Third, researchers tend to stem many words to remove their suffixes so that verbs of all tenses are reduced to their original form and nouns of either plural or singular forms are standardized to the singular form. Table 11.2 presents a revised table of term frequency representation after we remove the stopwords, normalize the terms, and stem them to their original forms.

These term frequency representations are called raw counts. Because documents are of different lengths, we sometimes perform normalization of the term counts relative to document length. Because longer documents have more words, and it is highly likely that they will have more word occurrences of the same words than shorter documents. These higher word frequencies in longer documents do not necessarily mean that these words are more important or relevant than the words that occur fewer times in shorter documents. To adjust the word counts in proportion to the document length, instead of using the raw word count, we normalize the term frequencies by dividing each by the total number of terms in the document.

Word clouds summarize keywords in a speech or text by giving greater prominence to words that appear more frequently and using word sizes and color schemes to illustrate their relative count frequency. In order to create a word cloud, we first convert letters to lowercase and remove common English words (stopwords), numbers, and punctuation. Word clouds generate a collection of words representing the relative prominence of different topics covered in the text using font sizes that are proportional to their relative frequencies (see chap. 4, fig. 4.17, for an example).

When calculating term frequency over a collection of documents, it is important to consider the number of documents. The same term frequency t would be more significant in a smaller corpus of documents than in a larger corpus. This is measured by the inverse document frequency IDF index for term t to gauge inverse document frequency (Provost and Fawcett 2013, 257; Silge and Robinson 2017).

$$IDF\ (t) = 1 + \log \left(\frac{n\ of\ documents}{n\ of\ documents\ containing\ t} \right) \qquad (11.1A)$$

or

$$IDF\ (t) = \ln \left(\frac{n\ of\ documents}{n\ of\ documents\ containing\ t} \right) \qquad (11.1B)$$

This index decreases the weight for terms that appear in more documents and increases the weight for words that are not used very much in a collection of documents. It can be seen as the boost for a term that rarely shows up in the corpus. When a term is rare, the IDF(t) is very high. It then declines quickly when the term t becomes more common. Words that are common and show up in every document have an IDF of 1.0 (11.1A) or 0 (11.1B).

In an attempt to find the words that are important in one document but not very common in a collection of documents, we calculate a joint index TFIDF (t, d), using both the term frequency for term t for a document d, TF(t, d), and inverse document frequency for this same term (t) in a corpus of documents IDF (t). The idea of TFIDF is to find the important words for each document by decreasing the weight for commonly used words in the document collection and increasing the weight for words that are rare in this corpus of documents. This index is a combined product of term frequency measuring how often a term occurs in one document TF(t,d), and the inverse document frequency indicating how rarely it is used in this collection of documents IDF(t).

$$TFIDF(t,\ d) = TF(t,\ d) \times IDF(t) \qquad (11.1C)$$

TFIDF enables us to find terms that are prominent for a single document within a corpus of documents. It provides insights into characterizing the major themes in a collection of natural language presented in a collection of documents.

The bag-of-words method is simple and effective in most cases. It does not require any sophisticated parsing ability or advanced linguistic analysis. It is usually the first-choice approach for a text mining task because it performs quite well on a variety of problems.

N-GRAM SEQUENCES

When the simple bag-of-words approach is not effective for analyzing complex problems, we must use more sophisticated methods. The n-gram sequences technique is one of them. When the word order is an important feature in text mining, we want to preserve that information in the representation. This is especially important when we analyze phrases wherein the sequence of words is meaningful but each single component word is not. Since the bag-of-words approach discards word order and treats each individual word as a term for study, it is an inadequate approach for such problems. We thus need to add complexity to the method by considering sequences of adjacent words, treating this collection of ordered words as terms. This approach is called n-grams. When n-grams consist of pairs of adjacent words, they are called bigrams. When n-grams consist of triple words adjacent to each other, they are called trigrams.

n-grams greatly increase the size of the term sets under consideration. The number of feature sets that are generated can quickly get very large as there are many bigrams, trigrams, four-grams, and so on to be considered. However, many of these n-gram feature sets can be rare, occurring only once or twice in the corpus.

We may also examine TFIDF of n-grams instead of individual words. Feature sets consisting of multiple consecutive words might capture language structure that is invisible when only single words are considered. Counting frequencies of n-grams may provide context that makes individual terms or tokens more understandable. However, the n-gram counts are also sparse, as word pairs or three-word sequences are rarer than their component words. Only when we are working with a very large text data set is consideration of n-gram frequency useful.

For people who are interested in conducting text mining in printed books, the Google Books corpus contains more than 500 billion words in English, French, Spanish, German, Chinese, Italian, Russian, and Hebrew. This corpus digitalized by Google and including one- to five-grams that appear over 40 times across the corpus is available for downloading (http://storage.googleapis.com/books/ngrams/books/datasetsv2 .html). Google also hosts another site to graph word usage over time from 1800 to 2008 (https://books.google.com/ngrams).

By analyzing the enormous corpus of Google Books, social scientists and humanists have been able to provide insights about cultural trends, including English-language lexicography, the evolution of grammar, collective memory, adoption of technology, pursuits of fame, censorship, and historical epidemiology (Michel et al. 2011). Sociologists have used this database to analyze the emergence and development of sociology as a discipline in the period 1850–2008 (Chen and Yan 2016b), and economic

TABLE 11.3 PRESENCE OF WORDS X AND Y IN N NUMBER OF DOCUMENTS

		Word Y		Total
		Present 1	*Absent 0*	
Word X	Present 1	n_{xy}	n_{x0}	n_x
	Absent 0	n_{0y}	n_{00}	$(n - n_x)$
	Total	n_y	$(n - n_y)$	N

performance and public concerns about social class in books of the twentieth century (Chen and Yan 2016a).

However, others call into question the vast majority of existing claims about cultural and linguistic evolution drawn from the Google Books corpus as its use to study trends in the popularity of terms or words suffers from a number of limitations (Pechenick, Danforth, and Dodds 2015). The corpus is overrepresented by prolific authors, is missing information on the books' popularity, and increasingly includes scientific texts of phrases typical to academic articles. These issues point to the need to fully characterize the dynamics of the corpus (data representation) before deriving broad conclusions about cultural and social trends.

PAIRWISE CORRELATIONS

When we are interested in words that tend to co-occur in particular documents, even if they are neither adjacent nor in a particular order, we analyze pairwise correlations of terms in a corpus of documents. Unlike in the bigram analysis, in which words are considered in an ordered sequence, the pairwise relationships are symmetrical rather than ordered or directional (where one leads to another).

We first identify words that co-occur with high frequency and then examine correlations among these words. A correlation indicates how often words appear together relative to how often they do not. To do so, we construct a measure for binary correlation, the phi coefficient. The focus of the phi coefficient is how much more likely it is that both words X and Y co-occur or both X and Y are absent than the likelihood that only one of them appears.

As shown in table 11.3, we use n_{xy} to represent the number of documents where both word X and word Y are present, n_{00} to represent the cases where neither X nor Y appears, n_{x0} and n_{0y} to represent the numbers where one of X and Y appears without the other, n_x and n_y to represent the total number of documents where X and Y are present, respectively, and N the total number of documents. The phi coefficient representing this pairwise coefficient is

$$\emptyset = \frac{n_{xy}n_{00} - n_{x0}n_{0y}}{\sqrt{n_x n_y \, (n - n_x) \, (n - n_y)}}$$

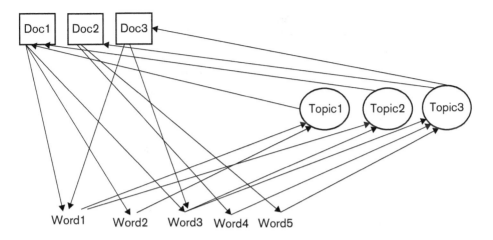

FIGURE 11.1
A Topic Model: Modeling Documents with a Topic Layer.

This approach can also be used to measure the similarity between two texts or two authors by analyzing the co-appearance of similar features between two texts or collections of texts.

TOPIC MODELS

Topic modeling is a method of unsupervised classification of a corpus of documents that we want to divide into natural groups to understand separately. This is similar to unsupervised clustering of numerical data that identifies "natural groupings" of cases even when we have no idea about the nature of such grouping. The main idea of topic model is first to model the set of topics in a corpus separately. Each document constitutes a sequence of words, and these words are used as inputs to a classifier to be mapped to one or more topics. These topics are learned from the word data via unsupervised data mining. Finally, documents are characterized in terms of these topics and the component words.

There are two general methods for creating topic models: *matrix factorization methods* (e.g., latent semantic indexing) and *probabilistic topic models* (e.g., latent Dirichlet allocation). Latent Dirichlet allocation (LDA) is a popular method for fitting a topic model. It sees each document as consisting of various topics, and each topic consists of various words. Using words and documents as input, LDA learns to identify the topics through unsupervised data mining. Instead of separating documents into discrete or crisp groups, LDA allows documents to consist of a mixture of topics, overlapping each other in content as measured in both words and topics. Figure 11.1 shows this relationship between words, documents, and topics.

LDA follows two principles. First, every topic is perceived as a mixture of words. For instance, we could imagine a topic model of two topics from a series of novels:

mystery and romance. The most common words in the mystery topic may be "missing," "murder," and "suspicion," while the words associated with the romance topic may be "love," "beauty," and "fond." These two topics may share a few words, such as "doubt" and "thought." Second, each document is seen as a mixture of topics. Each document contains many words, which in turn are from several topics in different proportions. For example, in a topic model of two topics, we can model Document A as consisting of 80 percent Topic I and 20 percent Topic II and Document B as 10 percent Topic I and 90 percent Topic II. LDA is a mathematical method for estimating both relationships: the words that are associated with each topic and the topics that describe each document.

APPLICATION OF TEXT MINING IN SOCIAL SCIENCE RESEARCH

Social scientists have captured this opportunity to use text data to mine knowledge about human nature, social interactions, and organizational structure. For example, researchers in economics and business have enhanced existing text mining methods to understand news and improve stock price prediction. They collected data from textual news that included corporate announcements from Germany and the United Kingdom published over fourteen years, from 1997 to 2011. They used features of two-word terms to represent attributes of texts, which were more expressive and accurate than one-word terms. They also employed market feedback in the feature selection process to best link characteristics of the market and text (Hagenau, Liebmann, and Neumann 2013).

Sociologists have investigated the mobility of fame using data from a large corpus of media sources (Van de Rijt et al. 2013). The Lydia text analysis system scanned personal names from approximately 2,200 U.S. daily newspapers, periodicals, and foreign English-language newspapers. It also performed named entity recognition, classification, and analysis of text corpora. Researchers discovered that the saying, "15 minutes of fame" only holds true for those at the bottom of the public attention hierarchy. For those in upper tiers, fame is far from fleeting. On the contrary, the media maintained stable coverage in time and intensity. The super-famous enjoy a self-reinforcing process that perpetuates their fame.

SUMMARY

The astronomical amount of data on the World Wide Web has made web mining and text mining some of the most important and fastest-growing fields of research. Web mining is the collection of data from the World Wide Web and application of data mining techniques to discover patterns from the web. Crawlers, scrapers, and browser automation are data extraction tools to collect information from websites. A web crawler is an automated program that methodically crawls through web pages to create an index of the data. Web scrapers extract content from the web pages they download.

Web mining consists of content mining, structure mining, and usage mining. Web content mining extracts data, mines information, and integrates knowledge from web page content. Web structure mining generates summary information about websites and web pages. Web usage mining applies data mining techniques to discover interesting usage patterns from web data to understand web usage patterns.

Text mining has revolutionized social science research by making it possible to quickly analyze a large amount of data on human information exchange. It handles text data retrieval and preprocessing before summarizing, representing, and finding patterns in the data.

The bag-of-words approach treats words as the basic feature of a document, converts entire documents into a collection of words without particular order, and carries out mathematical operations on either the presence of certain attributes or the frequency of terms. Word clouds summarize key words in a text by using the size of words in proportion to their frequencies. We use the IDF index to consider term frequency over a collection of documents. We also use TFIDF to find the most important words for each document by decreasing the weight for commonly used words in the documents and increasing the weight for rare words in these documents.

N-gram sequences add complexity by considering sequences of adjacent words and treating this sequence or order of words as terms, the basic unit of analysis. The n-gram method needs to deal with large number of features.

We use pairwise correlations to identify words that co-occur frequently. This co-occurrence of words is symmetrical. The two words could occur in different locations in the text, which is different from the ordered sequence of n-grams. The phi coefficient is a measure of binary correlation.

Topic modeling classifies a corpus of documents into natural groups in a similar method to the unsupervised learning of clustering analysis. The latent Dirichlet allocation (LDA) method sees each document as consisting of various topics, with each topic consisting of various words. LDA allows documents to consist of a mixture of topics that overlap in content.

PRACTICE QUESTIONS

1. What is web mining? What are the two steps involved in web mining?
2. What is a web crawler? What is a web scraper?
3. What are the three types of web mining?
4. What is web content mining? Describe some of the methods used in web content mining.
5. What is web structure mining? What can web structure achieve?
6. Describe web usage mining and what makes it a useful approach.
7. What is particularly difficult with text mining? In text mining, describe what stopwords removal, term normalization, and term stemming mean.

8. Using the following sentences, do the following:
   1) On a beautiful day in September, the family went on a 10-mile hike in the mountains.
   2) The family went to Europe in December and went on a 10-mile hike in the snow.
   3) A warm fireplace is a must-have for a family vacation in cold December.
   4) On a cold and snowing day in December, the family sat around the warm fireplace.
      a. Construct a table of term frequency representation.
      b. Conduct stopwords removal, normalization, and stemming, and revise the term frequency representation table.
9. What is a word cloud?
10. Explain what the IDF index is. What is TFIDF? What are IDF and TFIDF used for?
11. In what ways is n-gram sequence different from the bag-of-words approach?
12. What is pairwise correlation in text mining? Is this the same as bigram? What is phi coefficient?
13. What is a topic model? What is the relationship between words, documents, and topics in a topic model?
14. What is the latent Dirichlet allocation method?

R PACKAGES

Package readtext: https://cran.r-project.org/web/packages/readtext/readtext.pdf.
Pagkage quanteda: https://cran.r-project.org/web/packages/quanteda/quanteda.pdf.
Package topicmodels: https://cran.r-project.org/web/packages/topicmodels/topicmodels.pdf.

ADDITIONAL READING

Ignatow, Gabe, and Rada Mihalcea. 2017. *Text Mining: A Guidebook for the Social Sciences*. Thousand Oaks, CA: Sage. A very good book for the beginner. It covers the basics up to intermediate topics for both novice and intermediate students. It provides open source or free trial tools that can be applied to analyses. A companion website provides all the data used as examples: https://study.sagepub.com/textmining.

Silge, Julia, and David Robinson. 2017. *Text Mining with R: A Tidy Approach*. Sebastopol, CA: O'Reilly Media. Contains sample codes and simple explanations for complex problems such as comparing texts, graphing word connections and correlations, and clustering texts. Book Homepage to read the book for free: https://www.tidytextmining.com/; Book GitHub Repository for download code and data: https://github.com/dgrtwo/tidy-text-mining.

Zhai, ChengXiang, and Sean Massung. 2016. *Text Data Management and Analysis: A Practical Introduction to Information Retrieval and Text Mining*. San Rafael, CA: ACM Books. Covers the major concepts, techniques, and ideas in information retrieval and text data mining from a practical standpoint and includes many hands-on exercises designed with a companion software toolkit (i.e., META). It provides examples and illustrative figures from two massive open online courses (MOOCs) offered by Dr. Zhai on Coursera: https://www.coursera.org/learn/text-mining.

REFERENCES

Chen, Yunsong, and Fei Yan. 2016a. "Centuries of Sociology in Millions of Books." *Sociological Review* 64 (4): 872–93.

———. 2016b. "Economic Performance and Public Concerns about Social Class in Twentieth-Century Books." *Social Science Research* 59: 37–51.

Hagenau, Michael, Michael Liebmann, and Dirk Neumann. 2013. "Automated News Reading: Stock Price Prediction Based on Financial News Using Context-Capture Features." *Decision Support Systems* 55 (3): 685–97.

Kearney, Michael W. 2018. "We Put Data Science to the Test to Try to Uncover the Mystery Author of the Times' Op-ed." D. W. Reynolds Journalism Institute, Missouri School of Journalism, University of Missouri. September 6. https://www.rjionline.org/stories/we-put-data-science-to-the-test-to-try-to-uncover-the-mystery-author-of-the.

Michel, Jean-Baptiste, Yuan Kui Shen, Aviva Presser Aiden, Adain Veres, Matthew K. Gray, the Google Books Team, Joseph P. Pickett, Dale Hoiberg, Dan Clancy, Peter Norvig, Jon Orwant, Steven Pinker, Martin A Nowak, and Erez Lieberman Aiden. 2011. "Quantitative Analysis of Culture Using Millions of Digitized Books." *Science* 331: 176.

Pechenick, Eitan Adam, Christopher M. Danforth, and Peter Sheridan Dodds. 2015. "Characterizing the Google Books Corpus: Strong Limits to Inferences of Socio-Cultural and Linguistic Evolution." *PLoS ONE* 10 (10): e0137041. https://doi.org/10.1371/journal.pone.0137041.

Prabakaran, S., and Shilpa Mitra. 2018. "Survey of Analysis of Crime Detection Techniques Using Data Mining and Machine Learning." National Conference on Mathematical Techniques and Its Applications. IOP Conference Series: Journal of Physics, Conference Series 1000(2018)012046.

Provost, Foster, and Tom Fawcett. 2013. *Data Science for Business*. Sebastopol, CA: O'Reilly Media.

Robinson, David, and Julia Silge. 2017. *Text Mining with R: A Tidy Approach*. Sebastopol, CA.: O'Reilly Media.

Takhteyev, Yuri, Anatoliy Gruzd, and Barry Wellman. 2011. "Geography of Twitter Networks." *Social Networks* 34: 73–81.

Van de Rijt, Arnout, Eran Shor, Charles Ward, and Steven Skiena. 2013. "Only 15 Minutes? The Social Stratification of Fame in Printed Media." *American Sociological Review* 78 (2): 266–89.

Welbers, Kasper, Wouter Van Atteveldt, and Kenneth Benoit. 2017. "Text Analysis in R." *Communication Methods and Measures* 11 (4): 245–65. http://kenbenoit.net/pdfs/text_analysis_in_R.pdf.

Chapter 12

NETWORK OR LINK ANALYSIS

S OCIAL NETWORK OR LINK ANALYSIS provides a powerful group of tools for representing and analyzing relational data. Social network analysis is an interdisciplinary field focusing on the structure of relationships or connections within a set of social actors such as persons, groups, organizations, communities, nations, or human activities and creations. These methods have been applied to a wide variety of social phenomena ranging from research on international relations between nations to connections among websites, Facebook friends, WeChat moments, Twitter follows, coauthorships among researchers, character co-appearances in fiction or movies, correlations of textual terms or semantic concepts, and wars between nations (Wimmer and Min 2006).

Interesting examples abound that network analysis reveals interesting and surprising patterns undetected using conventional approaches. For example, multimedia researchers use a story-based movie analysis method that applies network analysis tools to investigate connections between characters and classify the roles and obtain the number of sequences (Park and Jo 2011). This method has been applied to the characters in the *Star Wars* movies and the ties among them. Using information from the *Star Wars* seven-movie cycle, social network structure has been extracted both within each movies and across the whole *Star Wars* universe. The thickness of the lines linking the nodes is proportional to the amount of time they speak together (analysis of seven episodes: http://evelinag.com/blog/2016/01–25-social-network-force-awakens/index.html#.XJlavndFxGs; analysis of six episodes: http://evelinag.com/blog/2015/12–15-star-wars-social-network/#.XJlZoXdFxGt; codes: https://github.com/evelinag/StarWars-social-network). This analysis reveals the relative importance of each character in the episodes and makes it possible to trace changes between the original trilogy and later episodes. Another example combines text mining and network analysis to demonstrate character co-occurrence in *Les Misérables* (https://bl.ocks.org/mbostock/4062045), thus greatly expanding our appreciation and creation of literature and arts, realms previously beyond the reach of quantitative analysis.

The origin of social network studies can be traced to anthropological observations of small village marriage and kinship ties in face-to-face groups and, later, to mathematical graph theory. More recently, particularly with the rise of online networks, the social networks under investigation are now very large, with some as large as millions of nodes or in the case of Facebook billions or tens of billions of nodes. In addition to their growing size, social networks are constantly evolving as relationships emerge, transform, and die off.

Social network analysis (SNA) provides a collection of methods for visualizing network configurations, describing network characteristics, and building mathematical and statistical models of network structures and dynamics. Unlike many other methods that analyze the relationships among variables as indicators of attributes, SNA evaluates influences between entities or cases such as people, organizations, words, fiction or movie characters, and websites. In general terms, any social process or structure that can be represented by lines connecting sets of units can be conceptualized as a social network. We thus also call it link analysis.

REPRESENTING THE NETWORK: GRAPH AND MATRIX

Social network analysis has its roots in graph theory, a field of mathematics that is concerned with discrete relational structure (Butts 2006, 13–15). It is thus natural to conceptualize a social network as a graph consisting of a set of nodes (vertices, units, or points) and a set of lines (edges) connecting them. The nodes represent social actors, entities, or objects, and the lines represent the relations among them. A network graph, sometimes called a sociogram, is a relational structure showing a set of entities and the ties connecting them.

Figure 12.1 is a graphic representation of a network. This is a diagram or sociogram of telecommunications (telephone) networks among fifty-one countries in 1992. The

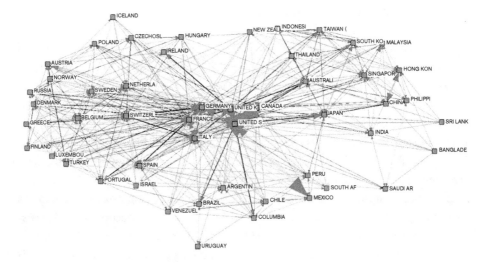

FIGURE 12.1
Telecommunications Networks among Nations.

data record the number of minutes of connections as well as the direction of these calls. In this diagram, nodes are squares representing countries. The lines connect two countries. The color and thickness of the lines represent the strength of the connection. The arrows indicate the direction of the connection, which of the pair placed the call and which was on the receiving end. The size of the arrows represent the total number of minutes arriving at the country to which they are directed. Larger arrows represent more minutes. The line between the United States and Mexico is the thickest, indicating the strongest connection by telephone between the two nations. The arrow directed at Mexico is the largest among all the arrows, showing that most of the connections originate from the United States.

The most common data representation of a social network is the adjacency matrix. It is an $n \times n$ matrix whose ijth cell indicates the edge from i to j. When there is a line starting from i and ending with j, then the value in the cell is 1. When there is no line between the two vertices or nodes, the value in the cell is 0.

1) For an undirected graph, the matrix A is symmetric with $A_{ij} = A_{ji}$ with all the diagonal terms 0.
2) When the diagonal term is 1, there is a loop connecting the node to itself.
3) For a directed graph, if the term $A_{ij} = 1$, there is an edge coming out of i toward j. If the $A_{ji} = 1$, there is an edge directing toward i coming from j. In the graph, we use arrows to represent directions.
4) For edges with values, we enter the values in the cell in the matrix instead of using 0 and 1.

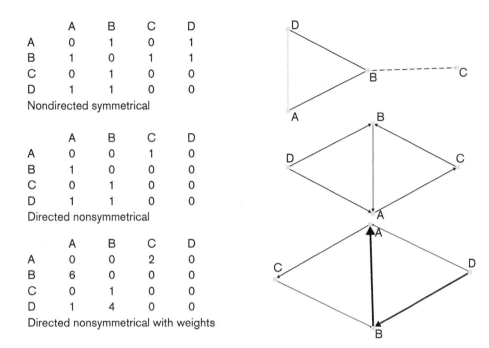

	A	B	C	D
A	0	1	0	1
B	1	0	1	1
C	0	1	0	0
D	1	1	0	0

Nondirected symmetrical

	A	B	C	D
A	0	0	1	0
B	1	0	0	0
C	0	1	0	0
D	1	1	0	0

Directed nonsymmetrical

	A	B	C	D
A	0	0	2	0
B	6	0	0	0
C	0	1	0	0
D	1	4	0	0

Directed nonsymmetrical with weights

FIGURE 12.2

Two Representations of SNA: Adjacency Matrix and Sociogram.

5) When there are multiple relationships in the same vertex set, we extend the adjacency matrix to include the adjacency array, such that the matrix becomes $m \times n \times n$ adjacency array.

Figure 12.2 demonstrates these two ways of representing a social network with four nodes. The left side uses an adjacency matrix, and the right side translates this relationship into a network diagram of vertices and lines. When the adjacency matrix is symmetrical, the diagram is nondirected, as shown in the network diagram at the top. When the adjacency matrix is nonsymmetrical and represented only by 0's and 1's, it is a directed nonsymmetrical diagram, as shown in the middle diagram. When the adjacency matrix is nonsymmetrical and represented by weights, it is a directed nonsymmetrical diagram with the value of the lines expressed by the thickness of the lines, as illustrated in the bottom diagram.

The adjacency matrix for the international telecommunication ties in figure 12.1 is nonsymmetrical, directed, with weights for the edges. Figure 12.3 shows this adjacency matrix.

There are a variety of approaches to illustrate a social network. Because graphic display networks are often drawn in a two-dimensional space, the location of a node or relation in the space is suggestive of the nature and prominent structure of the

	1 ARGE NTIN	2 BRAZ IL	3 CANA DA	4 CHIL E	5 COLU MBIA	6 MEXI CO	7 PERU	8 UNIT ED S	9 URUG UAY	10 VENE ZUEL	11 BELG IUM	12 DENM ARK	13 FRAN CE	14 GERM ANY	15 GREE CE	16 IREL AND	17 ITAL Y	18 LUXE MBOU	19 NETH ERLA	20 PORT UGAL	21 SPAI N	22 UNIT ED K	23 AUST RIA	24 FINL AND	25 ICEL AND	26 NOR WAY
1 ARGENTIN	0	13	2	10	0	2	2	28	21	0	0	0	3	3	0	0	8	0	0	0	9	2	0	0	0	0
2 BRAZIL	18	0	0	4	0	2	0	61	5	0	0	0	3	9	0	0	9	0	0	8	4	6	0	0	0	0
3 CANADA	0	0	0	0	0	13	0	1511	0	0	0	0	41	39	0	0	30	0	14	13	0	117	0	0	0	0
4 CHILE	9	3	1	0	1	1	2	15	1	1	0	0	1	2	0	0	1	0	0	0	3	1	0	0	0	0
5 COLUMBIA	1	2	1	1	0	3	0	50	0	9	0	0	2	2	0	0	2	0	0	0	3	2	0	0	0	0
6 MEXICO	3	3	9	0	4	0	2	610	0	2	0	0	4	5	0	0	4	0	0	0	8	4	0	0	0	0
7 PERU	1	1	1	0	1	1	0	15	0	1	0	0	1	1	0	0	1	0	0	0	2	1	0	0	0	0
8 UNITED S	0	145	2226	0	172	1277	80	0	0	76	0	0	240	563	0	0	208	0	93	0	105	734	0	0	0	0
9 URUGUAY	18	3	0	1	0	0	0	2	0	0	0	0	0	0	0	0	0	0	0	0	1	0	0	0	0	0
10 VENEZUEL	2	2	2	1	0	2	3	54	0	0	0	0	2	2	0	0	5	0	0	2	7	2	0	0	0	0
11 BELGIUM	0	0	0	0	0	0	0	31	0	0	0	8	221	119	9	5	47	28	185	10	27	83	7	0	0	0
12 DENMARK	0	0	0	0	0	0	0	21	0	0	9	0	19	78	0	0	11	0	16	0	9	47	4	9	0	44
13 FRANCE	0	0	32	0	0	0	0	153	0	0	216	0	0	303	0	0	217	0	80	114	157	275	0	0	0	0
14 GERMANY	0	0	0	0	0	0	0	235	0	0	115	0	318	0	77	0	288	0	250	0	18	287	329	0	0	0
15 GREECE	0	0	9	0	0	0	0	25	0	0	8	0	17	62	0	0	26	0	8	0	0	40	5	0	0	0
16 IRELAND	0	0	3	0	0	0	0	28	0	0	4	2	10	12	0	0	4	0	6	0	4	206	1	0	0	0
17 ITALY	0	0	17	0	0	0	0	155	0	0	44	0	209	227	23	0	0	0	32	0	56	56	39	0	0	0
18 LUXEMBOU	0	0	0	0	0	0	0	4	0	0	42	3	35	36	1	0	9	0	7	12	3	11	2	0	0	0
19 NETHERLA	0	0	12	0	0	0	0	66	0	0	189	17	87	264	0	0	37	0	0	0	31	147	17	0	0	10
20 PORTUGAL	0	0	4	0	0	0	0	9	0	0	8	2	45	21	2	0	8	0	7	0	33	23	0	0	0	0
21 SPAIN	14	0	0	0	0	0	0	75	0	8	27	8	139	112	0	0	58	0	32	31	0	115	0	0	0	0
22 UNITED K	0	0	95	0	0	0	0	575	0	0	79	47	269	325	43	218	135	0	134	36	115	0	0	0	0	42
23 AUSTRIA	0	0	0	0	0	0	0	23	0	0	8	0	19	33	0	0	35	0	17	0	0	23	0	0	0	0
24 FINLAND	0	0	0	0	0	0	0	14	0	0	0	7	6	19	0	0	4	0	4	0	4	13	0	0	0	7
25 ICELAND	0	0	0	0	0	0	0	6	0	0	0	3	1	2	0	0	0	0	1	0	0	3	0	0	0	2
26 NORWAY	0	0	3	0	0	0	0	24	0	0	4	45	10	23	0	0	5	0	0	0	6	40	2	8	2	0
27 SWEDEN	0	0	6	0	0	0	0	53	0	0	12	84	26	70	0	0	16	0	15	4	17	60	9	98	0	95
28 SWITZERL	0	0	12	0	0	0	0	65	0	0	27	0	264	358	0	0	224	0	37	59	53	82	69	0	0	0
29 CZECHOSL	0	0	2	0	0	0	0	11	0	0	3	0	6	44	0	0	9	0	4	0	0	7	20	0	0	0
30 HUNGARY	0	0	3	0	0	0	0	13	0	0	3	0	6	46	0	0	10	0	4	0	0	9	25	0	0	0
31 POLAND	0	0	6	0	0	0	0	25	0	0	5	4	13	63	0	0	9	0	6	0	0	12	9	0	0	0
32 RUSSIA	0	0	2	0	0	0	0	21	0	0	3	0	6	25	0	0	0	0	0	0	2	6	0	0	0	0
33 ISRAEL	2	0	5	0	0	0	0	48	0	0	4	0	12	11	0	0	6	0	4	0	0	15	0	0	0	0
34 SAUDI AR	0	0	0	0	0	0	0	38	0	0	0	0	9	0	0	0	0	0	0	0	0	21	0	0	0	0
35 SOUTH AF	0	0	4	0	0	0	0	18	0	0	0	0	4	11	0	0	4	0	0	0	0	37	0	0	0	0
36 TURKEY	0	0	0	0	0	0	0	16	0	0	5	0	15	83	4	0	8	0	11	0	0	18	7	0	0	0
37 AUSTRALI	0	0	16	0	0	0	0	184	0	0	0	0	0	17	12	0	19	0	0	0	0	112	0	0	0	0
38 BANGLADE	0	0	0	0	0	0	0	2	0	0	0	0	0	0	0	0	0	0	0	0	0	3	0	0	0	0
39 CHINA	0	0	5	0	0	0	0	30	0	0	0	0	4	5	0	0	3	0	0	0	0	3	0	0	0	0
40 HONG KON	0	0	57	0	0	0	0	80	0	0	0	0	0	0	0	0	0	0	0	0	0	45	0	0	0	0
41 INDIA	0	0	6	0	0	0	0	62	0	0	0	0	3	6	0	0	2	0	0	0	0	25	0	0	0	0
42 INDONESI	0	0	2	0	0	0	0	13	0	0	0	0	3	3	0	0	0	0	3	0	0	4	0	0	0	0
43 JAPAN	0	49	17	0	0	0	16	255	0	0	0	0	19	26	0	0	9	0	0	0	0	43	0	0	0	0
44 SOUTH KO	0	0	5	0	0	0	0	94	0	0	0	0	4	8	0	0	0	0	0	0	0	7	0	0	0	0
45 MALAYSIA	0	0	2	0	0	0	0	13	0	0	0	0	0	0	0	0	0	0	0	0	0	11	0	0	0	0
46 NEW ZEAL	0	0	3	0	0	0	0	16	0	0	0	0	1	2	0	0	0	0	1	1	0	16	0	0	0	0
47 PHILIPPI	0	0	7	0	0	0	0	54	0	0	0	0	0	1	0	0	2	0	0	0	0	3	0	0	0	0
48 SINGAPOR	0	0	0	0	0	0	0	35	0	0	0	0	8	9	0	0	0	0	0	0	0	22	0	0	0	0
49 SRI LANK	0	0	0	0	0	0	0	1	0	0	0	0	0	1	0	0	0	0	0	0	0	2	0	0	0	0
50 TAIWAN (	0	0	0	0	0	0	0	82	0	0	0	0	4	7	0	0	0	0	0	0	0	6	0	0	0	0
51 THAILAND	0	0	2	0	0	0	0	21	0	0	0	0	4	5	0	0	2	0	0	0	0	7	0	0	0	0

	27 SWE DEN	28 SWIT ZERL	29 CZEC HOSL	30 HUN GARY	31 POL AND	32 RUSS IA	33 ISRA EL	34 SAUD I AR	35 SOUT H AF	36 TURK EY	37 AUST RALI	38 BANG LADE	39 CHIN A	40 HONG KON	41 INDI A	42 INDO NESI	43 JAPA N	44 SOUT H KO	45 MALA YSIA	46 NEW ZEAL	47 PHIL IPPI	48 SING APOR	49 SRI LANK	50 TAIW AN (	51 THAI LAND
1 ARGENTIN	0	2	0	0	0	0	0	0	0	0	0	0	0	0	0	0	0	0	0	0	0	0	0	0	0
2 BRAZIL	0	4	0	0	0	0	0	0	0	0	0	0	0	0	0	0	4	0	0	0	0	0	0	0	0
3 CANADA	0	12	0	0	0	0	0	0	0	0	20	0	0	43	18	0	18	0	0	0	17	0	0	0	0
4 CHILE	0	0	0	0	0	0	0	0	0	0	0	0	0	0	0	0	0	0	0	0	0	0	0	0	0
5 COLUMBIA	0	0	0	0	0	0	0	0	0	0	0	0	0	0	0	0	0	0	0	0	0	0	0	0	0
6 MEXICO	0	0	0	0	0	0	0	0	0	0	0	0	0	0	0	0	2	0	0	0	0	0	0	0	0
7 PERU	0	0	0	0	0	0	0	0	0	0	0	0	0	0	0	0	0	0	0	0	0	0	0	0	0
8 UNITED S	0	94	0	0	0	0	138	0	0	0	114	0	0	114	98	0	367	208	0	0	200	0	0	163	0
9 URUGUAY	0	0	0	0	0	0	0	0	0	0	0	0	0	0	0	0	0	0	0	0	0	0	0	0	0
10 VENEZUEL	0	0	0	0	0	0	0	0	0	0	0	0	0	0	0	0	0	0	0	0	0	0	0	0	0
11 BELGIUM	12	24	0	0	0	0	0	0	0	0	0	0	0	0	0	0	0	0	0	0	0	0	0	0	0
12 DENMARK	76	10	9	0	7	0	0	0	0	5	0	0	0	0	0	0	0	0	0	0	0	0	0	0	0
13 FRANCE	22	196	0	0	0	0	0	0	0	29	0	0	0	0	0	0	0	0	0	0	0	0	0	0	0
14 GERMANY	0	315	96	0	104	0	0	0	0	295	0	0	0	0	0	0	0	0	0	0	0	0	0	0	0
15 GREECE	5	9	0	0	0	0	0	0	0	5	8	0	0	0	0	0	0	0	0	0	0	0	0	0	0
16 IRELAND	2	2	0	0	0	0	0	0	0	0	3	0	0	0	0	0	1	0	0	0	0	0	0	0	0
17 ITALY	0	149	0	0	0	0	0	0	0	0	0	0	0	17	0	0	0	0	0	0	0	0	0	0	0
18 LUXEMBOU	2	6	0	0	0	0	0	0	0	0	0	0	0	0	0	0	1	0	0	0	0	0	0	0	0
19 NETHERLA	18	32	0	0	10	0	0	0	0	28	0	0	0	0	0	0	0	0	0	0	0	0	0	0	0
20 PORTUGAL	3	12	0	0	0	0	0	0	0	0	0	0	0	0	0	0	0	0	0	0	0	0	0	0	0
21 SPAIN	13	30	0	0	0	0	0	0	0	0	0	0	0	0	0	0	0	0	0	0	0	0	0	0	0
22 UNITED K	54	86	0	0	0	0	0	0	39	0	90	0	0	35	53	0	43	0	0	0	0	0	0	0	0
23 AUSTRIA	0	53	23	24	16	0	0	0	0	22	0	0	0	0	0	0	0	0	0	0	0	0	0	0	0
24 FINLAND	89	4	0	0	0	12	0	0	0	0	0	0	0	0	0	0	0	0	0	0	0	0	0	0	0
25 ICELAND	3	0	0	0	0	0	0	0	0	0	0	0	0	0	0	0	0	0	0	0	0	0	0	0	0
26 NORWAY	90	5	0	0	3	0	0	0	0	2	0	0	0	0	0	0	0	0	0	0	0	0	0	0	0
27 SWEDEN	0	14	4	0	0	0	0	0	0	6	0	0	0	0	0	0	0	0	0	0	0	0	0	0	0
28 SWITZERL	16	0	11	0	0	0	0	0	0	29	0	0	0	0	0	0	0	0	0	0	0	0	0	0	0
29 CZECHOSL	2	6	0	8	7	7	0	0	0	0	0	0	0	0	0	0	0	0	0	0	0	0	0	0	0
30 HUNGARY	4	7	7	0	0	6	0	0	0	0	2	0	0	0	0	0	0	0	0	0	0	0	0	0	0
31 POLAND	9	3	5	0	0	15	0	0	0	0	0	0	0	0	0	0	0	0	0	0	0	0	0	0	0
32 RUSSIA	2	2	6	6	11	0	0	0	0	0	0	0	0	0	0	0	0	0	0	0	0	0	0	0	0
33 ISRAEL	0	5	0	0	0	6	0	0	3	2	2	0	0	0	0	0	0	0	0	0	0	0	0	0	0
34 SAUDI AR	0	0	0	0	0	0	0	0	0	12	0	0	0	0	24	0	0	0	0	0	13	0	0	0	0
35 SOUTH AF	0	0	0	0	0	0	4	0	0	0	5	0	0	0	0	0	0	0	0	0	0	0	0	0	0
36 TURKEY	0	9	0	0	0	5	0	4	0	0	0	0	0	0	0	0	0	0	0	0	0	0	0	0	0
37 AUSTRALI	0	0	0	0	0	0	0	0	0	0	0	0	0	28	0	11	32	0	0	90	14	20	0	0	0
38 BANGLADE	0	0	0	0	0	0	0	1	0	0	0	0	0	2	1	0	1	0	0	0	0	1	0	0	0
39 CHINA	0	0	0	0	0	0	0	0	0	0	6	0	0	412	0	0	57	9	2	0	0	7	0	47	4
40 HONG KON	0	0	0	0	0	0	0	0	0	0	34	0	535	0	0	0	45	0	0	0	34	34	0	68	0
41 INDIA	0	0	0	0	0	0	0	28	0	0	4	0	0	5	0	0	4	0	2	0	0	9	0	0	0
42 INDONESI	0	0	0	0	0	0	0	0	0	0	8	0	0	8	0	0	12	6	5	0	2	29	0	6	2
43 JAPAN	0	0	0	0	0	0	0	0	0	0	26	0	94	44	0	16	0	133	31	0	89	31	0	79	56
44 SOUTH KO	0	0	0	0	0	0	0	0	0	0	6	0	11	15	0	6	80	0	0	0	13	6	0	7	0
45 MALAYSIA	0	0	0	0	0	0	0	0	0	0	12	0	0	10	4	6	16	0	0	0	0	97	0	9	7
46 NEW ZEAL	0	1	0	0	0	0	0	0	0	0	72	0	0	4	0	0	4	0	1	0	0	3	0	2	0
47 PHILIPPI	0	0	0	0	0	0	0	3	0	0	6	0	0	12	0	0	21	3	2	0	0	4	0	4	0
48 SINGAPOR	0	0	0	0	0	0	0	0	0	0	17	0	10	34	14	40	34	0	118	0	12	0	0	0	19
49 SRI LANK	0	0	0	0	0	0	0	0	0	0	1	0	0	1	2	0	1	0	0	0	0	2	0	0	0
50 TAIWAN (	0	0	0	9	0	0	0	0	0	0	7	0	53	64	0	6	55	6	0	0	9	13	0	0	9
51 THAILAND	0	2	0	0	0	0	0	0	0	0	5	0	4	12	2	0	23	0	0	0	0	13	0	9	0

FIGURE 12.3

Adjacency Matrix of Telecommunication Ties between Countries.

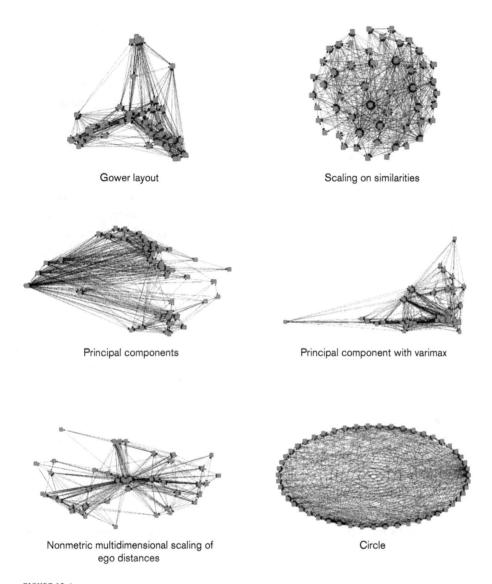

Gower layout

Scaling on similarities

Principal components

Principal component with varimax

Nonmetric multidimensional scaling of
ego distances

Circle

FIGURE 12.4
Different Sociogram Presentations of the Global Telecommunications Network.

network. Identical networks can be expressed in different ways by positioning the
nodes and edges differently, as shown in figure 12.4. These different configurations of
the same network present the full information about the network in different ways.
With choices of different graphic presentations, we can highlight different features of
the network structure. A lot of the work that we do with social networks is primarily
descriptive and/or exploratory rather than confirmatory hypothesis testing. Using
some of the tools described in this chapter can be particularly helpful because they
may let you see patterns that you might not otherwise have seen. These tools are very

helpful for dealing with the complexity of social network data, which may involve many actors, many ties, and several types of ties. Carrying out in insightful ways to highlight, hide, and locate parts of the data can be critical in making sense of the data, in understanding and describing the construction and evolution of the social structures. A good graphic is more effective in revealing hidden patterns in the data and sharing researchers' insights than numerical data or words.

DESCRIBING A SOCIAL NETWORK

Social network analysis describes mathematically the structure of the entire network and a node's characteristics within the network. Social network analysis formalizes the study of the structure of ties among social actors and offers several types of opportunities for systemic investigation and theorizing on actors and their connections as social systems. First, social network analysis provides data mining tools for describing overall network structure, revealing important network characteristics such as subgroups that have close ties with each other, hierarchical layers of networks, or holes in the network structure. Second, social network analysis provides a way to focus on individual nodes or actors and their immediate network context. This enables researchers to understand individual actors' behaviors and orientations as products of their network ties and the combined influence of their neighbors and communities.

NETWORK COHESION

Network cohesion refers to the sections in the network that are densely connected. When the ties are more frequent or extensive among certain nodes within a network, they are identified as a cohesive subgroup or a clique.

Clique. One strict definition is that all nodes are directly linked to each other. These maximally complete subgroups are called cliques.

N-Clique. This definition may be loosened up to allow the distance between any two nodes to be more than 1 by setting up a maximum value for the graph-theoretical distance between nodes.

In the global communications network, the United States, the United Kingdom, Germany, France, Italy, and Canada (all represented by black nodes) belong to a clique with direct ties to each other, as shown at the bottom of figure 12.5. If we extend to a 2-clique, we include Australia and Japan (represented by gray nodes), which are connected or have 1 and 2 direct ties with other members in this subgraph to form a cohesive subgroup.

K-Cores and K-Plex, M-Core or M-Slice. K-cores and k-plex define subgroups using the criteria minimum number, strength, or multiplicity of edges among nodes of subgroups. K-cores identify maximal subgraphs with a minimum number of k neighbors within the subgroup. K-plex defines maximal subgraphs with a maximum number of k nodes that are not adjacent. For networks with valued lines, the m-core or m-slice identifies maximal subgraphs connected with edges of minimum value m.

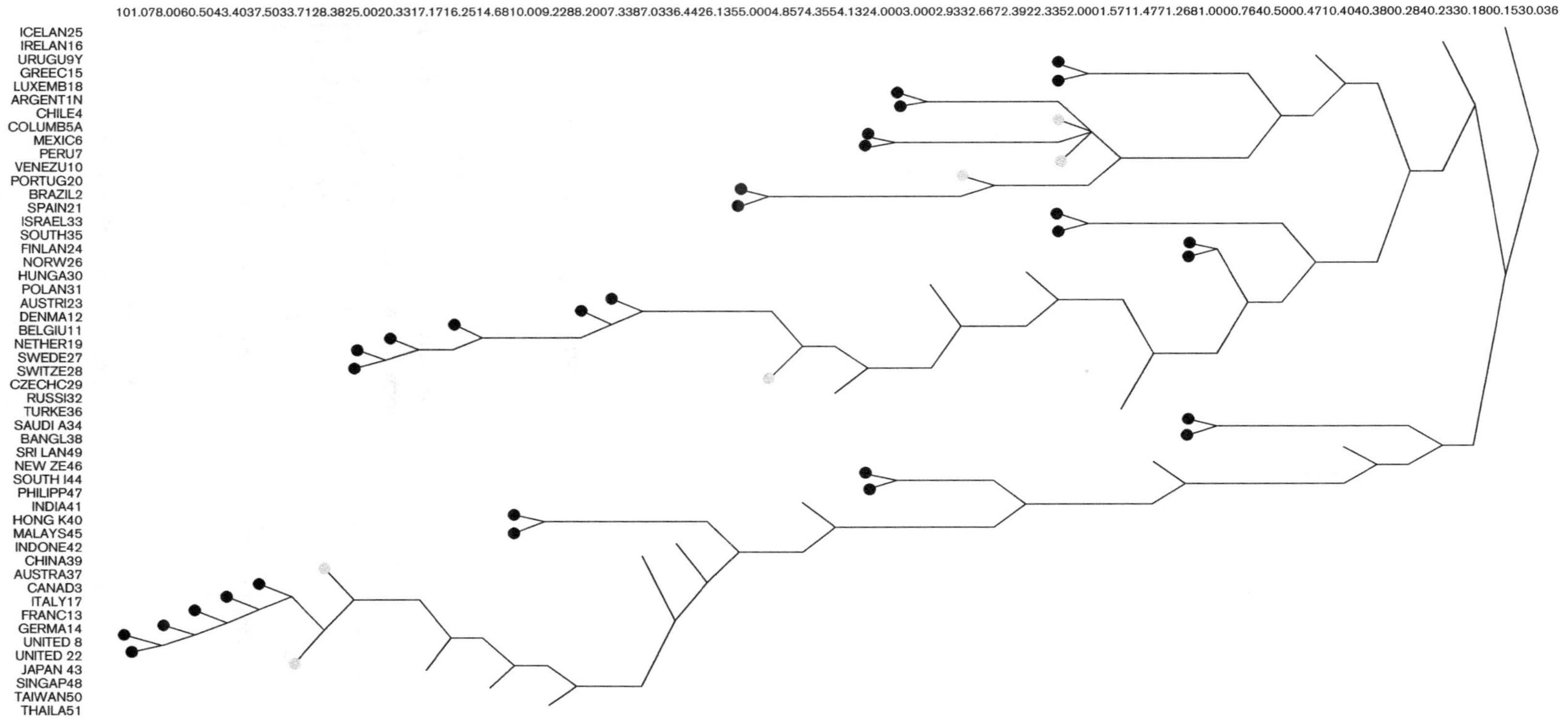

FIGURE 12.5

Clique and 2-Clique in Global Telecommunication Network.

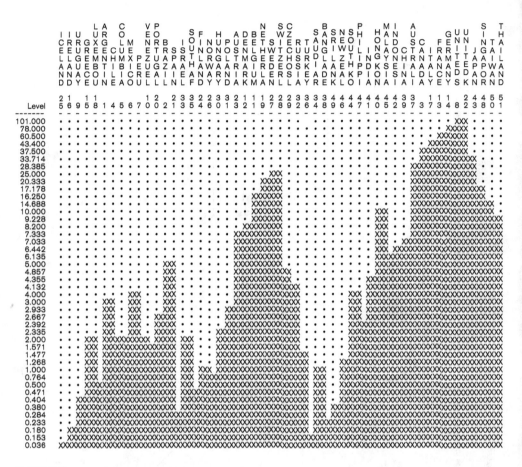

FIGURE 12.6

Blockmodeling Pattern of m-Core Schemes in Global Telecommunication Network.

Lamda Set. A lamda set focuses on the relative frequency of lines among subgraph nodes relative to outside nodes. It is a maximal subgraph with more ties among its member nodes than to nodes outside of it.

Since the global telecommunication ties are valued links, figure 12.6 provides various ways to slice m-core subgroups. If we want to be stringent and choose a relatively high value, 10K, we have three m-core subgroups with internal cohesion. The largest one consists of ten countries: the United States, the United Kingdom, Germany, France, Italy, Canada, Japan, Australia, Singapore, and Taiwan. The second largest m-core consists of four countries: Sweden, Switzerland, the Netherlands, and Belgium. The smallest m-core subgraph has two nodes, Hong Kong and Malaysia.

BLOCKMODELING

Blockmodeling is the method we use to analyze the adjacency matrix or sociomatrix to identify actors who have similar patterns of ties with other actors. The adjacency matrix is sorted intelligently so that a clear pattern emerges to reveal the relationships among the actors. The pattern is illustrated by classifying the nodes into clusters when actors with occupied rows belong to the same cluster. Empty cells show the absence of ties and thus the division of clusters.

Figure 12.6 is an example of using the blockmodeling method to classify countries into clusters based on the intensity of their telecommunication ties. The largest and most central cluster consists of the United States and the United Kingdom at the center with other wealthy European countries and Canada and with Asian countries at the periphery. The second cluster consists of other smaller European countries. A third cluster consists of Latin American countries. A fourth group of countries includes Saudi Arabia, Bangladesh, and Sri Lanka, which are predominantly Muslim countries that maintain few telecommunications ties with other countries.

NETWORK CENTRALITY AND PRESTIGE

The positions of nodes in the network are often described in terms of centrality. Centrally positioned individuals enjoy a position of privilege in the exchange of information, goods, services, favors, and so on. Centrally located actors are active, prominent, efficient, and important in a network compared to those relegated to the periphery. An actor who occupies a central location in the network is able to maintain numerous contacts and gain access to and/or influence over others. A central actor is a node in a structural position in the network that serves as a source or conduit for information exchange and resource transactions with other actors. Central actors are located at or near the center of a network with many ties to other actors. A peripheral actor maintains few or no relations and is located at the fringe of a network.

Researchers use graph theory in social network analysis to identify prominent and important actors. The centrality concept quantifies graph theoretic ideas about an individual actor's prominence within a network by summarizing structural relations among all the nodes. Group-level indices of centralization assess the dispersion or inequality among all actors in the network. The three main types of centrality are degree centrality, betweenness centrality, and closeness centrality. When the social network is a directed graph with relationships flowing from one vertex to another, we use the measure of prestige to differentiate from centrality, which is used for nondirected relations.

DEGREE CENTRALITY

An actor's degree centrality is the total number of direct ties in a nondirected graph. Because some networks are larger than others, a simple summation of total direct ties may not be able to provide information for comparison between networks. To standardize the degree centrality measure, we divide the degree centrality measure by the maximum possible direct ties a node can have.

To demonstrate the connection between network structure and an individual actor's degree centrality, we show three different network configurations in figure 12.7.

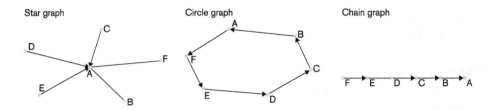

FIGURE 12.7
Centrality in Three Networks.

In the star graph, the most central actor A has a degree centrality score of 5 and a standardized centrality of 1.00. The five peripheral actors B, C, D, E, and F, each have degree centrality scores of 1 and a standardized centrality of 0.20. All six nodes on the circle graph have identical degree centrality of 2 with standardized scores of 0.4. In the chain graph, the two end nodes have smaller degree centralities of 1, while those in the middle have centralities of 2 with the respective standardized scores of .2 and .4.

CLOSENESS CENTRALITY

An actor in the network who can quickly interact and communicate with other actors without going through many intermediaries is also considered prominent in the network. To put this concept into a graph theory measure, an actor (ego) who has minimal path distances from all the other actors (alters) is considered to occupy a position of closeness centrality. Even if an actor is not directly tied to many other actors but it takes only a small number of steps to reach others, this actor attains higher closeness centrality. Closeness centrality is calculated as the inverse of the sum of geodesic distances from an actor (ego) to the other actors (alters). The closeness centrality is expressed as a proportion or percentage, with a high score indicating higher closeness centrality.

In the star graph in figure 12.7 actor A has a perfect closeness centrality score of 6/6=1, while the four peripheral actors B, C, D, E, and F have scores of 5/9=.56. In the circle graph, all actors have the same closeness centrality of 5/9=.56. In the chain graph, the middle two actors C and D have the highest closeness centrality of 5/9=.56. The two nodes B and E, next to the middle nodes, have the second high score of 5/11=.45. The two end nodes have the lowest closeness centrality of 5/15=.33.

A more sophisticated approach of measuring closeness centrality is the eigenvector approach. It aims to locate the most central actors in terms of the "global" or "overall" structure of the network and downplays patterns that are more "local." It uses the method of factor analysis to identify "dimensions" of the distances among actors. Eigenvalues indicate the location of each actor with respect to each dimension. The first dimension captures the "global" aspects of distances among actors while the second and further dimensions indicate more specific and local substructure.

BETWEENNESS CENTRALITY

Another form of network centrality stems from actors' "between" position on the geodesics connecting other actors in the network. Such a "between" actor plays a brokerage role and controls the flow of information or the exchange of resources among other actors. The actor betweenness centrality index is the sum of the proportions that an actor is involved in all pair of the other actors' geodesic(s). We normalize the betweenness centrality by dividing it by the maximum possible betweenness.

In the star graph in figure 12.7, actor A has a betweenness score of 10/10=1, while the five peripheral actors are 0/10=0. In the circle graph, all actors have the same betweenness score of 2/10=.2. In the chain graph, the two center nodes, C and D, have the highest betweenness centrality of 6/10=.6. The next two, B and E, score lower in betweenness centrality of 4/10=.4. The two end nodes of A and F have scores of 0.

PRESTIGE

Prestige is an attractiveness or popularity measure that counts asymmetrical ties in networks because social inequalities are created and reflected by asymmetrical ties. Prestige or attractiveness is measured as the number of incoming edges, or the "indegree" of a node or vertex, when the direction is positive, such as the most respected person. When the relationship is negative (e.g., criticizing or despising), prestige is then measured as the "outdegree" of a vertex. It is also labeled the popularity of a vertex. Therefore, prestige is a directed centrality degree.

Proximity prestige, a variant of closeness centrality, measures the average directed distance from all other nodes in the network. Proximity prestige takes into account both direct and indirect indegrees of a vertex.

SUMMARY

Social network analysis is an interdisciplinary research field focusing on the structure of relationships within a set of persons, groups, organizations, nations, and human activities and creations. Social network analysis has its origins in anthropological research on family and kinship ties and in mathematical graph theory. Social network analysis now uses very large data to analyze networks that are constantly evolving. Social network analysis can be broadly conceptualized as an approach to studying any social process or structure that can be depicted by lines connecting sets of units.

Social networks can be conceptualized as a graph consisting of a set of nodes and lines connecting them. The nodes are social actors, entities, or objects. The lines are relations among them. A network graph or sociogram is a visualization of the relational structure of a set of entities and the ties connecting them.

We use an adjacency matrix to represent a social network. We can represent directed relations, undirected relations, loop relations, relations with various values, and multiple relations.

Graphic representation of a social network is flexible and can be structured in an informative and suggestive way to show the nature and prominent features of the network. Using different configurations of an identical network, we highlight different dimensions of the structure of the network.

Social network analysis, as a formalized study of actors and their connections, focuses on two dimensions of social systems. It describes overall network structure. It also focuses on individual actors and their immediate network context.

Network cohesion refers to the sections in the network that are densely connected. We use concepts such as cliques, n-cliques, k-cores and k-plex, m-core/m-slice, and lamda sets to describe features of network cohesion.

Blockmodeling is a method for analyzing the adjacency matrix to identify actors who have similar patterns of ties with other actors. It sorts the adjacency matrix in an intelligent manner to reveal a pattern that illuminates the relationships among the actors. The pattern is illustrated by classifying the nodes into clusters.

Graph theory in social network analysis is used to identify prominent and important actors. Three types of centrality are considered. Degree centrality is the total number of direct ties in a nondirected graph. Closeness centrality is the average path distance from all the other vertices to the ego. Betweenness centrality is the sum of the proportions that the actor is involved in all pairs of the other actors' geodesics.

Prestige measures attractiveness or popularity and is measured as the number of indegree (positive) or outdegree (negative) relations of a vertex. Proximity prestige measures the average directed distance from all other nodes in the network and takes into account both direct and indirect indegrees of a vertex.

PRACTICE PROBLEMS

1. What constitutes a social network?
2. What are the two ways to represent a social network?
3. Use the adjacency matrices in table P12.1 to do the following:
   a) Construct a diagram (sociogram) to illustrate the graphic representation of the network;
   b) For those with nondirected and nonvalued edges, calculate degree centrality, closeness centrality, and betweenness centrality for all the nodes. You may use a computer program;
   c) For those with directed edges, calculate prestige and proximity prestige scores. Use a computer program if needed.
4. Write adjacency matrices based on these network diagrams in figure P12.1. How do we describe cohesion of a social network? What are cliques and n-cliques? What are k-cores and m-cores? What is a lamda set?
5. Using a network data set of an adjacency matrix and a computer software program of your choice, do the following:

TABLE P12.1   **ADJACENCY MATRICES**

	A	B	C	D
A	0			
B	1	0		
C	0	1	0	
D	0	0	1	0

	A	B	C	D
A	1	0	8	0
B	0	0	0	6
C	0	2	3	0
D	0	0	0	0

	A	B	C	D
A	0			
B	1	0		
C	1	0	0	
D	1	0	0	0

	A	B	C	D
A	0			
B	1	0		
C	1	1	0	
D	1	0	1	0

	A	B	C	D
A	0	0	2	0
B	0	1	0	0
C	6	0	5	9
D	8	1	0	0

	A	B	C	D
A	0	1	1	1
B	1	0	0	0
C	1	0	0	1
D	1	0	1	0

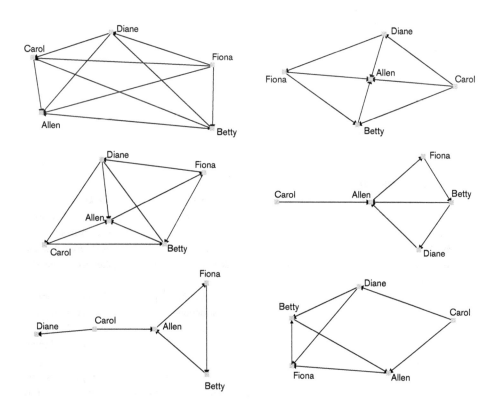

FIGURE P12.1
Network Diagrams.

a. Generate a sociogram of the social network;
b. Show the graph in the following layouts:
   i. principle component layout;
   ii. principle component with varimax; and
   iii. theoretical layout.
c. Use 1-core and 2-core to partition the network.
d. Find the actor with the highest degree centrality (nondirected) or prestige (directed). Calculate its closeness centrality and betweenness centrality (if nondirected) or proximity prestige (if directed).

SOFTWARE PROGRAMS

For SNA, widely used packages include

EgoWeb 2.0 (open source http://www.qualintitative.com/wiki/doku.php/egoweb_2.0_home),

GUESS (http://graphexploration.cond.org/),

NetMiner (http://www.netminer.com/product/overview.do),

UCINet (https://sites.google.com/site/ucinetsoftware/downloads),

Meerkat (https://www.scoop.it/t/sna-social-network-analysis/p/4003990028/2013/06/30/meerkat-social-network-analysis-tool),

Pajek (freeware http://vlado.fmf.uni-lj.si/pub/networks/Pajek/),

Visone (https://visone.info), and

Stata - nwcommandsa (https://nwcommands.wordpress.com).

R has several packages to conduct social network analysis:

Package "igraph" (https://cran.r-project.org/web/packages/igraph/igraph.pdf),

Package "statnet" (https://cran.r-project.org/web/packages/statnet/statnet.pdf),

Package "network" (https://cran.r-project.org/web/packages/network/network.pdf),

Package "sna" (https://cran.r-project.org/web/packages/sna/sna.pdf), and

Package "RSiena" (https://cran.r-project.org/web/packages/RSiena/RSiena.pdf and https://www.stats.ox.ac.uk/~snijders/siena/).

ADDITIONAL READING

Borgatti, Stephen P., Martin G. Everett, and Jeffrey C. Johnson. 2018. *Analyzing Social Networks*. 2nd ed. Thousand Oaks, CA: Sage. Focuses on collecting, visualizing, analyzing, and interpreting social network data with a particular emphasis on the software programs UCINET and Netdraw. A companion website provides supplementary materials to accompany the book, including data sets used, examples, and tutorials showing how to do each analysis included in the book: https://sites.google.com/site/analyzingsocialnetworks/.

Wasserman, Stanley, and Katherine Faust. 1994. *Social Network Analysis: Methods and Applications*. Cambridge: Cambridge University Press. A good reference and self-instruction manual for those who want to apply SNA methods in research. At more than 800 pages, it documents each subject area thoroughly, offers examples of application, presents the algorithms for most techniques, and provides further reading.

Yang, Song, Franziska B. Keller, and Lu Zheng. 2017. *Social Network Analysis: Methods and Examples*. Thousand Oaks, CA: Sage. A basic book on social network analysis without advanced statistics calculations. It is intended for undergraduate students and written as a textbook with history, scenarios, and review questions at the end of each chapter.

REFERENCES

Butts, Carter T. 2008. "Social Network Analysis: A Methodological Introduction." *Asian Journal of Social Psychology* 11: 13–41.

Park, Seung-Bo, and Geun Sik Jo. 2011. "Social Network Analysis in a Movie Using Character-net." *Multimedia Tools and Application* 59 (2): 1–27.

Wimmer, Adreas, and Brian Min. 2006. "From Empire to Nation-State: Explaining Wars in the Modern World, 1816–2001." *American Sociological Review* 71 (6): 867–97.

INDEX

NOTE: Page numbers in *italics* denote figures and tables.

29, 37; model complexity and completeness, 30, 33, 38; model prediction power as focus of data mining, 30, 33–34; nonlinear and joint effects, 30, 32, 38; opacity of mechanisms, as challenge in data mining, 36–37, 38; pros and cons of data mining vs. traditional statistical models, 29–30, 37–38; single causes (probability causality), 28–29, 29, 37; variety of data (text, images, video, voice, etc.), 30, 34–35, 38. *See also* complex causal heterogeneity

census, population, 35–36

centrality of nodes, 233–235, 234, 236

central tendency, measures of: box plots as illustrating, 75; replacement of missing data with, 46, 46; and replacement of missing data with random values, 46

centroid, 124, 127

CHAID (Chi-squared Automatic Interaction Detection), 31, 176, 181

chain graph, 234–235, 234

challenges of data mining, 35; causal mechanisms, 36–37, 38; convenience samples, 35–36, 38, 93–94

child mortality rate examples, 78–80, 79–80, 82, 83, 161–163

Chi-squared Automatic Interaction Detection (CHAID), 31, 176, 181

chi-squared tests: and decision tree analysis, 31, 176, 181–182, 183, 188; and logistic regression models, 168, 170; and parsimony, 33

Cios et al., KDP model (2007), 24–25, 26, 37

circle graph, 234–235, 234

classification: overview, 175–176, 187–188; bootstrapping and, 36; cluster analysis distinguished from, 118; combined with cluster analysis, 118; discrimination and, 44; and hierarchical cluster analysis, 127; imputed values for missing data, 47; linear discriminants for, 156; segmentation of data, 175, 179–180, 187; as supervised learning approach, 118; and target variables, 118; topic modeling, 35, 219–220, 219, 221. *See also* decision trees

Classification and Regression Tree (CART), 31, 32, 176, 183

clique, 230, 231, 236

closeness centrality, 234, 236

cluster analysis: overview, 116, 129–130, 133; binning variables by, 65, 66; and causal heterogeneity, separating, 30–31, 37; classification combined with, 118; classification distinguished from, 118; cluster cohesion and, 127–128, 130; cluster separation and, 127–128, 130; cross-validation of, 128–129, 130; definition of cluster, 116;

division of clusters, methods for, 124–127, 125–126, 130; exploratory analysis, as form of, 118; goodness-of-fit of, 127–128, 130; hierarchical cluster analysis, 125–127, 126, 130; and the linkage function, 125–127, 130; as maximizing similarity within the group while minimizing the similarity between groups, 116, 124, 129; model assessment and, 94; null hypothesis of, 127; pseudo-*F* test for optimal number of clusters, 127, 130; silhouette value measure, 127, 128, 128, 130; similarity measures, 118–119 (*see also* distance measures); standardizing numerical variables, 118; as unsupervised learning approach, 118; validation of model, 128–129, 130. *See also* K-means cluster analysis

coefficients of determination (R²): and linear regression model assessment, 158–159, 159, 164, 169; low, accepted in traditional statistical models, 34; values of, and strength of model, 159

cohesion of network, 230–232, 231, 236

collective memory, 217

colored nodes layout, network visualization, 82, 82

communication field, 109

complete linkage function, 126, 130

complex causal heterogeneity: overview, 30–31, 37; cluster analysis as separating, 116–117, 129

complex modeling, 10, 11

computational methods of statistics, 8, 9, 9

computational social science (CSS): overview, 10–11, 11, 14–15; big data as characteristic of, 10, 11; computer simulations, 11–12; definitions and conceptualizations of, 10–11, 11; emergence of, 4–5, 10; extraction of knowledge as characteristic of, 10–11, 11; instrumental dimensions of, 10; methodologies of, 10–12, 11; natural samples and, 10, 11, 35–36, 93–94; online experiments, 11, 12; social computing, 11; substantive/theoretical dimension of, 10. *See also* data mining

computer simulations, 11–12

confidence intervals, and replacement of missing data, 46

confidence. *See under* association rule mining

confusion tables: overview, 33; cost-benefit analysis, model assessment with, 94, 102–104, 103, 104, 110; model assessment and, 94, 110, 199, 200, 201

consent of informants, 44

Content Grabber (web scraper), 211

continuous variables: association rule mining and conversion of, 143, 150; decision trees and conversion of, 176, 178; definition of, 72;

continuous variables (*continued*)

histograms for single variable visualization, 73, *74*, 85; imputed values for missing data, 47; interval variables as, 72; linear function as default in traditional statistical models, 32; linear regression as supervised learning for, 156, 169; nonlinear effects and, 32, 38; scatter plots for, 95; transforming into discrete variables (*see* binning variables). *See also* linear regression

convenience samples (natural samples), 10, *11*, 35–36, 93–94

convergence criterion, 124–125

convolutional neural net (CNN), 196

co-occurrence grouping. *See* association rule mining

correlation matrix: association rules compared to, 144, 150–151; traditional statistical models and, 32

cosine distance, 122–123, *123*, 129–130

cost-benefit analysis, model assessment with, 94, 102–104, *103*, *104*, 110

cost-benefit matrices, overview, 33

country indicators, 49

criminal activities, and web usage mining by law enforcement, 212

cross-validation: overview, 33, 94, *95*, 109–110; of cluster analysis, 128–129, 130; definition of, 36; leave-one-out cross-validation, 96, 109–110; of regression models, 168–169, *170*; representative data sets, *95*; representative data sets, need for, 95; stratified holdout method, 95; tenfold cross-validation (holdout approach), 95–96, 109; three-fold cross-validation, 95; training and testing sets for, 36, 95–96, 109–110, 128–129, 168–169, *170*

CSS. *See* computational social science

Cukier, Kenneth, 6

cultural trends, and analysis of Google Books, 217–218

cumulative response curve, 104, *105*, 110

database extensions, 211

database systems: as foundation of data mining, 8–9, *9*; web scrapers exporting to, 211

data-driven research: distinguished from data mining, 18, 19, 22, 23, 37; Galilean approach to scientific research, 20, *20*, 22

data mining: overview, 18–19; data-driven research distinguished from, 18, 19, 22, 23, 37; defined as interchangeable term with knowledge discovery in this text, 10; definition (broader), 9–10, *9*; definition (narrower), 8–9, *9*, 14; as

dialectic process combining both deductive and inductive research, 19, 21–23, *22*, 37; and dialectic relationship between theory and data, 23–25, *26*; as multidisciplinary/interdisciplinary, 11, 19; as step in KDP model, 24; time and human resource savings provided by, 19. *See also* causality; challenges of data mining; data visualization; domain-specific knowledge; ethics and data mining; machine learning; model assessment; model predictive power; nonparametric methods; preprocessing of data; social network analysis (SNA); software programs; technology; text mining; web mining

data reduction, and KDP model, 24

data science/data studies majors, 5

data sets, and KDP model, 24

data transformation (normalization, standardization): overview, 48–49, *49*, *50*; decimal scaling, 52; range normalization, 51, 118, 129; Z-score standardization, 49–50, 118, 129. *See also* binning variables; normal distribution, transformation of

data visualization: overview, 8, *9*, 70–71, 85; of bivariate data, 76–78, 85; chain graph, 234–235, *234*; circle graph, 234–235, *234*; communication of values of data, 71, 85; decision trees and, 177–178, *178*; dendrograms, 125, *126*; discrete vs. continuous variables, 72, *72*; explanatory vs. exploratory, 71, 85; four steps of planning and implementation, 71, 85; and KDP model, 24; of multivariate data, 78–84, 85; network visualization, 80, 81–82, *82*, 85; nonlinear effects and, 32, 38; pie charts, 73, *74*, 85; qualitative vs. quantitative variables, 71–72, *72*; of regression models, and need to transform variables, 163–164, *164*; residual plots, 163; shedding light on new insights, 71, 85; significance of values in the chart, 71, 85; of single variables, 72–76, 85; star graph, 234–235, *234*; stem-and-leaf plots, 73, 75, *75*, 85; understanding the levels of data measurement, 71, 85; word clouds, 83–84, *84*, 85, 88–89, 216, 221. *See also* bar charts; box plots; histograms; map visualization; scatter plots; social network analysis (SNA)

decimal scaling, 52

decision rules, deductive method of applying, 23

decision trees: overview, 175–177, *177*, 187–188; advantages and disadvantages of, 176, 177–178, 187; branches (subtree), 176, *177*, 187; and causal mechanisms, opacity of, 36–37; chi-squared method, 31, 176, 181–182, *183*, 188; complexity of, 178, 187; conjunctive conditions and, 180; and continuous variables, conversion into discrete classes, 176, 178; data visualization and, 177–178, 178; decision node, 177; discrete nature of the outcome class, 175, 176, 178; Gini index method, 183, 188; information gain method, 183–184, 188; and joint effects of inputs, 201; leaf nodes (terminal nodes), 176, 177, 180, 187; missing data or outliers not constraining, 178, 187; neural networks compared to, 197, 201, 201, 202, 203; as nonparametric application, 36, 178, 187; overfitting of model as difficulty of, 178, 185–186, 188; parent/child nodes, 177; post-pruning, 186, 186, 188; predictive power of, 177, 187; preprocessing of data less extensive for, 178; pre-pruning (constraining tree size), 185, 188; programs for, 31; pruning, 177, 185–186, 186, 188; Random Forests (ensemble approach), 186–187, 188; as recursive procedure of divide and conquer, 178–179, 188; regression models compared to, 177, 187; and relationship heterogeneity, 177, 187; root node, 176, 180, 187; segmentation of data and, 179–180, 179–180; as sets of rules, 180–181, 188; software programs for, 31, 176, 179, 186, 187; splitting into subnodes, 176–177, 181–184, 181–183, 188; splitting, constraint of, 185, 188; as supervised learning problem, 155–156, 176, 187; target outcomes, as positive or negative, 175; training set for, 176; variance reduction method, 184, 188

degree centrality, 233–234, 236
degrees of freedom, 160, 168
dendrograms, 125, 126
descriptive objectives, 9, 9
deviance, 168, 170
Deza, Elena, and Michel-Marie Deza, 119
dichotomous variables, 143, 150, 165, 214
disability, discrimination based on, 44
discrete variables, 72, 85. *See also* binning variables
discrimination, ethics of data use and avoidance of, 44
distance measures: overview, 118–119, 119; cosine distance, 122–123, 123, 129–130; edit distance, 123–124, 130; Euclidean distance, 119–120, 120, 124, 129; Jaccard distance, 121–122, 122, 129; linkage function (distance function between clusters), 125–127, 130; Manhattan distance, 121, 129
divisive clustering method, 125–127, 126
divorce example, 181–184
domain-specific knowledge: data mining and need for, 5, 10, 11, 19–20; and KDP models, 23, 24; and

need for training in data mining, 14; and parameter learning, 156
dummy variables, 143

e-commerce applications, 212
economics: dual labor market structure, and immigration, 117; neoclassical models of, 117; text mining and, 217–218
edit distance, 123–124, 130
education examples, 103–104
EgoWeb 2.0 (software), 238
elections, Facebook and attempts to influence, 45, 212
English-language lexicography, 217
entropy, 183–184
epidemiology, historical, 217
ethics and data mining: overview, 43–44, 67; confidentiality of data and difficulty of anonymizing, 44; consent of informants, 44; discrimination, avoidance of, 44; integrity of data, 44–45; privacy of data, 44, 45; rights of human subjects, 44–45; scope of use allowed to apply data, 44; scraping data from web pages, 44–45
Euclidean distance, 119–120, 120, 124, 129
Exhaustive CHAID (software), 176
explanatory variables: joint effects among, association rule mining and, 31; nonlinear effects among, 32; and traditional statistical models, 30–31
explanatory vs. exploratory data visualizations, 71, 85
exploratory analysis: association rule mining as form of, 143–144, 150–151; cluster analysis as form of, 118
exploratory data visualizations, 71, 85
extraction of knowledge from previously hidden patterns, 9–11, 9, 11, 18–19. *See also* data mining; knowledge discovery process (KDP) model

Facebook: amount of data generated per day, 4; and associated rule mining, 136; and attempts to influence elections, 45, 212; and size of social networks, 225; web usage mining and advertisements on, 212; web usage mining and fake accounts on, 212
Facebook–Cambridge Analytica data scandal, 45
facial recognition, 196
false negatives vs. false positives: cost-benefit analysis as distinguishing, 102–104; proportion of (PFN), 102; rates of, 99, 101
false positives. *See* false negatives vs. false positives

job application example, 122–123
job openings in data analysis, 4

Kasparov, Gary, 5
k-cores and k-plex, 230, 236
K-means cluster analysis, 124–125, 130; algorithm
     for, and standardization of measurement
     scales, 49; binning variables with, 65, 66
knowledge: extraction of, from previously hidden
     patterns, 9–11, 9, 11, 18–19. *See also* data mining;
     domain-specific knowledge; knowledge
     discovery in database (KDD); knowledge
     discovery process (KDP) model; scientific
     research; social science research
knowledge discovery in database (KDD): broader
     definition of data mining as similar process to,
     9, 14; defined as interchangeable term with data
     mining in this text, 10; definition of, 7, 14; fields
     applied to, 7; narrower definition of data
     mining as seventh step in, 8, 14; nine-step
     process of, 7, 8. *See also* data mining
knowledge discovery process (KDP) model:
     backtracking steps, 25; Cios et al. (2007), 24–25,
     26, 37; Fayyad and colleagues (1996), 23–24, 37
Kolmorogov-Smirnov test, 52

lamda set, 232, 236
Laney, D., 5–6
latent Dirichlet allocation (LDA) method, 219–220,
     219, 221
latent semantic indexing, 219
law enforcement, and web usage mining, 212
Lazer, David, et al., "Computational Social
     Science," 10
Leaflet (software), 82, 87–88
least squares method, 157, 169
leave-one-out cross-validation, 96, 109–110
Les Misérables (film), 225
life curve, 104–105, 106, 110
life expectancy examples, 76–80, 157–159, 161–164
likelihood ratio test, 33
linear models: linear determinants, 156; parameter
     learning and, 156. *See also* linear regression;
     logistic regression
linear regression: overview, 156, 169; application of,
     157–158, 158; assumptions for, 160, 169;
     bootstrapping and, 36; for continuous output
     variable, 156, 169; cross-validation of, 168–169,
     170; equation for, 156; error term, 156, 165; least
     squares method, 157, 169; multiple regression
     model, 161, 162; regression slope, 161–162;
     simple regression (bivariate regression), 157;

sum of squared errors, 157, 169; sum of squares
     regression (SSR), 159; total sum of squares
     (TSS), 159. *See also* linear regression model
     assessment
linear regression model assessment: overview, 94,
     158; ANOVA (*F*-test), 160–161, 161, 162, 164, 169;
     assumptions, validation of, 160, 169; Box-Cox
     transformation, 164–165, 169; coefficient of
     determination, 158–159, 159, 164, 169; null and
     alternative hypotheses, 160–162; standard error
     of the estimate, 160, 169; transformation of
     variables to achieve linearity, 163–165, 164;
     t-tests, 161–163, 163, 169
linguistic evolution, analysis of Google Books and,
     217–218
linkage function (distance function between
     clusters), 125–127, 130
link analysis. *See* social network analysis (SNA)
listwise deletion of data, 45–46
logarithmic transformations (log), 54–56, 55–56
logical causes, 27–28, 29, 37
logistic regression: overview, 165, 169–170;
     calculation of, 167–168; for categorical outcome
     variable, 165, 169; and chi-squared test, 168, 170;
     combined with association rule mining,
     144–145; cross-validation of, 168–169, 170;
     deviance, 168, 170; error term of, 165; imputed
     values for missing data, 47; and *ln* odds ratios,
     transformation into, 165–166, 169–170;
     maximum likelihood estimation, 168, 170;
     model assessment, 168; neural networks
     compared to, 193, 197, 199–201, 200, 203; null
     hypothesis, 168; and odds, 166, 167, 170; and
     odds ratio, 166–167, 170, 199; and probability,
     167–168, 170; regression slope, 166–167; as
     supervised learning problem, 155–156
Lydia text analysis system, 220

machine learning: overview, 8, 9, 115–116, 129;
     definition, 115; and model predictive power, 34,
     38. *See also* supervised learning; unsupervised
     learning
McKinsey Global Institute, "Big Data: The Next
     Frontier for Innovation, Competition, and
     Productivity," 4, 6
Manhattan distance, 121, 129
Manyika, J., et al., "Big Data: The Next Frontier for
     Innovation, Competition, and Productivity,"
     4, 6
map visualization: overview, 82, 85; bubble maps,
     82; choropleth maps, 82, 83; connection maps,
     82, 83; network maps, 82; software for, 82

R (software): decision trees, 176, 186, 187; map visualization, 82, 83, 87–88; multiple imputation of missing data, 48; network visualization, 80, 82, 86–87; neural networks, 195, 205; Random Forests, 187; social network analysis, 238; text mining, 222; word cloud example of coding, 88–89; word clouds, 83–84, 84, 88–89, 216

R^2. *See* coefficients of determination

race/ethnicity, discrimination based on, 44

radial basis function (RBF), 205

Random Forests (ensemble decision tree approach), 186–187, 188

randomly placed vertices, layout of network visualization, 80, 81, 82

random values, replacement of missing data with, 46–47

range normalization, 51, 118, 129

RColorBrewer (software), 83

readtext (software), 222

recall precision curve, 108–109, 108–109, 110

receiver operating characteristics curve (ROC), 105–106, 107, 108, 110

recursive programming, imputed values for missing data, 47

recursive steps, agglomerative clustering method and, 125

reduced error pruning of decision trees, 186, 188

regression analysis: assumptions of, 160, 169; cross-validation of, 168–169, 170; decision trees compared to, 193, 197, 199–201, 200, 203; dichotomous variables in, 143, 165. *See also* linear regression; logistic regression

regression slope: for linear regression, 161–162; for logistic regression, 166–167

religion: discrimination based on, 44; missing data example, 46

replication, definition of, 36

residual plots, 163

rights of human subjects, 44–45

R igraph (software), 86

root mean squared error, 97

rpart (software), 176, 186

RSiena (software), 238

rule-based pruning of decision trees, 186, 188

samples: convenience samples (natural samples), 10, 11, 35–36, 93–94; population census, 35–36; probability samples, 35–36

scales of measurement. *See* data transformation (normalization, standardization)

scatter plots: 3D, 80, 80; for bivariate data, 78, 79;

85; and linear regression, 163–164, 164; for multivariate data, 78, 79–80, 80, 85

Science (journal), 6, 10

scientific research: cycle of data mining research, 19; deductive vs. inductive approaches, 19, 21–23, 22, 37; Galilean approach to, 20, 20, 22; grounded theory, 22–23, 37; as revolutionized by big data, 4–5, 14; seven stages of research, 20–21, 21; theory and research, relationship between, 21–26, 22, 26; theory-driven confirmatory hypothesis testing, 20–21, 20. *See also* causality; data mining; null hypothesis; statistical models, traditional

Scrapy (web scraper), 211

sensitivity, 100, 110, 197, 198, 203

sexual orientation, discrimination based on, 44

Shapiro-Wilk test, 52

sigmoid function (squashing function), 194–195, 195, 203

significance tests, not suitable for convenience samples, 36

silhouette value measure, 127, 128, 128, 130

single linkage, 125–126, 130

skewness: defined, 52, 54; and need for binning variables, 62; standard error for the skewness score, 54. *See also* normal distributions, transformation of

SKICAT (Sky Image Cataloging and Analysis Tool), 7

Skocpol, Theda, 28

Sky Image Cataloging and Analysis Tool (SKICAT), 7

Sloan Digital Sky Survey, 5, 14

Smyth, Padhraic, Fayyad KDP model, 23–24, 37

SNA (software), 86–87, 238

SNA. *See* social network analysis

social class, discrimination based on, 44

social computing, 11

social network analysis (SNA): overview, 13, 80, 82, 85, 224–225, 235–236; adjacency matrix, 226–227, 227, 228, 232–233, 235, 236; betweenness centrality, 235, 236; blockmodeling, 232–233, 232, 236; centrality of nodes, 233–235, 234, 236; clique, 230, 231, 236; closeness centrality, 234, 236; cohesion of network, 230–232, 231, 236; and complexity, 229–230; definition of, 225; degree centrality, 233–234, 236; dimensions of, as overall structure and individual actors, 230, 236; and graph theory, 225, 233, 235, 236; and instrumental dimension of computational social science, 10, 11; k-cores and k-plex, 230, 236; lamda set, 232, 236; lines, 225, 226, 235; link analysis as alternative term for, 225; m-core or m-slice, 230, 232, *232*, 236; n-clique, 230, *231*, 236; network graphs (sociograms), 80, *81–82*, *82*, 225–226, *226*, 227, *227*, 229, *229*, 235–236; nodes, 225, *226*, 233, 235; origin of, 225, 235; prestige (attractiveness), 235, 236; relational data applications, 224–225; size of networks, 225; software programs for, 80, 82, 86–87, 238

social science research: single causes and, 28–29, *29. See also* computational social science (CSS); data mining; domain-specific knowledge; scientific research

socioeconomic attributes, examples of, 119–122

Socio-GIS, 10, *11*

sociological studies, explanatory variables as focus of, 30–31

sociology, emergence of, 217–218

software programs: association rule mining, 145–149; binning variables (optimal binning), 32, 62, 64–67; Box-Cox transformation, 60, 62; causal mechanisms, 36–37; computer simulations and, 11–12; map visualization, 82, 87–88; multiple imputation of missing data, 47–48; neural networks, 195, 205; number of, in Internet Archive, 4; range normalization, 51; social network analysis (SNA), 80, 82, 86–87, 238; standard error for the skewness score, 54; text mining, 222; web mining, 210–211; word cloud example of coding, 88–89; word clouds, 83–84, *84*, 88–89, 216; Z-score normalization, 50

specificity, 100–101, 110

sphere layout of network visualization, 80, *81*, 82

sports, 7

SPSS (software): automatic binning, 32; Box-Cox transformation, 60, 62; and causal mechanisms, 36–37; decision trees, 176; multiple imputation of missing data, 47; neural networks, 195, 205; optimal binning, 62, 67; range normalization, 51; visual binning, 62, 64–66; Z-score normalization, 50

square root transformation, 56, *57–58*

stacked bars (chart), 80, *81*, 85

standard deviation: binning variables by, 65–66; and replacement of missing data with random values, 46; standard error of the estimate compared with, 160; Z-score standardization to values based on, 49–50, 118, 129

standard error for the skewness score, 54

standard error of the estimate, 160, 169

standard error of the sampling distribution, and replacement of missing data, 46

standardization. *See* data transformation (normalization, standardization)

star graph, 234–235, *234*

Star Wars movies, 225

Stata (software), 47, 238

statistical models, traditional: association rule mining compared to, 144–145; linear main effects as focus of, 30, 32; non-numerical data not addressed by, 30, 34–35; one or few theories as focus of, 29–30; parsimony and, 30, 33, 38, 97; predictor coefficients as focus of, 30, 33–34; probability causality, 28–29, *29*, 37; role of, data mining as complementary to, 30; simple main effects as focus of, 30–31; time-consuming nature of, 19, 32, 34; variance and, 33, 34, 38

statistics: computational methods of, 8, *9*; as foundation of data mining, 8. *See also* data visualization; statistical models, traditional

statnet (software), 238

stem-and-leaf plots, 73, 75, *75*, 85

stock market, 35

student examples: campus ID cards, 44; course taking patterns, 137–143

sum of squared errors (SSE), 157, 169, 195–196

sum of squares regression (SSR), 159

supervised data classification. *See* classification

supervised learning: overview, 115–116, 129, 155–156, 169; deductive method applying decision rules produced with, 23; definition of, 155; and detection of causal heterogeneity, 31; parameter learning, 156, 169. *See also* classification; decision trees; linear regression; logistic regression; neural networks

target variables, 96–97, 118

teaching plans for this text, 13–14; Chapter 5 and, 12

technology: adoption of, 217; advent of, as allowing extraction of knowledge from previously hidden patterns, 18–19; as foundation of big data, 6–7, *7. See also* artificial intelligence (AI); data mining; software programs

telecommunications networks example, 225–229, 230–232, 233

tenfold cross-validation, 95–96, 109

term frequency representation, 214–217, 218

testing sets. *See* training and testing sets

text analysis: deep learning neural networks and, 196; edit distance measurement, 123–124; of *New York Times* anonymous op-ed, 209–210; as qualitative analysis (traditional), 213; word

Founded in 1893,
UNIVERSITY OF CALIFORNIA PRESS
publishes bold, progressive books and journals
on topics in the arts, humanities, social sciences,
and natural sciences—with a focus on social
justice issues—that inspire thought and action
among readers worldwide.

The UC PRESS FOUNDATION
raises funds to uphold the press's vital role
as an independent, nonprofit publisher, and
receives philanthropic support from a wide
range of individuals and institutions—and from
committed readers like you. To learn more, visit
ucpress.edu/supportus.

www.ingramcontent.com/pod-product-compliance
Lightning Source LLC
Chambersburg PA
CBHW080551060326
40689CB00021B/4816